SAMUEL THE SEER

THE LAST OF THE JUDGES AND THE FIRST OF THE PROPHETS AFTER MOSES

BY

SHEPHERD CAMPBELL

Published by Karyn Rae Publishing
ISBN: 978-0-9960922-2-7

Visit Shepherd Campbell's official website at www.israel-a-history-of.com for the latest news, book details, and other information.

Edited by: Salvatore Borriello
Cover Design by: Humble Nations, www.goonwrite.com
Ebook Formatting by: Guido Henkel

A study of the first book of Samuel using the *NASB Hebrew-Greek Key Study Bible* by Dr. Spiros Zodhiates as the English translation of Scripture

To my parents, Louis and Ila Campbell,
for raising me in the Word of God,
for always being an encouragement,
and for always loving me in spite of me.

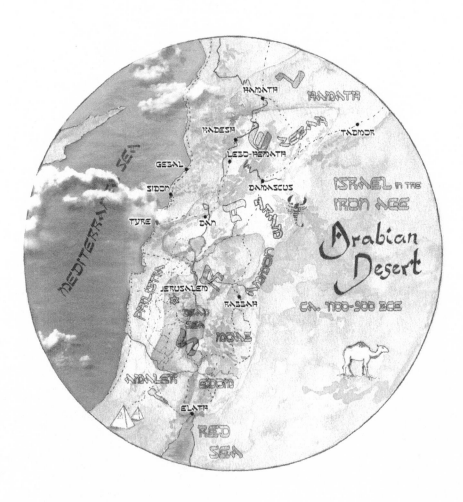

ISRAEL IN THE
IRON AGE

Arabian
Desert

CA. 1100-900 BCE

MEDITERRANEAN SEA
HAMATH
HAMATH
KADESH
ZOBAH
TADMOR
LEBO-HAMATH
GEBAL
SIDON
DAMASCUS
ARAM
TYRE
DAN
PHILISTIA
JERUSALEM
AMMON
RABBAH
DEAD SEA
MOAB
AMALEK
EDOM
ELATH
RED SEA

EXPANSION BY DAVID

EXTENT OF SAUL'S KINGDOM

EXPANSION BY SOLOMON

1 SAMUEL 1

THE FIRST AND SECOND BOOKS OF Samuel are combined as one book in the Hebrew Bible. Also, 1 and 2 Kings are one book and follow Samuel chronologically. This period of Israel's history was occupied with fending off foreign threats, namely the Philistines, and the evolution from a band of tribes (the amphictyony) to a monarchy. The fledgling nation was little more than a band of loosely confederated tribes, united by their belief in the One God Almighty, Elohim. They had yet to unite under one governmental authority since the death of Moses and Joshua, and they joined forces when needed throughout the random and chaotic time of the Judges.

The name "Samuel" translates as "asked of God." Samuel's mother, Hannah, asked God for a child, in return for which she would place him in the service of God Almighty. Samuel was God's answer. Hannah faithfully gave Samuel to the service of God under the direction of the old priest Eli, judge and leader of Israel, in the opening chapters of Samuel. Samuel's biological father was Elkanah, the son of Jeroham, the son of Elihu, the son of Tohu, the son of Ziph. His family descended from the tribe of Ephraim. Elkanah lived in the city of Ramathaim-zophim, located in the hill country of Ephraim, in the western mountains of Canaan.

When Hannah turned him over to Israel's priest, Eli, in a sense, the old priest became Samuel's earthly spiritual father. Eli, however, had two biological sons of his own in Hophni and Phineas.

This priestly family dwelt in Shiloh, the location of the ark of the covenant in this period of Hebrew history. The Lord of Hosts called Shiloh home as Shiloh was the first permanent site of the tabernacle in ancient Israel. Jerusalem at this time was called Jebus and was under the rule of the Jebusites. Interestingly enough, just as the case was with Abraham and Sarai, and Jacob and Rachel, Hannah's womb was originally barren, closed by God. The story of Samuel would begin with the faithfulness of God.

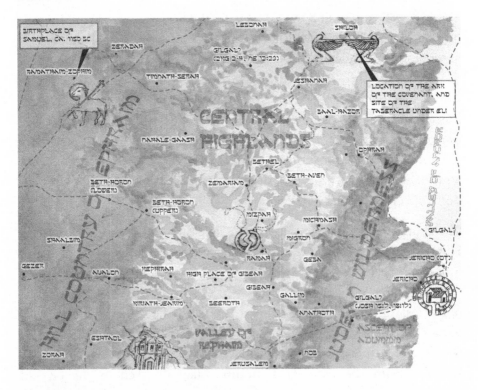

The Test

God will test your faith. Just as he tested the great patriarchs, Abraham and Jacob, so will he test all his people. Hannah, the soon-to-be mother of Samuel, was about to undergo such a test. It is interesting to point out a female plays the lead role in this narrative, as opposed to the male-dominated narratives of Abraham and Jacob, though those do possess females of exceptional character and ability. God Almighty seeks the heart of an individual, not the race, sex, or ethnicity. He seeks those hearts inclined toward him, and he found one in his servant Hannah.

Hannah, in 1 Samuel 1:6, falls victim to her "rival," who "would provoke her bitterly to irritate her." This was done because "the Lord had closed [Hannah's] womb."

This story harkens us back to Leah and Rachel, the two wives of Jacob. Rachel was the most loved of the two, yet her womb was closed. Leah, the less loved of the two, was quite fertile and produced Jacob's first four sons. In Genesis 30:8, Scripture implies a struggle between Rachel and Leah as a result of Rachel's barrenness and Leah's fertility. Hannah, in the same way, was provoked by whomever this unnamed rival was. In 1 Samuel 1:9, Hannah is in Shiloh. Eli the priest was sitting "on the seat by the door post of the temple of the Lord" when Hannah entered and began to pray to the Lord.

Exercise: Read 1 Samuel 1:10.

- What state of mind or emotional state was Hannah in, according to Scripture, when she arrived at the temple?
- Hannah is recorded doing two things in the temple. What were they?

In her brokenness, Hannah made a vow to God. This was a promise or an act of verbally consecrating a request to God. This word, *nadar*, is used thirty-one times in the Old Testament, and it appeared in the Dead Sea Scrolls. It was an ancient act of dedication to God. Numbers 30 gives more insight into laws concerning vows.

Hannah's vow called for God "to look on the affliction" of her situation. A similar plea is heard from Leah when she called for God to look upon her affliction in Genesis 29:32. God's answer to Leah was the birth of Reuben, Jacob's firstborn son. Likewise, God's answer to Hannah was Samuel.

God sees our situations! He will look upon our affliction if we ask him with a sincere heart and genuine motives. He will bring about a solution if we trust him. God will not simply give without our trusting him. He will likely require patience and persistence on our part in the form of praying and asking of him in faith.

Too often we want it *now*. Instant gratification is the way of today's society and culture. Information is given to us in seconds, and our patience has worn thin as a people. God, however, works in a much different way. God often operates in seasons, though he can, and has, operated in milliseconds as well. He is not limited or restrained. His seasons can be seen in the lives of Abraham, Isaac, Jacob, Joseph, Moses, David, and Daniel. He moves over aeons of human history and time. Then, in a split second, he raised Jesus Christ from the dead (Matthew 28:6; Mark 16:6; Luke 24:6-7). Abraham was seventy-five when God promised him a son through Sarah, thus an heir. Abraham was one hundred when Isaac was born.

We know of at least twenty-five years Abraham prayed and visited with God about the birth of a son. Jacob dwelt with Laban for several years to obtain the wife he originally loved and sought after, Rachel. He then labored for many more years under Laban's cruel hand.

Joseph was imprisoned for years, falsely accused by his master, enslaved for decades before God propelled him to second in all of Egypt!

Hannah's vow also called on God to not only look upon her affliction but to remember her and not forget her. God will always be aware of what we, his creation, are doing. He does not forget the good, nor does he overlook and forget the bad.

Exercise: Passage

A clear example of this is found in Genesis 11:5. Turn and read this passage.

- What situation is being discussed in this passage?
- Was God unaware of their activity?

God "came down to see the city and the tower which the sons of man had built." They were not seeking for God to come down and look upon their project. They did not ask God to come down. Yet, he knew what they were up to under the leadership of Nimrod. He had not forgotten, nor had he overlooked.

Jesus Christ assures us we are remembered in Matthew 10:30-31 and Luke 12:7. The very hairs on our heads are counted by him who sees all. It was God who saw Hagar fleeing from Abram and Sarai through the desert. Hagar harkened to him as "a God who sees." As El-Roi (literally, "God who sees") saw Hagar's distress, Nimrod's evil, and Hannah's desperation, so he sees us today. Jesus reminded us we are more precious than the sparrows.

Hannah pled her case before God and begged of him to give her a son. If he blessed her with a son, she would give that son to God "all the days of his life."

Exercise: Read the last half of 1 Samuel 1:11.

- What did Hannah say would never touch her son's head?

This was the Vow of a Nazirite. It is dealt with specifically in Numbers 6. It was a vow of separation. Scripture calls the Vow of a Nazirite a "special vow" or more accurately a "difficult vow" in Numbers 6:2.

The Vow of the Nazirite

This vow of separation was symbolic of one separating himself or herself as a dedication to God. One dedicates or separates his or her life for a specific period of time. Some made the vow for life. One of the requirements of the Vow of the Nazirite, as handed down by Moses via

God, was that a razor should not touch one's head during the duration of the vow. The interesting part of a Nazirite was that he or she did not become a hermit but, rather, remained within society. So, though the Nazirite lived among society, he or she remained separate from society.

Samson was a Nazirite, though a bit of a playboy as well. Samson drew his strength from God by fulfilling his vow of not cutting his hair with a razor (Judges 13:5; 16:7). John the Baptist may have been a Nazirite. Also, the Vow of a Nazirite may have been the vow associated with Paul in Acts 21:23.

Exercise: Compare Luke 1:15 with Numbers 6:3-4, 26.

Hannah singled out Samuel's life to God, if God would first grant her a son. She was specific in her requests before God. She was earnest and bold in her approach to God, yet humbled in spirit.

Hannah's earnestness and sense of urgency in prayer can be seen by carefully reading 1 Samuel 1:12-14.

- How is Hannah praying in this passage?
- Who is watching her pray? What does he think of Hannah?
- What are your impressions of Hannah based on these two verses?

Hannah's earnestness can be seen in the physical manifestation of her prayers, evident by her lips moving. Scripture informs us she was praying "in her heart," yet so intense were her prayers that her lips moved! This is just one example of direct communication with God in the Old Testament without the assistance of a priest. Her heart was talking to God's. Her sincerity was such that her lips moved. She did not care about anything or anybody around her. Hannah was in the direct presence of God, and she was 100 percent focused on being in his presence at that moment.

Eli, the old priest, had been watching Hannah closely and noticed her lips moving but no words coming out. He thought she was drunk, as indicated by his words in 1 Samuel 1:14.

Even the holiest of men can misunderstand one's intent toward God. Hannah was sincere and honest in her heart and worship of God, yet Eli misunderstood her for being drunk. He misunderstood the extent of her devotion. This is a good reminder that it is ultimately God's opinion that matters. The opinion of man should be insignificant to us in comparison with that of God. If you are pursuing him, and your heart is in the right place, don't let others discourage you, regardless of their titles or reputations. A Sunday school teacher once told one of her young, unfortunately unwed pregnant pupils God would not bless her baby out of wedlock. Ludicrous! God can and will bless whomever he pleases, especially one of his precious little ones—regardless of his or her parent's indiscretions. Concern yourself with the thoughts of God. Seek him and he will give you all the guidance you need. It is so hard to follow and submit—but so worth it if we just will.

Exercise: Read 1 Samuel 1:15.

- How does Hannah defend herself to Eli?
- How does Hannah describe her state of being to Eli?

Fulfillment

Hannah was so distressed that she "poured out her soul" to God. She was "oppressed" in her spirit.

The Hebrew word for "oppressed," *qasheh*, translates as "severe, grievous, heavy, or sad in spirit." God would prove faithful to Hannah, as he had previously been with Sarai, Hagar, Leah, and Rachel. Samuel was born in 1 Samuel 1:20, and Hannah remembered to give thanks to God. She weaned the child, then brought him "to the house of the Lord in Shiloh" (1 Samuel 1:24). God delivers his people from oppression, both physical oppression and emotional oppression. He lifts the yoke of hardship and trial, and bears it willingly. Hannah's faith and persistence, like that of Abraham and many, many others, paid off.

"For Thou shalt break the yoke of their burdens and the staff on their shoulders" (Isaiah 9:4).

"Take My yoke upon you, and learn from Me, for I am gentle and humble in heart; and you shall find rest for your souls" (Matthew 11:29).

"Thus says the Lord; Stand in the ways and see and ask for the ancient paths, where the good way is, and walk in it; And you shall find rest for your souls" (Jeremiah 6:16).

Hannah sought God intently and earnestly. She held fast to the words of the future prophet Jeremiah. In 1 Samuel 1:19, we are told Hannah arose early and went to worship again. This was a habit, a lifestyle for Hannah. She consistently spent time with God. She continuously sought his presence.

She likely petitioned God thousands of times. In 1 Samuel 1:20, God delivered a baby boy to Hannah.

Exercise: Read 1 Samuel 1:20.

- Why did Hannah name her baby Samuel?
- What is the implication of Hannah's words?

God fulfilled his promise to be faithful by giving Hannah a son. Yet, Hannah's role must be carefully observed as well. She was patient, persistent, bold, and specific in her approach to God. She approached God as an individual who really believed and had faith. She did not waver or doubt but prayed earnestly and intently. We must copy Hannah's faith. God hears our requests, and he also sees our hearts and motives. Are we pure in our motives? Are we selfish in our requests? God was preparing his people for another chapter in their history. Samuel was to be the man who led this band of tribes into the United Monarchy under Saul and then David. Hannah left Samuel with these words in 1 Samuel 1:28:

"So I have dedicated him to the Lord; as long as he lives he is dedicated to the Lord."

1 SAMUEL 2

THE FIRST TEN VERSES OF 1 Samuel 2 are the words to Hannah's song of thanksgiving to God. These verses sound like many of the Psalms. She is rejoicing in God's faithfulness. Time and again, God provides for his people. God provides for us in ways we do not see, such as strength in a desperate time or situation; the will to move forward despite all the resistance that oftentimes comes with it; the ability to lead people through difficult times, perhaps a death. God provides the strength to persevere, to make life changes, to simply get through today.

Read 1 Samuel 2:2.

It was Hannah's faith that paid off for her, not her money or status. It was her heart that God desired, not her position in society. In 1 Samuel 2:9, we learn that "it is not by might that man shall prevail." However, Samuel was soon to be in the grips of peer pressure to deviate from God's plan. This is a situation we can all relate to. One would think Samuel's upbringing in the temple would shelter him from certain evils. However, 1 Samuel 2:12–17 sheds insight into the wickedness of Eli's two sons. Nobody is sheltered from the attempts of the enemy, not even within the confines of God's temple.

Read the narrative concerning Eli's two sons.

- What does 1 Samuel 2:12–17 say about their sin?
- What is it Scripture states the young men "despised"?

Eli, though the priest for God's people for quite some time, failed to raise his sons in an upright manner. They were wicked priests. They violated the statutes and laws God had given concerning the sacrifices and what the priests were allowed to obtain and eat. Leviticus 7:29-34 describes the process by which priests would obtain food and minister the sacrifices. Eli's sons have total disregard for God's law. In essence, they were strong-arming and embezzling more than their share of the sacrifices. They were performing these sins in blatant disregard for YHWH. This is the environment young Samuel was being brought up in within the temple precincts. He would have been exposed to their wicked influence at an early and impressionable age.

In 1 Samuel 2:18, however, Samuel kept his distance. He was devoted to "ministering before the Lord." Samuel wore a "linen ephod," a sign of his commitment given to him by his mother. As Samuel had been set apart by his mother, in this instance we see him separating himself from the evil practices of Eli's two sons. So, while Samuel lived among his colleagues, and dwelt in the temple precincts, his service and life was separate from the self-serving evil of Hophni and Phineas.

Samuel simply ministered before God. Samuel kept his focus on God, not on personal gain or glory, not on popularity or fame. Young Samuel would have surely been pressured by the two sons of Eli to partake in their wickedness. We see in this instance the development of the young boy who would become the old prophet, the Seer, the servant of the Most High God who would anoint kings and then strip them of their kingdoms.

Read 1 Samuel 2:21.

- How does God further prove his faithfulness to Hannah?

In 1 Samuel 2:21, the Lord "visited" Hannah. As she had proven faithful with her son Samuel, so God once again proved he is capable of much more than we can imagine. Not only did Hannah willingly fulfill her promise, but she brought robes to her son Samuel every year. She proved a faithful servant and mother, fulfilling whatever role God required of her. God thus rewarded Hannah's obedience with more children. God Almighty is not an unfair God. He demands obedience, then gives us the strength to obey. He will prove faithful as he did with Hannah. Not only did she receive other children, but Samuel "grew before the Lord." God fathered him, and young Samuel served him faithfully.

THE MAN OF GOD

In 1 Samuel 2:27, a mysterious figure is introduced in the narrative. Scripture notes "a man of God" visited Eli one day. Who is this man of God? We hear of a similar incident in Judges 13:6.

Exercise: Turn and read Judges 13:6.

- Who is the woman talking in Judges 13:6?
- What did the "man of God" who appeared to her look like?
- What type of vow did she make regarding her son?
- Who was her son?

Samson was a Nazirite just as Samuel, though one of a much different nature, as the Bible clearly relates. Samson was known as somewhat of a ladies' man. The Bible does not hide Samson's desire for Philistine women.

A similar phrase is used of the great leader Moses. Moses lived approximately 250 to 300 years before Samuel. In Deuteronomy 33:1, Moses is called a "man of God." Moses, indeed, was a righteous and holy man, a friend of God. In Joshua 14:6, Moses was called "the man of God." The identity of this man of God in 1 Samuel is never stated. It could simply be a priest of unknown identity living nearby or something more mysterious, such as Melchizedek—who appeared out of nowhere in the Abraham narrative (Genesis 14). Or, perhaps this is a manifestation of Jesus, as has often been argued about the identity of Melchizedek as well as the frequent appearances in the Old Testament of "the angel of the Lord"—distinct from other angels that appear in the Old Testament. Regardless of identity, the man of God pointed out the sin of Eli and his sons.

ELI'S SIN

Eli's sin is indicated in verse 29. He knew his sons were doing evil, yet he did nothing to correct the situation.

Exercise: Read 1 Samuel 2:29.

- Who is Eli accused of honoring above God?
- What is God's punishment for Eli's sin?

Eli's situation parallels the words of Christ in Luke 12:53.

"They will be divided, father against son, and son against father; mother against daughter, mother-in-law against daughter-in-law, and daughter-in-law against mother-in-law."

Perhaps Christ thought of Eli and his sons when speaking these words. He may have been present in the form of the mysterious "man of God" during the time of Eli. Regardless, Eli had been convicted and condemned by God for his waywardness and sin. The question is, where does God fit within your heart?

Eli placed his children above God. This stands in stark contrast to where our priorities should lie. Abraham offered up his only son, Isaac. Abraham's act of faith was a crystal-clear example of the kind of dedication God seeks. Isaac was spared, of course—but the message was sent and received. Honor God above all else. He must be first in our hearts, ahead of family. In Eli's case, it was his family that dragged him into wickedness and evil. Family can be hard to run from sometimes. Family can be hard to confront with tough truths oftentimes. Our family exerts a powerful influence on us. The message here is God, in extreme situations, may call us to flee even our own family. In times of desperation, we must trust and obey God alone. Scripture shows us time and again that he comes through in the end.

Exercise: Read 1 Samuel 2:26.

- How does Scripture record the life of young Samuel?
- In your own words, describe what Samuel may have been like according to this description in the Bible.

Standing as direct opposites of Eli and his sons are Hannah and her son Samuel. Through Hannah and Samuel, God is showing us both his faithfulness and how to be faithful to him. Hannah had chosen God over family by following through in her vow to give up her son to the Lord. It could not have been easy relinquishing Samuel to the service of the temple. She was constantly thinking of her son, evident in the robes she handmade and delivered to her son every year. God granted her more children to replace Samuel, and Samuel gained favor in both the eyes of God and man.

We cannot imagine what God has in store for us if we step out in faithful obedience. We are given two stories, one of a priestly family seen in Eli and his two wicked boys contrasted with the second story of a Nazirite vow to God made by a barren mother. Hudson Taylor would say Hannah stepped out in fearful obedience in giving her son to God as she had promised. Though Hannah was not from a priestly family, God raised up a prophet, priest, judge, and ruler of his people in Samuel.

Samuel became the last of the Judges and the first of the Prophets of God. He would become the king-maker of Israel by anointing the first two kings in Israel's history. His heart was pure, and his eyes were focused only on God. Samuel is further proof that God seeks hearts, not bloodlines, fame, fortune, race, or any number of other such qualities so valued by the world of man.

1 SAMUEL 3

THESE WERE DARK DAYS IN ISRAEL. Though the time frame of Samuel is not widely agreed upon in certainty, dates tend to be relatively close to one another. One must keep in mind that dates concerning the Old Testament, and indeed the Bible in general, are highly controversial topics, and each event may vary widely in dating. The dates given are simply views and theories of others. *Young's Analytical Concordance* places Samuel circa 1171 B.C.–1060 B.C. David's reign is generally believed to have occurred circa 1000 B.C. Many scholars place the period of the Judges between 1200 B.C. and 1000 B.C.

The date of these events is determined by one's view of when the Exodus occurred—yet another contested topic. Samuel would have come at the tail end of this period, as he ushered in the time of the United Monarchy. The people of Israel were a generation or two into the settlement of the land their fathers had invaded and conquered after coming out of the wilderness. Israelites had fought many battles throughout all of Canaan since Joshua led the first excursion into Canaan after Jericho.

Scripture seems to indicate Israel had already strayed from God. Under the wicked leadership of Hophni and Phineas, it is not hard to believe.

Exercise: Read 1 Samuel 3:1.

- What was rare in those days?
- What does Scripture say was infrequent?

The Israelites had forgotten the mighty acts of God during the reign of Moses and Joshua. This is the case with mankind. We are quick to forget and move on with our daily lives. These Israelites were likely no different from you and me. They had heard of the miracles of their ancestors. They, though, had seen no such miracles, and fell into a state of spiritual stagnation. Their faith had diminished to the point that miracles and visions were rare. God requires faith to reveal himself to his people. Rather, faith is required by people to see him revealed. Unfortunately, Scripture does speak of those who will willingly harden their hearts to God.

Exercise: Turn and Read Ezekiel 7:25-26 and Amos 8:11-12.

- Does God seem to be with his people in these days?

Scripture does indicate that God may withdraw himself from his people in times of their rebellion, wickedness, and idolatry. He seeks out the righteous and obedient.

It is significant to take note of Samuel's actions in 1 Samuel 3:1.

Exercise: What does the Bible say Samuel was doing?

Samuel was in the temple faithfully performing his tasks before the Lord. Samuel was faithful and obedient. Little did he know God was about to speak directly with him.

Samuel was about to receive God's call for his life because of his faithful obedience and willing heart. Though Samuel had never heard from God, or seen God, he remained steadfast in his tasks and obedience. Though tempted to participate with Eli's sons in their sin, Samuel had refused, and offered his service to the Lord wholeheartedly and with purity.

Though these were not spiritually strong days in Israel, as their spiritual leader, Eli, was weak and permissive, God was raising a giant. Samuel remained faithful to God, thus God could use him mightily.

GOD'S CALL TO SAMUEL

This is an interesting encounter between God and his people. In 1 Samuel 3:4, God literally calls out to Samuel. As previously mentioned, visions and messages from the Lord were rare in those days. Samuel, thus, mistakes the voice of God for the voice of the old priest, Eli! Twice more this happens, and twice more Eli tells Samuel, "I did not call, my son."

Exercise: Read 1 Samuel 3:7-9.

- What do you think Scripture means when it says, "Samuel did not yet know the Lord"?
- What had not been revealed to Samuel?
- Who finally discerned what was happening to Samuel?
- What were the words Samuel was instructed to say if the voice called to him again?

It would seem that Samuel, having grown up in the temple, would have perhaps recognized the voice. However, it must be kept in mind that such occurrences were very rare, and Samuel likely did not expect God himself to call out directly to him. The Hebrew word translated as "know" in 1 Samuel 3:7 is used in a wide variety of senses. It has also been translated as "be aware, acquaint, discern, understand." In essence, Samuel knew who God was, but he was not aware of God's presence. In the Old Testament, God communicated through the priests in most cases. Direct revelation to people not of the priesthood was rare. Samuel, thus, had no concrete experience with God, until now. His training was complete, and God was calling his servant to action at this crucial time in Israel's history. God's sovereign plan dictated Samuel to fulfill his role.

Samuel's response is also insightful. Eli instructs the lad to say, "Speak Lord, for thy servant is listening." The operative word is, of course, "listening." We must listen to God. Even though he calls us and speaks to us, he waits until we initiate our search for him. Three times he called Samuel, yet Samuel did not know who he was. In 1 Samuel 3:10, Scripture presents a fascinating picture. It says, the "Lord came and stood and called as at other times." Within the walls of his house in Shiloh, he manifested himself to Samuel.

Samuel realized, at last, that the God of Abraham, Isaac, and Jacob was calling him.

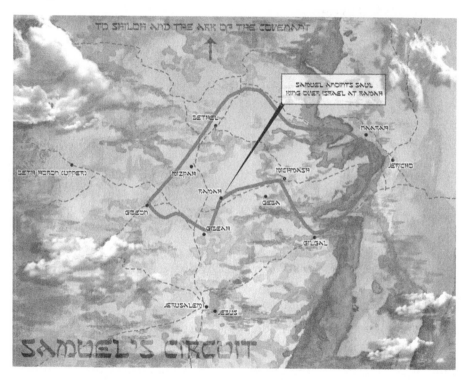

Exercise: Read 1 Samuel 3:10.

- What was Samuel's response this time to God's voice?

This is a glimpse of God's way of reaching out to us. God speaks, and we must listen to hear his voice. How many times do we want God to hear *our* complaints? *Our* needs? Listen! God promises to act faithfully.

God promises to exact his plan upon the house of Eli. He never ceases from tending to his creation, including us, created in his image. God's ways, too, are mysterious. Why did God, who had been so silent during these years, reveal himself to Samuel? He saw Samuel's heart.

God physically came and stood before his servant to draw Samuel's attention. This act of physically manifesting himself seems to indicate God *will* accomplish his purposes. Despite the inattentiveness of the current priesthood, God saw the heart of one young lad he could and would use. It took God physically coming as himself to get Samuel's attention—as the old priest, Eli, was too distant to see God and his sons too wicked to care.

The Jews were faced with extermination during the time of Esther—the Jewish queen of the Persian Empire. She lived when Jews were granted the right to move back and forth from Persia to Israel, during the reign of Xerxes I (485–465 B.C.). She had an opportunity to save the Jews—her people. She wavered briefly, until her Uncle Mordecai straightened her out. Mordecai spoke bluntly to Queen Esther in Esther 4:14.

"For if you remain silent at this time, relief and deliverance will arise for the Jews from another place and you and your father's house will perish. And who knows whether you have attained royalty for such a time as this?"

We have a choice to answer God's call or not. If Samuel, who presumably was a bit frightened by the voice, had shrunk from God's call, he would not have had the special privilege of anointing kings Saul and David. Samuel ushered in a new era of history for God's people. Mordecai reminded Esther if she would not plea for her people before the king of Persia, she and her father's house would be destroyed. God will accomplish his will. His purpose will be established. Are we ready to participate in his bidding? As Hudson Taylor put it, are we ready "to step out in glad obedience to the Master?"

Samuel stood up and spoke. He listened to the voice of God and answered his call. The young servant was to play an integral role in God's plan for Israel. He stepped out in fearful obedience, and God put him over kings.

Exercise: What are some things God may be calling you to "step out in glad obedience" for?

- Is our response like Samuel's, in which Samuel told God to "speak, for thy servant is listening?"

The section at 1 Samuel 3 ends with God appearing once again to Samuel. The Hebrew word *raah* is translated as "appeared." It literally means "to see, to see intellectually, to look at, to view, to inspect." God appeared to Samuel again, inspecting Samuel, looking his heart over intently, and approving of his servant. Samuel, thus, was confirmed in 1 Samuel 3:20 in the sight of Israel, for "all Israel, from Dan even to Beersheba knew that Samuel was confirmed as a prophet of the Lord."

The boy given to God through a vow was now God's mouthpiece to Israel. Times were dire for the Israelites, as their main enemy pressed in from all sides. The mighty Philistines awaited Samuel and the Israelites. Their presence is felt immediately in the opening verses of 1 Samuel 4.

1 SAMUEL 4

IN THE OPENING VERSES OF 1 Samuel 4, the Israelites are engaged in a battle with the Philistines. In addition, 1 Samuel 4:1 informs that "all of Israel" was now aware of Samuel. The timing of the two events is not a coincidence. As previously stated, Samuel's visitation and calling in 1 Samuel 3 was a rare occurrence in Israel. A prophet had not been seen in decades, thus any anointing or visitation by YHWH was sure to garner a lot of attention and inspire a lot of hope throughout all of Israel. High expectations would have been placed upon young Samuel.

Samuel's significance, however, was lost on the Philistines. They simply sought to annihilate Israel and take over the Israelite territory. The mighty Philistine Army had marched from their coastal strongholds into the mountains of Israel seeking a fight with the tiny nation.

THE PHILISTINES

Not much is known regarding Israel's primary threat during this period. Historically, these events took place during the Iron Age. At one point, some critics denied the Philistines had ever existed. Archaeology had yet to produce evidence confirming their existence. Time has changed that, and we now know they existed *precisely* as the Bible said they had, and *exactly* where the Bible said they had been.

The Philistines are believed by many scholars to have belonged to that mysterious group of people known as the Sea Peoples. These were an unknown and mysterious conglomeration of peoples most likely from the Aegean Sea region. One scholar claimed the Philistines "used the most advanced weapons and military equipment of their time." The Aegean Sea was home to ancient Greeks, Etruscans, Minoans, Mycenaeans, and Cycladic peoples, as well as others.

In brief, it is generally accepted that the Philistines may have developed from this group, participated in a failed invasion of Egypt, then settled along the western shores of Canaan. In a Roman attempt to humiliate and mock the Jews, Caesar renamed the whole land of Canaan "Palestine" after these Philistine warriors.

These people became the most feared enemy of ancient Israel. Goliath was a Philistine. The Philistines were known for their giant size and fierce ability in combat. Goliath was a giant, and it is commonly believed he was a giant even among his own people. This, however, may not necessarily be the case. Scripture states he was a "champion" among his own people (1 Samuel 17:4). These were a fierce and powerful people of great size, stature, strength, and ability. They were giant warriors and regularly oppressed the Israelites.

The Philistines created a miniature empire along the western shores of the region. The Philistine Pentapolis was made up of five cities, each ruled by a Philistine king. These cities were united militarily, governmentally, and culturally. The five cities of Gaza, Ashdod, Askelon, Ekron, and Gath made up this pentapolis, and together they dominated the lowlands. They would often push into the central mountains occupied by the Israelite clans and tribes, coming into conflict repeatedly with the disadvantaged Israelites.

The Philistines possessed iron and chariots, making them technologically more advanced than Israel. The advantage in size and weaponry made them even more powerful and threatening to Israel's security. Samuel found himself on the front line of this battle between God's people and the mighty Philistines.

APHEK

In 1 Samuel 4, the Philistine Army encamps at Aphek, and Israel encamps beside Ebenezer. Decades earlier, in Joshua 3:4 and 12:18, under Joshua's leadership, the Israelites had subdued the king of Aphek, then under Amorite rule. Like the Philistines, the Amorites were a giant people, as tall as oak trees in ancient depictions. Aphek would also come to be the site where Elisha told King Joash he would defeat the Arameans in 2 Kings 13:17.

In this particular instance, Aphek would come to represent a dire turning point for the Israelites against the Philistines. God would fulfill his prophecy concerning the fate of Eli and his sons as spoken of in 1 Samuel 2:34.

Exercise: Read 1 Samuel 4:2-4.

- What was the result of the battle at Aphek between Israel and the Philistines?
- What was the solution to the problem in the eyes of Israel?

Scripture makes no mention of the elders seeking or inquiring after God. It simply states they took the ark from Shiloh and marched it to the battlefield. The priests would have been the ones to order the ark moved. In 1 Samuel 4:17, Eli's sons, Hophni and Phineas, were the priests at the battle in Aphek. These two men, as we have already learned, were guilty of using their positions for selfish gain. God, through the mysterious "man of God," had already condemned Eli and his sons for their sin. It was likely these men did not seek the Lord, but rather sought to use his power manifested through the ark. In their minds, the ark of the covenant would be enough to propel them to victory over the Philistines.

Exercise: Read 1 Samuel 4:7-11.

- What was the result of the battle at Aphek with the ark present?
- How many men did Israel lose, according to Scripture? What else did they lose?

- What happened to Hophni and Phineas, the priests and sons of Eli?

- What did the Philistines say concerning the ark in verse 8?

- In your own opinion, why do you think the ark failed to bring Israel victory over the Philistines? Why were the results so disastrous?

The Philistines were clearly aware of the ark's power and that Israel's God was the one who "smote the Egyptians with all kinds of plagues" (1 Samuel 4:8). The power of God was clearly capable of destroying the Philistines completely and totally. The Philistines recognized such, yet rose up and defeated Israel regardless. Though Scripture is silent as to the exact reasons God would allow such to happen, one may presume the spiritual state of Israel had fallen once again into idolatry.

As recorded earlier, visions and messages from God were rare in those days, and the priests Hophni and Phineas were in clear violation of their duties. God was displeased with his people and exacted his punishment at Aphek by the mighty hands of the Philistines. His people had attempted to use him for their own selfish gain. They were not pure in their hearts and motives and sought the ark's presence simply for physical victory.

We may glean an important lesson from the battle of Aphek. Hophni and Phineas were no different than the many frauds we find today among the church. They had all the appearances of godliness. They brought the ark, the manifestation of God's power, to the front lines, and expected God to work his might. They likely spoke all the right words, performed all the right rituals, yet their actions were meaningless. No power was found in them. God's power was not found in the ark.

The object is not what made it powerful, nor was what was inside responsible for its power. Just because they brought forth the ark does not mean they brought forth God. God is to be found in the heart of man, and Phineas and Hophni had proven their hearts were only concerned with themselves. Religion without God is powerless. False religion is detestable in the sight of God.

Jesus spoke of such men in the New Testament when he addresses the scribes and Pharisees of his day. He called them "whitewashed tombs" in Matthew 23:27.

"Woe to you scribes and Pharisees, hypocrites! For you are like whitewashed tombs which on the outside appear beautiful but inside they are full of dead men's bones and all uncleanness."

Hophni and Eli were the Old Testament equivalent of these scribes and Pharisees, exploiting their position for personal gain. Thus, despite the ark's presence that day on the battlefield, God was not with Israel and "the slaughter was very great; for there fell of Israel thirty-thousand foot soldiers" (1 Samuel 4:10).

The actions of evil rulers have far-reaching consequences. The people under them perish and suffer. Those in positions of power have the added burden to wield their power for the benefit of others. Unfortunately, this is not the case in much of today's culture. Politicians lie for reelection. Despots wage civil wars to maintain power. Global "peace keeping" entities sit idly by while millions starve and die.

Israel, under the weak spiritual guidance of Eli and the corrupt influence of his sons, had not only been soundly defeated by the Philistine Army, but their most coveted possession, the ark of the covenant, had been captured and taken by the enemy. God, it seemed, had departed from Israel, abandoned his people who had previously turned on him. As God had predicted, Hophni and Phineas died in the battle.

Upon learning of their fate, Eli stumbled over backward on his stool, broke his neck, and died as well. Eli and his two sons, the spiritual "leaders" of Israel, were dead. Israel had suffered massive casualties in its defeat by the Philistines. The ark of the covenant—the symbol of Israel's relationship with God—had been looted by the enemy.

To the Israelites of this time, it must have seemed as if God had left them. They were leaderless, with a severely crippled army, at the mercy of fierce warriors and enemies, and without their God. Enter Samuel.

1 SAMUEL 7

FOR THE BACKGROUND LEADING UP to 1 Samuel 7, take the time to read chapters 5 and 6. These two chapters detail the travels of the ark through Philistine territory.

In the waning verses of 1 Samuel 6, the ark was sent back to Israel, to Beth-shemesh. Each Philistine city that housed the ark suffered plagues and curses sent from God Almighty. As a result, the ark was returned to Israel. From Beth-shemesh, it was moved to Kiriath-Jearim, a town of Israel since Joshua's campaign in Canaan (Joshua 9:17). The ark was to stay there until David's accession to the throne of Israel (1 Chronicles 13:5-6).

The Philistines were highly organized, militarily strong and efficient, and technologically superior to Israel. They ruled a unified network of five main cities, the Philistine Pentapolis, located along the coast. They were the first in Canaan to use iron weapons and tools. They had a significant and skilled chariot force. They were massive in size and strength. They constantly sought to expand into the hill country, thus bringing them into conflict with the Israelites.

The Israelites were pastoral. They were farmers and shepherds, and they raised cattle. The Bible declared at one point the Philistines had a monopoly on the blacksmiths, overcharging the Israelites for their services and preventing them from obtaining weapons. During one battle, Israel fought with pitchforks and shovels for the most part.

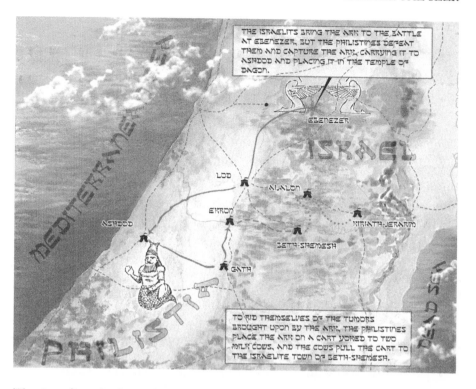

The Israelites had no chariot force, no organized network of cities, and certainly no professional standing army. They fought with whatever weapons they had managed to loot. Their main weapons included spears, knives, slingshots, and at times, shields. Most had no significant armor. They fought as tribes, loosely ruled by priests and/or Judges.

Ancient Israel faced desperate conditions during these perilous years. With the death of Eli, Israel was left leaderless. Its most sacred object had been taken by its most feared enemy. Upon the return of the ark, however, some hope was restored. Samuel used this opportunity to address the people. Despite the odds, Samuel knew where to turn for strength and deliverance.

Exercise: Turn and read 1 Samuel 7:3.

- What was the first thing Samuel mentioned the Israelites must do?
- What detestable practices had Israel fallen into? What did Samuel instruct them to do regarding these practices?

Samuel's message was simple and to the point: *God will deliver you.* Alone, the Israelites were sure to fall to the more powerful Philistines. Yet, their deliverance was waiting. Samuel, as the Judges before him and the prophets after him, spoke the message he was given by God. The nation of Israel as a whole had fallen into idolatrous practices. This is a repeated theme throughout the Old Testament.

Exercise: Read Judges 2:13-14.

- What was the state of Israel's heart in Judges 2:13–14?
- Describe what happened to the Israelites because of their actions.
- In your own words, relate this passage with the current text.

Canaanite influences and corruption had infiltrated Israel early in its development. Despite brief periods of righteousness, Samuel's speech indicated circumstances had regressed to a state of idolatry. Canaanite religion included sacred prostitution and, in some cases, human sacrifices. There have been discoveries of ancient jars with infants inside of them in what is believed to be proof of infant sacrifice. It was a polytheistic system of immorality, and it was detestable in the eyes of God.

BAAL

The Canaanite pantheon was a complex system of gods and deities. It likely finds its origins in the ancient cults of Sumeria. The ancient religions of Egypt and Mesopotamia dominated the region of Canaan. Baal was one of the major gods in the pantheon. He was the divine executive to El. El was the father of the gods and ruler of the divine assembly on the mountain of the gods. Whereas El was aloof, yet benevolent, Baal represented the royal power and authority.

Baal is depicted as a warrior-god, bearing a spear and mace. He was called prince, master, and rider of the clouds in the Ras Shamra texts.

He was also known as Baal Hadad, the storm god. In this capacity, he was the bringer of rain and fertility. The Phoenicians referred to him as Baal Shamen. The Old Testament indicated that Baal worship was mixed with the worship of the one true God, oftentimes represented by the term "Yahweh," the name of God. These mixed practices were what Samuel was referring to in his speech to the Israelites. Saul and Solomon both worshiped these foreign gods.

Many of the other kings of Israel and Judah instituted worship of foreign gods during their reign. They would construct high places of worship, or altars for these gods, on the hillsides. During the reigns of Ahab and Jezebel, the great prophet Elijah defeated, then slaughtered, one thousand priests of Baal and Ashtoreth.

ASHERAH

Asherah/Ashtaroth, mentioned in 1 Samuel 7:3 as Ashtaroth in the NASB or Ashtoreth in the NIV, was a marine goddess. She was El's counterpart and consort. She was the creator of creatures, the mother goddess. The Ras Shamra texts indicate she bore El seventy divine sons. There is yet another Asherah in the pantheon, a separate yet connected goddess. This Asherah is often seen as the tree of life, giving sustenance to the animals on either side of her. This goddess was often worshiped as queen of heaven. She was represented by a sacred wooden pole or pillar, symbolic of the tree of life. These poles were called Asherah, after her, and appeared frequently in the Old Testament. A third goddess, Anath, or Anat, was a goddess of war and love.

These three goddesses were frequently merged as one and worshiped as one—though technically they were three distinct goddesses. Such confusing names and similarities are common in many of the ancient religions and cosmologies. The Israelites merged these religions and traditions into their worship of Yahweh, as stated above.

Samuel, thus, faced difficulties on two fronts. The physical front faced imminent extermination at the hands of the mighty Philistines; and the spiritual front was confronted with apostasy and idolatry that had crept into Israelite society. Times were indeed desperate. A closer look at Samuel's message will reveal how God uses desperate times for his glory.

SAMUEL'S MESSAGE

1. Return to the Lord with All Your Heart
   The Israelites had only given God part of their hearts. How many of us are guilty of the same? Samuel said they must return with *all* of their hearts. This sentiment echoes the words of Jesus in Matthew 26:39. This is a fascinating glimpse into Jesus's mind-set immediately before his crucifixion. He prayed that the "cup pass from Me; yet not as I will, but as Thou wilt." Jesus had the will of the Father before all of his actions, thoughts, and words. He had given all of his heart to the Father, indeed their heart was one. Jesus exemplified selfless and complete service. That is what Samuel was calling for from Israel. Their idolatrous practices had no place with God.
   King Solomon would address Israel in similar fashion in 1 Kings 8:48. It was a continual call echoed throughout the Old Testament.

2. Remove the Foreign Gods and the Ashtaroth
   We may feel as if this is not relatable to us today. After all, society today does not worship multiple gods as the ancients did. Though many practices exist today, those are not in the mainstream. However, in America's culture today, Baal and Ashtaroth exist in the form of new cars, big homes, bigger salaries, fancy toys, expensive vacations, drugs, alcohol, sex, fame, and

popularity. Our gods are the same in spirit as the ancient ones—selfishness, greed, corruption, and immorality—though different in names.

Exercise: What are some of your Ashtaroths?

- o   What are some of the Ashtaroths and Baals set up by society?

3.   Samuel calls for the removal of anything that prevents total and complete submission and reliance on God. Our worship and love cannot be shared. God is looking for hearts totally dedicated to him. He is not looking for perfection, because he knows the flesh is corrupted. Jesus was the only one found perfect in the flesh. David, though an adulterer and murderer, was called a man after God's own heart.

Though far from perfect, David tried his best to be completely dedicated to God. Samuel is telling Israel that by removing the foreign gods, they will be taking the right steps toward complete dedication and reconciliation to God.

Exercise:

- o   Why was Samuel able to fully give himself to God in a time when the majority of Israel was mired in pagan religious practices? What was special about Samuel?

4.   Direct Your Hearts to the Lord and Serve Him
Within Canaanite society, immorality flourished. Scripture speaks of King Manasseh and his human sacrifices to the Canaanite deities. God's people would continually struggle to follow this simple directive. However, this time, the people seem to have answered Samuel's call. In 1 Samuel 7:4, the "sons of Israel removed the Baals and Ashtaroth." They turned from their idolatrous ways and "served the Lord alone."
Samuel was quick to turn to the Lord in prayer. He was unproven in roles of leadership. The elders and people had just rededicated themselves to the Lord by destroying their idols and

high places, enemies still lurked nearby, and Samuel knew he needed help. His trust in the Lord never wavered.

Exercise: Read 1 Samuel 7:5-6.

- o   Why did Samuel gather Israel together, and where did he gather them?
- o   What do you think Samuel prayed to God about on behalf of the people?
- o   How did the people of Israel respond to Samuel's urging?

5.   It is interesting that immediately after the confession of the Israelites for their sins, God brought forth a test to challenge their sincerity. Did they really believe in Samuel's promise of deliverance, or were they just paying lip service to God Almighty?

Exercise: Read 1 Samuel 7:7.

- o   How did God test the faith of the Israelites?

6.   Samuel's decision to pray for Israel's deliverance turned out to be their deliverance. The word translated as "prayer" is an interesting word in Hebrew. The Hebrew word is *palal*, pronounced *paw-lal*. It means "to judge, to decide, to punish, to act as a mediator, to pray." This word is found eighty-four times in the Old Testament.

It is commonly translated as "pray." Mostly, it reflects the idea of praying on behalf of others. *Palal* has a reciprocal meaning between its subject, the one praying, and the object, the one being prayed to. The word paints a beautiful picture of prayer where it is a two-way street of communication between God and man. We pray and entreat God through our prayers. He hears, thinks, deliberates, judges, then acts how he sees fit to act. Samuel exemplifies this type of relationship when he prays and intercedes on behalf of Israel as God's mouthpiece.

With the death and resurrection of Jesus, we have an intermediary with God today as well. He personally carries our prayers to the Father. Christ's death and resurrection allowed us to approach God the Father through prayer and entreat him directly and without need of assistance, save Jesus alone! We can talk to God. We can move people through faithful prayer, not because of who is doing the prayer but because of the recipient of the prayer, God Almighty. God shows his power in response to Samuel's prayer for Israel.

God tested their faith by sending the Philistine Army against Israel. When prayer is offered, God will test the one praying. We are to ask without doubt. Samuel prayed for deliverance, and God sent the Philistine Army! The greater the test, the greater his glory and honor, and the greater his power. Despite Samuel's prayer, the Israelites became afraid and urged Samuel to pray further for their deliverance.

Exercise:

- o In life, we all have our Philistines we face and fear. How can you give your Philistines to God? Use Samuel and Israel as a model.

- o In 1 Samuel 7:8, the Israelites cry to Samuel to pray further. How do you respond when faced with overwhelming problems, odds, and trials? Do you let fear paralyze you? Or, do you seek God with a sense of urgency?

- o List some examples of how God delivered you over the course of your life.

7.   When faced with seemingly impossible odds, Israel turned to God in earnest. The Israelites had to go through Samuel, their Judge and Prophet. Samuel's job included offering the sacrifices necessary to God Almighty on behalf of the people. Not only would he offer sacrifices, but he would take the requests of the people before God in earnest prayer. Now was a time when such actions were most necessary, in times of distress and threat. Notice the urgency with which Samuel approached God in

1 Samuel 7:9. Scripture says he "cried to the Lord for Israel."

Exercise: Read 1 Samuel 7:10-14.

- o   What was God's response to Samuel's prayer?

- o   How did God answer Samuel?

8.   God's response in 1 Samuel 7:10 was to "thunder with a great thunder" against the Philistine Army. His answer was over-whelming and majestic. Yet, what does Scripture mean when it says he "thundered with a great thunder"? How did God reach down and confuse (1 Samuel 7:10 NASB) the Philistines? Scripture has a number of passages associating God with thunder. In this instance, an alternative translation interprets the second "thunder" as "voice." Thus, it reads, "But the Lord thundered with a great voice."

God directly interceded on behalf of Israel by uttering some word or words from his heavenly throne upon the Philistine camp.

Exercise: Read the following passages that associate God and thunder:

1. "Those who contend with the Lord will be shattered; Against them He will thunder in the heavens" (1 Samuel 2:10).

2. "The voice of the Lord is upon the waters; The God of glory thunders, the Lord is over many waters. The voice of the Lord is powerful, the voice of the Lord is majestic" (Psalm 29:3-4).

3. "The Lord also thundered in the heavens, and the Most High uttered His voice, hailstones and coals of fire" (Psalm 18:13).

4. "At Thy rebuke they fled; at the sound of Thy thunder they hurried away" (Psalm 104:7).

5. From Elihu, Job's wisest friend: "Listen closely to the thunder of His voice, and the rumbling that goes out from His

mouth... After it, a voice roars; he thunders with his majestic voice; and he does not restrain the lightnings when his voice is heard. God thunders with his voice wondrously, doing great things which we cannot comprehend" (Job 4–5; 37:2).

9.   Thunder is associated with the voice and power of God. From 1 Samuel 7:10, it is clear he dealt wondrously with the Philistines. In response to Samuel's prayer, God's voice thundered down from heaven, and the Philistines were routed.

Interestingly, the word "thunder" from the passage in Job 37:2 translates from the Hebrew as "commotion, restlessness, crash, anger, fear, rage." It stems from the Hebrew *ragaz*, which means "to quiver with any violent emotion, be afraid, stand in awe."

We learn from this passage in 1 Samuel that God is not a distant and aloof figure. He is active, and the picture of him in 1 Samuel 7 is not one of an aged grandfather; rather, he is seen as a warrior-king. A force to be reckoned with and feared. The rage of God struck fear and awe in the Philistine camp. God's presence *is* all-powerful and not to be taken lightly. When we encounter God, we know it!

Whether one believes in God or not, our souls are shaken when we encounter God or have a divine experience. The believer hears the voice of God and recognizes his touch. The unbeliever may become confused or unsure of the experience, and perhaps misinterpret the message.

We see an example of this in Daniel 10:1-8.

Exercise: Read this passage and take notice of the reaction of the men with Daniel in Daniel 10:7.

- o   Why do you think they reacted as they did?
- o   What does this tell us about God?
- o   Does this picture of God conform to the picture of God taught in churches today? Why or why not?

1 SAMUEL 8

THE PHILISTINES HAD DEFEATED ISRAEL in a number of battles throughout the region. They were militarily superior to Israel and possessed a large chariot force, placing Israel at a decided disadvantage. As a result, the Israelites primarily dwelt in the mountainous regions, where the chariots were less effective, while the Philistines occupied the coastal plain, ideal terrain for chariot warfare. Even though God had delivered Israel in the previous engagement of 1 Samuel 7, the Philistine threat was still imminent and dangerous. Israel was under constant alarm and threat.

The Israelites felt they needed a king to oversee and protect them, just as the Philistines and the other nations surrounding them. In 1 Samuel 8–9, Israel pleads for a king. This led to a new era in Israelite history, that of the United Monarchy. During the United Monarchy, Israel was united as one nation, under one king. This period would last for approximately one hundred years.

However, their desire for an earthly king went against God's desire to be their heavenly king. Nevertheless, he granted them this request through the leadership of Samuel. God's desire for his people is seen in Exodus 19:5-6.

"Now then, if you will indeed obey My voice and keep My covenant, then you shall be My own possession among all the peoples, for all the earth is Mine; and you shall be to Me a kingdom of priests and a holy nation. These are the words you shall speak to the sons of Israel."

These were Moses's words to Israel at Mount Sinai upon leaving Egypt. Again, in Deuteronomy 4:39-45, God expressed through Moses his desire to lead and father the Israelites as their king. God had intended for his people to be led by him alone. How did Israel respond to Moses's words? In Exodus 32, the Israelites made the golden calf and worshiped it instead. They forsook the God that had delivered them out of Egypt, out of Pharaoh's grasp and slavery, and bowed to the very gods that had enslaved them. Similar disobedience is seen here in 1 Samuel 8:4-6 when the Israelites sought a human king to lord power over them. Listen to the plea of Israel's elders in 1 Samuel 8:4-5.

"Then all the elders of Israel gathered together and came to Samuel at Ramah; and they said to him, 'Behold, you have grown old, and your sons do not walk in your ways. Now appoint a king for us to judge us like all the nations."

Exercise:

- Where is your faith? Just as the Israelites chose a man over God, so we too often put stock in men and things. Why do we reject the grace and love of God?

Read these words of Jesus in Matthew 6:24.

- Whom do you serve? What do you serve?
- Are you a slave to schedules, appointments, and meetings?
- Is it more important to "keep up with the Joneses" by buying the newest and latest things than to give to those in need?

Why do we choose the stresses and demands of gain over the mercy and love of God? We must be ever watchful of what we pursue and how we pursue it. The Israelites sought security and protection from their Philistine enemies. This, in itself, is not evil but a natural need. However, the Israelites put their faith not in God, but in man. This would prove to be a fatal mistake.

Samuel's response in verse 6 was to pray to God. He understands they have rejected God as their king, and he seeks wisdom as to how to respond to his compatriots.

Exercise: Read 1 Samuel 8:7.

• What was God's answer to Samuel's prayer?

Search Scripture for a verse that promises God's faithfulness and deliverance, and set your mind and heart to live by it. The commands given to the Israelites through Moses, passed down from generation to generation, had been disobeyed by Israel. The Israelites sought to be like everybody else. They sought that which was popular, not that which God had instructed of them. This is an example of an age-old problem. Oftentimes, seeking God's will may not be the popular thing to do. In fact, God's word is adamant that to live a godly life is to be in conflict with what this world tells us.

Exercise:

• Name a time you sought something because it was the popular thing to do.

• Was it also a godly and righteous thing to do?

• If not, then why did you do it?

Samuel warned Israel of what a king would do to them and require of them in 1 Samuel 8:10–19. Nevertheless, the people wished to be subject to the demands of a man and the system of government he would establish. The yoke of a king would be burdensome on his subjects. The people would personally suffer at his expense. This moment was one of the most critical moments in all of the Old Testament. Israel officially chose man over God, and this would echo throughout the ages.

Moses warned Israel of such an action centuries prior to Samuel, in Deuteronomy 28:48.

In 1 Kings 12:4 are the words of the northern tribes to King Rehoboam. Rehoboam was the son of Solomon, the son of David, the second king of Israel after Saul.

"Your father [Solomon] made our yoke hard; now therefore lighten the hard service of your father and his heavy yoke which he put on us, and we will serve you."

King Rehoboam foolishly refused to listen to these words.

The result of this particular passage was the splitting of Israel into two kingdoms, Israel in the north, and Judah in the south. Solomon had burdened the northern tribes with the brunt of the forced labor and high taxes to finance his building projects, including the first temple. The load for the southern tribes had been significantly less than that of the northern tribes. This caused a civil war, which in turn caused the schism into two kingdoms. The words of Samuel in 1 Samuel 8:10-22, and those of Moses in Deuteronomy 28, were coming to fruition.

In Isaiah 10:24 and 27, Isaiah prophesied during the Divided Monarchy, in the eighth century B.C.

"Therefore, thus says the Lord God of hosts, 'O My people who dwell in Zion, do not fear the Assyrian who strikes you with the rod and lifts up his staff against you, the way Egypt did... So it will be in that day, that the Assyrian burden will be removed from your shoulders and his yoke from your neck, and the yoke will be broken."

The northern kingdom of Israel was conquered and exiled by the Assyrian war machine in 722 B.C. Isaiah speaks of this yoke. Northern Israel was totally destroyed, and only Judah in the south remained. The northern tribes came to be known as the lost tribes of Israel.

In Jeremiah 28:14, nearly two hundred years later in 586 B.C., the Babylonians under Nebuchadnezzar would lay siege to Jerusalem. The Babylonians would burn the temple, looting its treasures, carrying the people off to Babylon in exile, and burning the city. Thus, Judah, too, was no more, and the nation of Israel was no longer a state or country.

"For thus says the Lord of hosts, the God of Israel, 'I have put a yoke of iron on the neck of all these nations, that they may serve Nebuchadnezzar king of Babylon; and they shall serve him. And I have also given him the beasts of the field.'"

What we see in these passages is the fulfillment of God's words through Moses. God's discipline played out over hundreds of years, when the full weight of Israel's ill-fated decision to seek an earthly king fully manifested itself. The kings of Israel, for the most part, sought their will, not God's. Consequently, first Israel and then Judah were given over to the conquering armies of Assyria and Babylon. The demands of kingship first split the nation in two, then ultimately doomed her. Their refusal to heed Moses, then Samuel, led to God's punishment.

Exercise: *Turn and read Matthew 11:29-30.*

- Which yoke would you rather bear: The yoke of society placed on us through the demands of gain, prosper, bigger and better, achieve, acquire? Or, the yoke of Christ?
- What does the yoke of Christ consists of?
- Why do we choose willful enslavement?

Forming the basis for Christ's words in Matthew 11, Jeremiah reads as follows:

"Thus says the Lord, 'Stand by the ways and see and ask for the ancient paths, where the good way is, and walk in it; And you shall find rest for your souls.' But they said, 'We will not walk in it.'"

Unfortunately, we oftentimes refuse to walk in it as well.

The second part of 1 Samuel 8:7 confirms this. God tells Samuel, "For they have not rejected you, but they have rejected Me from being King over them."

This passage resonates throughout the rest of the Bible. God demonstrates through his people the consequences of disobedience and the blessings of obedience. However, the wayward choices Israel repeatedly made were not wasted; he exhibits his patient love and grace through his continual forgiveness and mercy. It is along these ancient paths

(Jeremiah 6:16) of the Old Testament we see the good way leading to Jesus, and the full redemption and salvation of all who walk them.

1 SAMUEL 9

THE SELECTION OF SAUL AS the first king of Israel seems, at first, an unlikely choice. Physically, however, he had that presidential look. In 1 Samuel 9:2, Saul is said to be a head and shoulders taller than everybody else in Israel. He was "a choice and handsome man," kingly looking by all physical standards. Saul was tall and impressive, presidential, definitely an imposing figure and easily recognizable in a crowd. He had all the appearances of a great king.

THE JOURNEY

Saul and a family servant set out to find his father's lost donkeys. They set out south from Saul's home, through the hill country of Ephraim. After a thorough search, the servant advises Saul that they seek out Samuel, "a man of God." Saul's servant says, "Perhaps he can tell us about our journey."

Oftentimes, what we think our journey is about, or where we think our destination is, does not work out like we had planned. This is the case many times with God. Saul is searching for lost donkeys. His goal is to find them; thus, he is hoping his journey ends with the lost donkeys in hand. The last thing on his mind would have been becoming king of Israel! In reality, Saul had no clue as to where his journey would go. In Mark 6:8, Jesus instructed his disciples to take nothing with them on their journey. In this instance, Saul fully expected to be home by dark, thus he had no provisions.

In the desert, with Moses, the Israelites had no compass, no GPS, no map. The provisions they had were short-lived, as they quickly ran out of water and food. However, Exodus 40:38 states, "For throughout all their journeys, the cloud of the Lord was on the Tabernacle by day, and there was fire in it by night in the sight of all the house of Israel."

Just as God led the Israelites through the wilderness in these ancient days, so he leads you on your journey today. Our cloud and our fire is found in the Holy Spirit of God. It is the Spirit, our Counselor as called by Christ, who guides us, instructs us, and watches out for us. Often-times, we simply need to be still and listen to God. He promises this to us in a number of verses, both in the Old and New Testaments.

Exercise: Turn and read Psalms 40:2.

- Where was the author of this Psalm when the Lord "brought" him out? Of what is this symbolic?
- Where does God place our feet, according to this verse? What is the meaning of this phrase?

Exercise: Turn and read Jeremiah 29:11.

- What does God promise us in this remarkable verse?
- Restate this verse in your own words.

We must submit to the journey, and God's leadership in it, just as Saul did in 1 Samuel 9. Saul and his servant traveled to the city of Samuel's location. As they enter the city, Samuel is preparing to offer sacrifices to God on behalf of the city. Verse 15 paves the way for Samuel and Saul to meet.

"Now a day before Saul's coming, the Lord had revealed thus to Samuel saying, 'About this time tomorrow I will send you a man from the land of Benjamin, and you shall anoint him to be prince over My people Israel'" (1 Samuel 9:15-16).

We also learn in this verse that God reveals things to us as we need it. He knew Saul would be coming, and Saul was his choice to be king. Thus, God instructs his servant Samuel as to how it will happen. God gives us revelations and words when we need them, not necessarily when we want them. He has the big picture in mind; we only have a very small fraction of it. This is echoed in the New Testament.

Exercise: Read the words found in 1 Corinthians 13:12.

Saul was looking for donkeys. He had no idea what was about to happen. Saul's only concern was with his lost family donkeys—not the daily affairs of the nation of Israel. Saul becoming King was likely the very last thing on his mind—in fact, it had probably never even occurred to Saul because of the tribe he was from. Donkeys were far more important to him.

His servant's idea to stop in and ask the man of God, Samuel, seemed like a good idea. In Saul's mind, they had nothing to lose. He was oblivious to what awaited. We must keep in mind that God appoints and directs everything in this world. Listen to the words of Daniel speaking to King Belshazzar in Daniel 5:18.

"O king, the Most High God granted sovereignty, grandeur, glory and majesty to Nebuchadnezzar your father."

God did not just direct Israel's path, but also the nations surrounding her, just as he continues to do today. The same holds true for your life.

Looking back, think of a time when now you can clearly see the hand of God directing your life, whereas at the time perhaps you could not see God's hand working. Perhaps you didn't understand why things were happening as they were—only to look back now for that past situation to make perfect sense. That is God.

Exercise: Read Psalms 103:19.

In 1 Samuel 9:20, Samuel spoke words to Saul that indicated wealth, power, and esteem.

"And as for your donkeys which were lost three days ago, do not set your mind on them, for they have been found. And for whom is all that is desirable in Israel? Is it not for you and for all your father's household?" (1 Samuel 9:20).

In other words, Samuel says why be bothered with donkeys, Saul, when you're the king of Israel and can have whatever you want? Samuel was indicating to Saul that all of Israel's resources as a nation were at his disposal. This obviously made no sense to Saul. It is interesting to note Saul's reaction. At this stage in his life, Saul was cloaked in humility. His response was one of a humble man, not thinking himself worthy of such a position.

Exercise: Read 1 Samuel 9:21.

- What tribe did Saul belong to?
- What is the implied status of this tribe in relation to the other tribes of Israel?
- Where did Saul's family stand within their tribe?
- What was Saul's reaction to Samuel's words?

Saul did not believe the Seer's words! His question reveals his attitude.

"Why then do you speak to me in this way?"

- Did you ever shrink from something because you didn't feel worthy?
- Why didn't you feel worthy, or capable, or deserving of the task?

In Judges 20, we learn why Saul's tribe was looked down upon. The Bible depicts one of many unflattering episodes in Israel's history. A civil war breaks out between the tribe of Benjamin—Saul's tribe—and the remaining eleven tribes of Israel. The resulting civil war leaves Benjamin with only six hundred men. The tribe, in effect, was on the verge of extinction. With only six hundred men and no women, there was no way to further the tribe after the present generation.

49

Obviously, a solution was reached; however, the tribe of Benjamin was still suffering from this episode during the time of Saul. It remained the smallest tribe in Israel. The rest of Israel marginalized the tribe and deemed it insignificant. It seemed Saul had an inferiority complex because of it. When we feel as Saul did, it is best to keep in mind the words of Paul found in 2 Corinthians 12:9.

Exercise: Read these words and jot down how they can help you overcome times you feel inadequate or unworthy.

- Name one specific area of your life you can apply these words to.

Despite Saul's reluctance to take Samuel at his word, Samuel placed Saul at the head of the table at the city's feast, in front of the city elders and leaders. This feast came after Samuel offered the sacrifice on behalf of the town (1 Samuel 9:12), and the Bible tells us in 1 Samuel 9:22 there were about thirty men present. These men would have been the leaders and officials of the town. They would have been surprised to look up and see a big, strapping young man sitting at the head of the table with Samuel the Seer. One can imagine these elders looking around at one another in a puzzled state, frantically trying to figure out who this young man was, and a bit intimidated, likely, by Saul's huge size.

Saul, too, would have been wondering what he was doing at the head of the table. One can imagine Saul, as most young men around older strangers, feeling awkward, embarrassed, keeping his gaze down, feeling very inadequate and out of place. The event has the feeling of solemn awkwardness. Only Samuel and God knew the details. So it is with the mind of God.

Exercise: Read Isaiah 55:8–9; Micah 4:12; 1 Corinthians 2:11.

- What are these verses saying about man's relationship with God?

Samuel possessed the Spirit of God, which enabled him to hear the words of God and commune openly with God. This was reserved solely for the prophets in the Old Testament. From the moment Samuel answered the call of God, even though he didn't recognize the voice (1 Samuel 3:1-10), he was a faithful and powerful prophet. He founded a school of prophets, evident in a number of passages throughout the Bible (1 Samuel 10:10; 1 Samuel 19:20; 2 Kings 2:3, 5, 15). Samuel would mentor and bring Saul along according to the Word of the Lord. Spiritual mentors are vital to the growth and development of our relationship with God.

Exercise:

- Who is your spiritual mentor?

If you do not have one, think of the people you know, and perhaps you will discover a good candidate. If you cannot think of a person, perhaps you should find a church, group, author (dead or alive), or simply pray to God to bring a person into your life. The Bible is an excellent mentor, when coupled with diligent effort and prayer.

Perhaps God is calling you to be a mentor to another. We must initiate the search for Christian friends and support. Take the initiative. Reach out. Spiritual mentors and teachers help guide us along the way. One can envision the scene as it unfolds in 1 Samuel 9:27.

The strange old man grabs the strapping young lad by the shoulder, looking him square in the eyes with an intensity and purpose that made Saul squirm.

Samuel then begins to speak, "Say to the servant that he might go ahead of us and pass on, but you remain standing now, that I may proclaim the word of God to you." (NASB)

Sit quietly now and listen to what the Word of God says to you. You never know when the search for donkeys will lead to the discovery of kingship. Oftentimes, we simply need to be still and listen.

1 SAMUEL 10

AS 1 SAMUEL 10 OPENS, Samuel pulls Saul aside while sending the servant on ahead. The tribe of Benjamin—the smallest, least wealthy, and most insignificant of the twelve tribes—was about to take the reins of Israel. Samuel instructs Saul to listen to the words of God. The last two days must have left Saul uncomfortable and uncertain. He felt he wasn't up to the task, and he was afraid.

At this point in the narrative, Saul seems to be the gentle-giant type of person. He possessed a very lowly view of himself, his father's house, and his tribe. Though he was physically superior to those around him, he lacked confidence and was a bit insecure about his personal identity and that of his tribe. Not only had the tribe of Benjamin suffered severely from a civil war, but Saul's father's house was the least of the families within the smallest and least of the twelve tribes of Israel. In this aspect, the choice of Saul as king seems highly unlikely. He was from the least of the least. He was of such insignificance the very thought of becoming king would have been fantastical daydreaming. In fact, it is quite probable the thought itself never even crossed Saul's mind!

However, Samuel quickly made it clear God had chosen him.

Exercise: Read 1 Samuel 10:1.

- What symbolic act did Samuel perform on Saul?

- What word did Samuel use to indicate Saul had been chosen by God?

- Whose kingdom was it that Saul was placed in charge of?

The word "anointed" is a powerful word in this passage. God had not only chosen Saul, but had anointed him as king. By implication, the word meant to consecrate. It is used over 140 times in the Old Testament, yet not every time refers to the act of consecration. The word and act played an important part in Jewish ceremony. It was a formal way of inducting leaders into office, much like coronation, especially when referring to kings. In the United States, the president puts his hand on the Bible as he is sworn in. This was the same type of act as anointing with oil in Bronze Age Israel.

Exodus 29:7 and Numbers 35:25 state how the High Priest and other priests were anointed. Both 1 Kings 19:16 and Isaiah 61:1 make mention of prophets being anointed. This act signified the anointed individual was separated for God's service, by God himself. He was chosen by God, and the Spirit of God would accompany the anointed throughout his life. Only God could sanction one to be anointed.

After Samuel anoints Saul, he instructs him on future events that would take place that day. In 1 Samuel 10:6, Samuel tells Saul the following:

"Then the Spirit of the Lord will come upon you mightily, and you shall prophesy with them and be changed into another man."

THE MESSAGE

The Spirit of God transforms!

Exercise: Read the following passages taking note of the Spirit's presence in each.

1. "Then the Lord came down in the cloud and spoke to him [Moses]; and He took of the Spirit who was upon him and placed Him upon seventy elders. And it came about that when the Spirit rested upon them, they prophesied. But they did not do it again" (Numbers 11:25).

2. "But Moses said to him, 'Are you jealous for my sake? Would that all the Lord's people were prophets, that the Lord would put His Spirit upon them'" (Numbers 11:29).

3. "And the Spirit of the Lord came upon him, and he judged Israel. When he went out to war, the Lord gave Cushan-rishathaim king of Mesopotamia into his hand, so that he prevailed over Cushan-rishathaim" (Judges 3:10).

4. "So the Spirit of the Lord came upon Gideon; and he blew a trumpet, and the Abiezrites were called together to follow him" (Judges 6:34).

5. "And the Spirit of the Lord came upon him [Samson] mightily, so that he tore him as one tears a kid though he had nothing in his hand; but he did not tell his father or mother what he had done" (Judges 14:6).

   o What is the common denominator in each passage?
   o What do you gather about the nature of God through these passages?

Samuel was imparting God's Spirit to Saul, per God's instruction, by the anointing of oil. This Spirit would change Saul from an insecure man to a bold and fearless leader of men. Notice 1 Samuel 10:7, "And it shall be when these signs come to you, do for yourself what the occasion requires, for God is with you."

When we have God as our focus, we are free to act because he guides our steps. We are free to be bold because he gives us strength and courage. This is what Samuel meant when he said, "do for yourself what the occasion requires." Why did he give Saul such freedom of choice? Because "God is with you." When God is with us, and we have given him control, our steps are his steps. Saul departs from the old prophet in 1 Samuel 10:9.

Exercise: Read 1 Samuel 10:10.

- What happened to Saul?
- What did Saul do in response?
- According to 1 Samuel 10:11, who witnessed this event?

What is this "Spirit" that repeatedly descended upon his people in the Old Testament? Jesus left us with a Counselor, being the Holy Spirit of God, upon his ascension. Is this the same Spirit talked of in the Old Testament? Let us take a closer look at this word and its usages throughout the Bible.

SPIRIT

The Hebrew word used here is *ruwach*. It literally means "wind, breath, a sensible or even violent exhalation." Figuratively, it indicates life. By extension, the word signifies a region of the sky, or the spirit of only a rational being. It is translated variously throughout the Bible as "air," "anger," "blast," "breath," "tempest," or "whirlwind."

Ruwach stems from a primitive root meaning "to blow, to breathe." This word occurs 387 times in the Old Testament. The basic and general meaning is air in motion.

Exercise:

Read the following passages in which the word is used and underline the word you believe to have been translated from *ruwach*:

1. "And at the blast of Thy nostrils the waters were piled up, the flowing waters stood up like a heap; the deeps were congealed in the heart of the sea" (Exodus 15:8).

   In this instance, the word translated "blast" is also *ruwach*.

2. "And they heard the sound of the Lord God walking in the garden in the cool of the day, and the man and his wife hid themselves from the presence of the Lord God among the trees of the garden" (Genesis 3:8).

   In this verse, the word translated "cool" is also *ruwach*. In some manuscripts, "cool" is also translated as "wind," both taken from the Hebrew word *ruwach*.

3. "And behold, I, even I am bringing the flood of water upon the earth, to destroy all flesh in which the breath of life, from under heaven; everything that is on the earth shall perish" (Genesis 5:17).

   Here, the word "breath" is also *ruwach*, the vital spirit of life.

4. "Restore to me the joy of Thy salvation. And sustain me with a willing spirit" (Psalms 51:12).

   In this instance, "spirit" is also *ruwach*. David speaks of *ruwach* as the sustaining spirit of God, similar to the prophet Isaiah below.

5. "But they rebelled and grieved His Holy Spirit; Therefore He turned Himself to become their enemy. He fought against them. Then His people remembered the days of old, of Moses. Where is He who brought them up out of the sea with the shepherds of His flock? Where is He who put His Holy Spirit in the midst of them?" (Isaiah 63:10–11).

   Here, *ruwach* is God himself. He is a presence, a power. In the days of Isaiah, he was hard to find.

In 1 Samuel 10:6, 10, it is *ruwach* that empowered Saul to prophecy and changed his heart. We will encounter this *ruwach* many times in 1 Samuel. The Spirit of God was mightily at work within Israel during these ancient times. We will see him working constantly throughout the lives of Samuel, Saul, and David.

As Saul turns to leave Samuel in verse 9, the Bible says, "God changed his heart." Saul is empowered by God, and in verse 1 Samuel 10:10, he prophesies with the prophets. The power of the Spirit is such that when people encounter God's Spirit they are changed. The next day they may go back to their old ways, but they know deep down something is different.

Exercise: Read 1 Samuel 10:17-27.

- Think of a time when you encountered God. Has it permanently changed you? Or, was it only temporary?

- Is he tugging on your soul right now?

Saul was publicly chosen as king before all of Israel at Mizpah. Saul was named king in the first place because the people had complained to Samuel that they, like all of the other nations surrounding them, needed a king. By so doing, the Israelites rejected God as their King. Though Saul had boldly prophesied with the prophets in the previous verses, and Scripture indicates he had been changed by God's Spirit, Saul did not hold fast to his boldness of Spirit. We see his fear of being king creep in at Mizpah.

Exercise: Back up two verses and read 1 Samuel 10:15-16.

- Why do you think Saul chose not to tell his uncle what Samuel said? Does this show a lack of faith, in your opinion?

Read Saul's statement in 1 Samuel 9:21.

- Do you think, based on these two verses, Saul really believed he would become king of Israel?

- Is it hard for you to *really believe* God wants something good for you?

Perhaps Saul didn't really believe it, and who could blame him? Samuel's anointing seemed ridiculous to Saul. However, in 1 Samuel 10:17, Samuel has gathered all of Israel together in Mizpah to announce Saul's anointing. Reality was quickly setting in for young Saul. He really was the first king of Israel.

"Therefore Samuel called the people together to the Lord at Mizpah."

Mizpah in Judah was the ancient assembly place of Israel, pre-Jerusalem. When important matters were discussed and important decisions made regarding Israel, the people gathered at Mizpah. There were three cities designated as Mizpah in the Bible. One was located east of the Jordan, one was located in the plain of Judah, and one was located within the tribe of Benjamin. It was at the Mizpah within the tribal allotment of Judah that Samuel gathered all of Israel together in this verse.

In Judges 20:1, "all the sons of Israel" gathered in Mizpah to decide the fate of the tribe of Benjamin, Saul's tribe. The outcome of that assembly was near annihilation of all of the Benjamites. The people, thus, knew when an assembly was gathered in Mizpah important decisions were to be made. Little did they know, however, that the tribe of Benjamin would be at the center of this meeting as well. In 1 Samuel 10:18-19, Samuel addressed Israel according to the Word of the Lord.

"And he said to the sons of Israel, 'Thus says the Lord, the god of Israel; I brought Israel up from Egypt, and I delivered you from the hand of the Egyptians, and from the power of all the kingdoms that were oppressing you. But you, today, rejected your God, who delivers you from all your calamities and your distresses; yet you have said; No, but set a king over us!' Now, therefore, present yourselves before the Lord by your tribes and by your clans."

Exercise: Read Judges 6:8–10 and 1 Samuel 8:6–7.

- What do these passages tell you about God's nature?
- What do these passages reveal about the nation of Israel?
- Were they consistent in their obedience to God?
- Now apply these two passages to yourself and your life. How are you alike and/or different from these ancient Israelites?

Samuel then brings each tribe before the assembly, and each tribe is brought clan by clan within that tribe. The people knew a king would be selected, and they likely expected that king to be from the tribe of Judah, or one of the more prominent tribes. The expectation of Judah stems from the blessing Jacob gave his son, Judah, in Genesis 49. Most Israelites would have been readily familiar with this passage.

Exercise: Turn and read Genesis 49:10.

- How would you interpret this blessing by Jacob to his son Judah?

The anticipation of Judah would have been in accordance with the Word of God. However, as 1 Samuel 10:20 indicates, this was not to be the case. Instead, the least likely of all the tribes was selected. It often seems God chooses to operate in this manner, thus we need to always have an open mind, even when things don't look or feel as we think they should. The tribe of Benjamin was not too far removed from annihilation during the time of the Judges. Their selection by Samuel would have sent ripples of disbelief throughout the crowd. Leaders from the tribe of Judah would have likely been upset. Questions would have abounded as to what Samuel was up to.

Exercise: Turn and read 1 Samuel 10:21.

- What strange incident is recorded in this verse? Who does it involve?

Saul and Samuel were the only two individuals who knew God's selection for Israel's first king. Saul had already expressed doubt to Samuel and hid the news from his family. Now it comes about he is hiding from Samuel during his own coronation ceremony! Perhaps Saul had doubted the reality of Samuel's word up until the tribe of Benjamin was selected.

Scripture does not give details as to when he hid, or why. It would seem the reality finally hit home with Saul, and it was too much for him to bear, thus he hid himself in hopes another would be selected. This, of course, is just a theory, because Scripture is silent as to why Saul hid among the baggage. The context of the situation would seem to imply he was afraid of being king.

It is plainly evident that Saul was still battling the task of being king. Despite God's Spirit empowering him two verses earlier to prophesy with the prophets, Saul still possessed doubt and fear. Now, he hid like a child. The message is clear; we must strive daily to live in faith. Saul failed to exhibit that faith, and he hid from his calling. It was a dubious beginning to his reign.

One can imagine the spectacle as it plays out in 1 Samuel 10:22-23. Saul was found hiding himself among the baggage!

God's response in verse 1 Samuel 10:23 possesses a hint of exasperation. God plainly states, most likely to Samuel, "Behold, he is hiding himself by the baggage." Thus the people "ran and took him from there" and placed him at the head of the assembly. The entire scene is ridiculous. God and Samuel probably looked on in dismay as the people lifted up their choice for a king—a coward hiding among the bags! All the while, the Creator of the universe desired to be their King.

Exercise: Read 1 Samuel 10:23.

- How is Saul described in this verse?
- Does his appearance seem to fit with his behavior in 1 Samuel 10:22?
- What are your impressions of Saul based on these verses?

Interestingly, the people seemed to overlook this somewhat embarrassing episode. Samuel seemed to be reinforcing the choice as he stressed Saul's stature and physical appearance to the people. Their response in 1 Samuel 10:24 was to shout, "Long live the king!" It was as if Saul never hid himself from being king. The people refused to see the flaw in Saul's behavior. God had seemingly taught them a lesson about appearance, yet they ignored it and celebrated the choice of Saul as king. Saul's appearance weighed more with the people than his actions.

- Would you want a president who hid himself among the baggage at his own coronation ceremony?

One may not want the task that God has called him or her to. Yet, it is an exercise of faith and obedience to accept that task and fulfill it to the best of one's ability. Centuries later, Jonah would shrink from his assignment and attempt to hide from God.

Exercise: Read Jonah 1:1-3.

Most are familiar with what happened to Jonah. Saul's reluctance to be king was noble to an extent, but his actions indicated a lack of faith that would manifest itself during his reign. The people, though, looked at his outward appearance and stopped there. God teaches his people a lesson in appearances throughout all of 1 Samuel, starting with the selection of Saul as king.

Read carefully the following verses:

1. "But the Lord said to Samuel, 'Do not look at his appearance or at the height of his stature, because I have rejected him; for God sees not as a man sees, for man looks at the outward appearance, but the Lord looks at the heart'" (1 Samuel 16:7).

2. "Do not judge according to appearance, but judge with righteous judgment" (John 7:24).

3. "We are not again commending ourselves to you but are giving you an occasion to be proud of us, that you may have an answer for those who take pride in appearance, but not in heart" (2 Corinthians 5:12).

- Do you think society has changed in this regard from when these words were written?

- What do you think of a leader when he or she appears on TV confident, sharply dressed, and speaking with grace and eloquence?

- Why is it we pay so much attention to what the rich and famous have to say or think?

- What are your initial thoughts when you pass by a homeless person, or a person of lower socioeconomic status?

We should not shrink from people, nor should we put instant faith in people, because of their appearance, credentials, bank account, or title. The sons of Eli the old priest had the appearance of holy men; they were descended from Aaron, the brother of Moses; they were sons of the high priest Eli; and they were caretakers of God's House in Shiloh. They had priestly bloodlines and were raised according to the duties and obligations of priests. However, they were corrupt and wicked.

Samuel, on the other hand, was the product of a barren woman, a commoner in Israel. Hannah possessed no significant title or position that we are aware. A thankful and faithful woman had given Samuel to God. He was given out of an act of faith and love. Samuel possessed no sacred lineage or priestly bloodline. He was, simply put, a faithful and obedient servant. God seeks hearts! Saul's impressive appearance hid a stubborn heart.

"For the eyes of the Lord move to and fro throughout the earth that He may strongly support those whose heart is completely His" (2 Chronicles 16:9).

"Where is the wise man? Where is the scribe? Where is the debater of this age? Has not God made foolish the wisdom of the world?" (1 Corinthians 1:20).

Exercise:

- Why would Saul hide?
- Is it a sign of a lack of faith? A character flaw?
- Did Saul not want the job to begin with, or was he just scared?
- Is the fact that the first king of Israel was from the tribe of Benjamin a coincidence given the tribe's past (see Judges 20)?
- What do you think Samuel thought about God's choice?

- If you had been an ancient Israelite in Mizpah on that day, what would you have thought about Saul's selection? About Samuel, the man anointing Saul?

- Do you think any political jealousies began to form because of the selection?

1 SAMUEL 11

IN ANTIQUITY, LEADERS GENERALLY HAD to prove themselves worthy of their position through battle. Empires rose through conquest and expansion. Glory by bloodshed. Conquering nations looted and exploited their foes, enlarging the royal treasuries and bringing fame to their names and their homelands. A leader who proved successful in combat solidified his hold on the kingdom. To fail in such exploits showed weakness. Weakness invited rebellion. Rebel leaders, and those in opposition to the authorities, sought such opportunities to overthrow the king and set themselves in positions of authority.

Though Samuel selected Saul, some did not agree with the selection. God's people were not above such political intrigues and rebellions. This is made plain in 1 Samuel 10:27:

"But certain worthless men said; 'How can this one deliver us?' And they despised him and did not bring him any present. But he [Saul] kept silent."

Though Scripture does not indicate who these men were, it would seem possible at the very least that some of them came from the tribe of Judah or those men loyal to the tribe of Judah. As previously noted, Genesis 49:10 indicated that Judah was to be the royal tribe, the leader of Israel.

The fact Saul came from the tribe of Benjamin was problematic to many. The situation could be likened to a president of the United States being elected from the Libertarian Party, or as an Independent. The establishment, like the other eleven tribes of Israel, deems these parties in the United States today insignificant, just as the tribe of Benjamin was. Thus, leadership arising from these ranks is highly unlikely and not seriously considered. If it does happen, it upsets and threatens many people.

These men questioned how one from the least of all the tribes of Israel could be king and effectively lead the people. Saul needed something to get the people behind him. He needed a chance to prove his worthiness as king. He needed a crisis to galvanize the country behind him. God would provide that opportunity in 1 Samuel 11.

THE AMMONITES

The Ammonites were common enemies of Israel in the Old Testament. They primarily dwelt on the eastern border of the Transjordan, the land which lies east of the Jordan River. Their capital was Rabbath-ammon. The ruins of Rabbath-ammon are in modern day Amman, Jordan. Rabbath-ammon was the ancient capital of the Ammonites, just as Amman is the capital of Jordan today.

The Ammonites were a mostly nomadic people. They lasted for many centuries and possessed an extensive and connected history with Israel. Their territory consisted of steep ravines and wilderness. They were hemmed in to the south and east by the tribes of Gad and Reuben, and to the west and north by desert wilderness. Their only hope of expansion lay in conquering the tribes of Gad and Reuben. Barren wilderness was in the other direction for hundreds of miles. Conflict, thus, was inevitable.

During the reign of King David, Uriah the Hittite died in battle near Rabbath-ammon, opening the door for David's marriage to Bathsheba. In Roman times, Amman stood as an outpost fending off desert invaders, mostly from the powerful Arabian tribes of the desert regions. In the opening verse of 1 Samuel 11, the Ammonites march from their capital in Rabbath-ammon and lay siege to Jabesh-gilead, an Israelite city belonging to the nearby tribe of East Manasseh.

KING SAUL'S TEST

Though Saul had been anointed king by Samuel and had prophesied with the prophets in front of some of the people, his hiding among the baggage and tribal identity left many skeptical about his abilities. Israel's transition from the tribal confederacy, or amphictyony as it is termed by scholars, to a monarchy was a huge political shift that also likely drew resistance from some of the people. Change, after all, often faces stiff resistance from many directions.

The amphictyony allowed the tribes to retain their individual sovereignty. However, now all of Israel fell under the leadership of one man. The young nation was ripe with division and uncertainty. The Ammonites, perhaps sensing such division within Israel, seized the opportunity to pounce on their neighbor's instability. Scripture relates in 1 Samuel 11:1 the Ammonite King Nahash and his army "came up and besieged" the city of Jabesh-gilead. They surrounded the city, cutting off all supplies from entering the city gates, and began to starve the inhabitants into submission. These were dangerous and precarious times for God's people.

Exercise: Read 1 Samuel 11:1-3.

- What were Nahash's terms of surrender?
- How many days did the men of Jabesh-gilead petition for before they said they would surrender to Nahash?
- What does this lead you to believe about the conditions of the city during the siege, if they would submit to such horrendous terms of surrender?

One must remember that Israel had suffered a terrible and crushing defeat in 1 Samuel 4 by the hands of the Philistines. Though God miraculously delivered them from the Philistines in 1 Samuel 7, they were still in a weakened and vulnerable state, ripe for invasion from hostile neighbors. The inhabitants of Jabesh-gilead faced dire consequences if captured, including the gouging out of their right eye, slavery, and possible execution. The situation was bleak in 1 Samuel 11.

Often it is during these times of utmost desperation and helplessness that God *will* act. He knows in advance what must be done! God already knew the Ammonites would invade Jabesh-gilead. He knew in advance the demands Nahash would make and the response of the Israelites. God had anointed Saul at just the right time to respond to this situation.

Such a task was what Saul needed to unite the country and legitimize his rule.

Exercise: Read 1 Samuel 11:4-11.

- Have you experienced such an instance of desperation, where in the end you recognized how God had foreseen it and prepared you for it? If so, write it down and remember it for future crises.
- What city did the messengers come to in 1 Samuel 11:4? Was Saul present initially to hear the plea of Jabesh-gilead?
- Where was Saul and what was he doing when the messengers arrived?
- Do you find this strange in that Saul was king of Israel? What does this say about his kingship in its early stages?
- What happened to Saul upon learning of the situation?
- How does the end of 1 Samuel 11:6 describe Saul's emotional state?

Despite being king of Israel, Saul found it necessary to continue working in his father's fields! Saul showed much promise in the early phases of his kingship. Despite being king over all the land, he maintained a sense of humility and perspective about himself and his place within his family. He had previously overlooked the criticism of those "worthless men," showing a side of mercy and forgiveness few kings of antiquity possessed. Now he worked the oxen in his father's fields.

His heart remained humble before God in these early days.

As the Spirit had previously filled him to prophesy, now the Spirit filled him with righteous anger and indignation. His reaction to the plight of Jabesh-gilead at the hands of the Ammonites is that of a king rising to the occasion. Once again, we encounter the *ruwach* of God empowering an individual. In 1 Samuel 11:6, Saul "became very angry." A literal translation is that Saul's "anger burned exceedingly." Righteous anger is what the Bible depicts Saul as experiencing.

Exercise: Turn and read Matthew 21:12.

- Who is the one in this passage exhibiting righteous anger? What is the reason for such anger?

- How are the situations with Saul and Jesus alike? What is the common denominator in these two instances?

- Describe the actions taken by Jesus because of his anger and then describe those taken by Saul.

- What does the Bible indicate through these two passages about anger? Is it always a sin to be angry, or to manifest anger?

In 1 Samuel 11:7, Saul's action brought the "dread of the Lord" on Israel. This, however, is not to be mistaken as a negative fear. The result of such dread was to bring Israel together "as one man." Saul was an extremely charismatic leader, and he manifested this charisma by rallying Israel together. In the face of adversity, division, doubt, and overwhelming odds, he managed to bring all of Israel together as one nation, with one purpose—to free the men of Jabesh-gilead.

God's Spirit empowered Saul. God had enabled Saul to prophesy with the prophets, and now he would enable Saul to rally the men of Israel and defeat the Ammonites. So confident is Saul that he tells the messengers to return to Jabesh-gilead with the following message:

"Tomorrow, by the time the sun is hot, you shall have deliverance."

Saul did not waver, did not doubt, and did not hesitate. We already see a maturation of the man who had previously hidden himself among the baggage. Saul alone seemed to possess a soft-spoken, gentle-giant type of personality. However, Saul, empowered by the Spirit, is a fearless warrior-king, afraid of nothing. Thus in 1 Samuel 11:11, he leads the army of Israel "into the midst" of the Ammonite camp. The result is that he "struck down the Ammonites until the heat of the day," delivering Jabesh-gilead from its perilous siege. The men of Jabesh-gilead would align themselves with the house of Saul because of this, as Scripture later indicates.

An interesting change takes place within the people of Israel because of Saul's victory. As stated at the beginning of this chapter, military accomplishment is vital to the legitimacy of a king's reign. Whereas at the end of 1 Samuel 10, doubters of Saul voiced their discontent, in 1 Samuel 11:12 the people approached Samuel with the desire to put these men to death. This victory had justified Samuel's anointing and solidified Saul's rule.

Exercise: Read 1 Samuel 11:13.

- What was Saul's reaction to the people's request of Samuel?
- Whom does Saul credit with the victory?
- In your own words, describe the state of Saul's heart and his relationship with God.

Saul humbly and graciously gave the Lord all credit for his signature victory. He refused to take vengeance on his opposition, rather taking the opportunity to glorify God Almighty. The old prophet Samuel must have looked on with great satisfaction and pride as his pupil Saul proved to be the right man to lead God's people. The questionable start to his kingship forgotten, Saul now had the respect, loyalty, and admiration of the people.

Despite overwhelming odds and adversity, the young nation showed promise under the charismatic and righteous leadership of King Saul.

In 1 Samuel 11:14, Samuel led the people to Gilgal to "renew the kingdom" under Saul's now unquestionable leadership. In 1 Samuel 11:15, Scripture indicates a joyful celebration at Gilgal:

"And there Saul and all the men of Israel rejoiced greatly."

1 SAMUEL 12

IN 1 SAMUEL 12, SCRIPTURE contains some great truths about a great God. After Saul's confirming victory over the Ammonites, the prophet Samuel takes the occasion to gather Israel one last time. This was the common practice of prophets throughout the Old Testament. On important occasions, or when important decisions had to be made, they would gather the people together, or gather the assembly, and speak the words God had given them. The prophets would remind the people of God's great name and his special relationship with them, the people of Israel, his chosen nation. In 1 Samuel 12:6, Samuel does just this.

"Then Samuel said to the people, 'It is the Lord who appointed Moses and Aaron and who brought your fathers up from the land of Egypt.'"

If the Old Testament seems repetitive at times, that is because God's people needed constant reminding! How often do you need to be reminded of God's greatness and what he has done for you and your family? The ancient Israelites did not have a "Bible" as we know it today. Even with the sacred Scriptures Israel possessed, it was unlikely each family had a copy to read for themselves. The oral tradition of those narratives was critical to the spiritual wellbeing and instruction of Israel. The prophets were the oral transmitters of God's will.

Exercise: Turn to and read the words of Paul to the Christians in Rome found in Romans 12:2.

- How did the prophets meet this need of the ancient Israelites?
- In your own words, why is what Paul talks about in this verse so important?
- How can you apply this verse to your life?

Samuel gathered the people to renew their minds in God's greatness, to remind them of his control over their lives and the course of their country. It is interesting to note that some manuscripts substitute the word "made" for "appointed" in verse 6, thus reading: "It is the Lord who made Moses and Aaron."

Exercise: Turn now and read Exodus 3:10-12 and Exodus 4:11-12.

Centuries later, the prophet Micah echoed these same words to Israel and Judah. Micah was a contemporary of the prophet Isaiah. Take notice of the words in Micah 6:4.

"Indeed I brought you up from the land of Egypt and ransomed you from the house of slavery, and I set before you Moses, Aaron and Miriam."

Again, we see God constantly reminding his people of his power and deliverance. Samuel continues his sermon to Israel in 1 Samuel 12:7-8.

"So now, take your stand that I may plead with you before the Lord concerning all the righteous acts of the Lord which He did for you and your fathers. When Jacob went into Egypt and your fathers cried out to the Lord, then the Lord sent Moses and Aaron who brought your fathers out of Egypt and sitted them in this place."

Samuel gave the people a history lesson recounting the events that had shaped their history as a nation. I can remember as a child during holidays with our extended family, Mamaw Murphy would pray with the whole family present, and us kids would take our stands because the prayer was going to be a long one. Such is the case in this instance with

Samuel and the assembly. Samuel asserted, "Now take your stand, that I may plead with you."

Exercise: Turn and read the following passages.

1.   Ezekiel 20:35-36
     Ezekiel prophesied around the beginning of the sixth century B.C., in the last days of the kingdom of Judah. These were also to be the last days of Jewish identity and sovereignty as an independent nation for the next twenty-four hundred years. Ezekiel was deported to Mesopotamia by the Babylonians in 597 B.C. Eleven years later, in 586 B.C., the Babylonians would destroy Jerusalem, burning the first temple to the ground. The nation of Israel would not regain complete sovereignty over itself again until 1948 of the Common Era.

     God addressed his people through his prophet Ezekiel. He promised them judgment. The situation of Israel under Babylon was similar to that of the Hebrews under Egypt in that they were forced to live in a foreign land, under foreign rule. The people under Babylon had lost their identity, homeland, and temple. They had been exiled and lived in a foreign land. Many had fallen into slavery. Though centuries separated the passages in 1 Samuel and Ezekiel, God's message remained the same, and remains the same today—He will deliver you.

2.   Micah 6:1-5
     Micah was a contemporary of Isaiah, living and teaching in the last third of the eighth century B.C. (ca. 740-700 B.C.). Micah foretold the fall of Israel to the Assyrians (722 B.C.) and the fall of Judah (586 B.C.) to the Babylonians.

     In this passage, God was upset about the actions of Israel and, through Micah, sought to get their attention. Notice the Lord once again reminded them of his deliverance from Egypt.

3.   Deuteronomy 32
     The NASB titles this chapter "The Song of Moses." The date of Moses and the Exodus is a hotly debated topic. *Young's Analytical*

Concordance to the Bible puts the birth of Moses around 1571 B.C. This, though, is far from certain. Moses constantly prayed on behalf of the wayward Israelites he led through the desert. The generation of Moses is the generation spoken of as "your fathers and forefathers" in the later books of the Old Testament. This was the defining moment in Israel's history.

It was the watershed event. Moses was the very first prophet, though his role included much more than simply being a prophet. He was commander, priest, judge, president, and prophet to the wandering Israelites. Moses was one of the greatest leaders to have ever lived upon the face of the earth.

• Read each of the three above passages once again, noting the similarities found in each passage. Note similarities in language, situations, and actions.

Has God changed? It becomes evident that people have not changed either. After Samuel reminded the people of Israel about God's deliverance, he then turned to the actions of their fathers in 1 Samuel 12:9.

Exercise: Read carefully 1 Samuel 12:9-11.

• What does Samuel accuse the Israelites of doing in verse 1 Samuel 12:9?

• How did God respond to their actions?

Read Deuteronomy 32:18-19 and Judges 3:7–8.

• What is the accusation against God's people in Deuteronomy 32:18–19?

• How does God respond?

• What does Scripture record about "the sons of Israel" in this instance?

• Whom did they serve?

• How did God respond to their actions?

The message is clear and just as true today as it was thousands of years ago. The Baals and Ashteroths of antiquity exist in our lives today. We serve Baal and Ashteroth through our lifestyles, our excesses, our rationalizations, and justifications. The disobedience of Christians today echoes throughout all of history. The anonymous author of Ecclesiastes states the following in Ecclesiastes 1:9:

"That which has been is that which will be, and that which has been done is that which will be done. So, there is nothing new under the sun."

Samuel continues to retell the story of the Israelites' ancestors in 1 Samuel 12:10. He tells how they "cried out to the Lord." This phrase appears throughout the pages of the Old Testament.

Exercise:

- What kind of image do you get when you hear the phrase "cried out to the Lord"?

- Can you think of a time when you cried out to the Lord? If yes, really focus on the details of that time. Take a few minutes to revisit, however painful, that event. What was the cause of your cry? How did God answer you? What did God show you?

The book of Judges presents many such cries by God's people (Judges 3:9; 3:15; 4:3; 6:6; 10:10). Cries such as these oftentimes followed an extended period of disobedience, at which point the Israelites were oppressed by a foreign threat. Yet, as Samuel made evident, God repeatedly delivered them through the different Judges. Samuel listed the Judges Barak, Jephthah, Gideon, and Samson as examples of godly providence. The people of Israel would have been very familiar with these names and the stories associated with them. They would have been familiar with the oppression associated with each Judge. They would have recognized the chief sin, the worshipping of foreign gods, as also being prevalent in their time. Samuel points out another sin in 1 Samuel 12:12.

Exercise: Read 1 Samuel 12:12.

- What is the sin of the people Samuel hints at in this verse?

By choosing a king, they rejected God, their true King and deliverer. Samuel, however, assured them there was still hope. They could still please God and he would still bless them and the king. God is bigger than our plans, and he knew Israel would choose a king one day, just as he knows our choices for tomorrow. God is never surprised.

He sees the big picture, and despite the attempts of the ancient Hebrews, our attempts today, and the attempts of the enemy, God's plans will not be hindered.

Listen to the words found in Hebrews 4:12-13.

"For the word of God is living and active and sharper than any two-edged sword and piercing as far as the division of soul and spirit, of both joints and marrow, and able to judge the thoughts and intentions of the heart. And there is no creature hidden from His sight, but all things are laid bare to the eyes of Him with whom we have to do."

Despite their lack of faith in God manifested in their request for a king, God would still use his people mightily. He saw it coming and already had his plan in mind. The final part of Samuel's address to Israel included a message of hope, and a dire warning as well. Samuel reiterated God's desire for his people and the consequence of neglecting his words.

Exercise: Read 1 Samuel 12:14-15.

- What are the Israelites commanded to do?
- What are the consequences if they obey God?
- What are the consequences if they do not obey God?
- Who is mentioned as an example of disobedience, and what was their punishment?

Scripture lends insight into the time of year Samuel addressed the assembly in 1 Samuel 12. The Bible indicates it was the day of the wheat harvest, which would place these events in June or July. The wheat harvest was a critically important day to the Israelites. It was the culmination of months of hard work. Israel possessed an agriculture-based economy, thus harvest day meant food. Wheat was an important staple in their diet. God used this harvest day, however, to send a message.

Exercise: Read 1 Samuel 12:16-19.

- What was the sign Samuel would send?
- Why was this significant in relation to the wheat harvest?
- How did Samuel achieve this feat?
- What was the reaction of the people?
- Can you think of a wheat harvest in your life that did not work out as planned? Why did it not work out? Was God's hand involved?

No rebellion goes unpunished, and God wanted his people to understand that Samuel only spoke on the authority of God Almighty. He would punish them if they disobeyed. To emphasize his point, he sent a rainstorm, characterized by a booming thunder. This storm would have smashed the wheat harvest, leaving much of the crop destroyed. The Israelites would have been shocked to see such a storm in the harvest month. A storm like this would have been extremely rare for this time of year—and incredible bad luck and timing to happen on harvest day. This was a national tragedy. Yet it was not bad luck, but God's timing. God used it to display the seriousness of Samuel's words, and to show the assembly disobedience would have consequences. The storm worked, for the people turned to Samuel and urged his prayers to God "so that we may not die."

Fortunately for us today, God's desires have not changed for humanity. Thus, we can turn to the pages of the Bible and learn from previous generations how we should act and respond to God's desires. The Bible is full of both good and bad examples. Read Samuel's instructions to the people in the closing verses of 1 Samuel 12:

"And Samuel said to the people, 'Do not fear. You have committed all this evil, yet do not turn aside from following the Lord, but serve the Lord with all your heart'" (1 Samuel 12:20).

"Only fear the Lord and serve Him in truth with all your heart; for consider what great things He has done for you" (1 Samuel 12:24).

Samuel was speaking around the eleventh or twelfth century B.C. (1100-1000 B.C.). Read what others in the Bible have said, and then notice the dates (though oftentimes debatable) given for each. Compare these passages with each other and to 1 Samuel 12.

Moses (ca. 1575–1455 B.C. or 1300s B.C.):

"And you shall love the Lord your God with all your heart and with all your soul and with all your might" (Deuteronomy 6:5). Jesus called this the greatest commandment.

"Beware, lest your hearts be deceived and you turn away and serve others gods and worship them" (Deuteronomy 11:16).

Joshua (ca. 1400–1200 B.C.)

"Now, therefore, fear the Lord and serve Him in sincerity and truth; and put away the gods which your fathers served beyond the River and in Egypt, and serve the Lord" (Joshua 24:14). The phrase "beyond the River" indicates the Euphrates River. Joshua, who is speaking here, was the successor to Moses and led the Israelites on the conquest into Canaan.

The Prophet Micah (ca. 740-700 B.C.):

"He has told you, O Man, what is good; and what does the Lord require of you, but to do justice, to love kindness, and to walk humbly with your God?" (Micah 6:8).

Jesus Christ (ca. 4 B.C.-33 A.D.):

"And He said to him, 'You shall love the Lord your God with all your heart, and with all your soul, and with all your mind. This is the greatest and foremost commandment. The second is like it, 'You shall love your neighbor as yourself.' On these two commandments depend the whole Law and the Prophets" (Matthew 22:37–40).

Men such as Jeremiah, Elisha, Elijah, Isaiah, Ezekiel, and the other great prophets of the Old Testament would repeat the preaching of the prophet Samuel over the next several centuries. Samuel followed Moses, who followed Abraham, who followed Noah and his sons—all separated by great distances of time, yet all with the same message from the same God. Jesus Christ would bring forth a new era of God and man. His sacrifice opened the way for everybody, not just the Hebrews, to commune with God Almighty. The steady and consistent message of God reverberates across the millennia, and his message is as true today as back in the day. Love and serve him with all your heart.

Exercise:

- What do these passages lead you to believe about the church today?

- Is God concerned with Methodist, Baptist, Catholic, Episcopalian, Presbyterian, Nondenominational, or any other such label?

- The timelessness of God is seen in his instructions and desires for us. In your own words, write down those instructions. Have they changed since the days of Moses and before? Will they change in the future?

- How does our society today seek to change God's commands to us?

- Who should be your ultimate authority? Your priest or pastor? Your husband or wife? Your family? Your God?

In 1 Samuel 12, we learn a great deal about the history of Israel. Samuel reiterates many fundamental truths about God. The nation of Israel was undergoing a significant change in government and everyday life by converting to kingship. Divided attitudes existed in Israel as to having a king, though Scripture indicates a great majority seemed to have wanted one. Their choice went against the will of God, yet he did not abandon them. They needed the constant message of what God's desires were, and the constant reminders of his repeated deliverance. Times were precarious for these Israelites, as they are for us today.

Samuel, their spiritual and national leader, was old in age, enemies were pressing in from all sides, and a new form of government was being implemented. The future of the young nation of Israel and her king was uncertain at best.

Yet, Samuel's sermon of God's consistent deliverance, and the consistency of God's commands, provided a steadying foundation for Israel during these turbulent times of change and uncertainty. Much would be required of King Saul as Samuel faded into the background of Israel's day-to-day operations. Saul emerged as the new leader, the first king of Israel. This second anointing by Samuel paves the way for the official beginning of Saul's reign. Obedience to God's commands would be essential to Saul's success.

1 SAMUEL 13

THE EARLIER PHILISTINE VICTORY OVER Israel at Aphek in
1 Samuel 4 had enabled the Philistines to further encroach upon Israelite territory in the mountains. The Philistines had fortified a garrison of
soldiers in Geba. Geba's proximity to Israelite villages and fields created an imminent threat. The Philistines also had access to the high-
land routes now and could threaten Israel from a number of different
positions. Despite Israel thwarting an advance in 1 Samuel 7, the Philistine threat still loomed large and dangerous.

What this amounted to was the potential threat of Israel being pushed
all the way east of the Jordan River, consequently losing the promised
land their ancestors had fought for under Joshua's leadership. If they
were to lose their mountain villages and towns it would threaten their
very existence as a nation. It seemed only a matter of time before Israel
was either under the Philistine yoke or wiped out altogether.

In 1 Samuel 13:1, Scripture seems to suggest that although Saul had
been anointed king some time earlier, it was only after Samuel's sermon
in 1 Samuel 12 that all of Israel recognized Saul as king. He was thirty
years old when he became king, and he would rule for forty-two years
as king of Israel. This, however, was in question during the early periods of his reign. Though he had defeated the Philistines earlier, that
was only a skirmish, which served to intensify the ongoing battle. The
hornet's nest had been stirred up, and the Philistines gathered for war.

The book of Samuel informs us Saul's army consisted of three thousand total men. The Israelite forces were divided in two.

Two thousand men were with King Saul in Michmash. One thousand men were under the command of Saul's son, Jonathan, at Gibeah of Benjamin.

"Now the Philistines assembled to fight with Israel, 30,000 chariots and 6,000 horsemen, and people like the sand which is on the seashore in abundance; and they came up and camped in Michmash, east of Beth-aven" (1 Samuel 13:5).

Chariots were cumbersome when used in mountainous warfare. They were better suited for battles in the plains and along the coastal region. Nonetheless, Israel was heavily outnumbered and badly out-matched in weaponry. The sizes of the forces mentioned in the Bible are debated issues. Translations and interpretations of certain words lead to these debates. Regardless, the Philistines had cavalry and chariots, a much larger force than Israel, and a technological advantage in iron.

As if these advantages were not enough, in 1 Samuel 13:19, the Bible reveals the Philistines had a monopoly on iron, a new resource at the time. The blacksmiths in the region were under Philistine control and refused to produce spears and swords for Israelites. Israel's soldiers, thus, were armed with pitchforks, shovels, axes, and hoes—farming equipment. Combined with the superior weapons, monstrous size, and fierce cruelty of the Philistines, one could not blame the Israelite forces for doubting their chances of survival.

Exercise: Turn and read 1 Samuel 13:6-7.

- How does Scripture record the reaction of the Israelites?
- To where did many of the Israelites defect?
- How does Scripture record Saul as reacting?

Saul's army was fleeing and hiding from the enemy! Saul, however, stood his ground, and the ones who stayed with him were still "trembling." For the most part, it seemed the people lost heart. Saul's young kingdom was in danger of slipping from his grasp. This would have been the end of Israel, perhaps for good.

Exercise: Turn and read Matthew 26:69-75.

- Can you think of a time in life when you "were in a strait"?
- Did your situation appear helpless, like Israel's here?
- How did you respond?
- How did Peter respond to being "in a strait"?

In 1 Samuel 13:8-15, we see Saul's reaction. He was the king, the people's representative before Samuel and God. His actions were to be in accordance with God's will. Samuel had told Saul to wait seven days for him to arrive, at which point Samuel would offer the burnt offerings and the peace offerings for the people. Samuel did not show, however, on the appointed day. A test of faith and obedience sat before Saul. Did he trust God? How would King Saul—overcome with seeing his army abandon him in increasingly large numbers, the mighty Philistines standing at the doorway, and without prophet Samuel—react to this hopeless situation? Would he react in obedience?

Exercise: Turn and read Psalms 34:17.

- The author of this Psalm is David. What was the righteous pictured doing in Psalms 34:17? What was the outcome?

Read 1 Samuel 13:9-10.

- How did Saul respond?
- In your opinion, was this the right response? Why, or why not?

Saul took matters into his own hands. Nowhere does Scripture record him stopping and inquiring of God. He foolishly rushes to action. Notice Saul's excuses to Samuel for his disobedience.

Exercise: Read 1 Samuel 13:11.

- What were the three excuses Saul gave Samuel?

Not all of us have waged war with the Philistines, but we all wage war against our own version of Philistines in everyday life. Our excuses sound a lot like Saul's, focused on worldly appearances and circumstances rather than godly perspective. Saul needed the advice of James, as we do, too, in James 1:5.

"But if any of you lacks wisdom let him ask God, who gives to all men generously and without reproach and it will be given to him."

Saul's actions drew the reproach of Samuel. Dr. Spiros Zodhiates made the statement that Saul showed no regard for God's will. He did not seek God's counsel nor did he follow God's commandments. In fact, up to this point in the narrative, Scripture has yet to depict Saul in prayer. He did spare the lives of men in God's honor in 1 Samuel 11:13; however, we get none of the heartfelt cries we see from David. Samuel sensed such as well, and he addresses Saul's impulsive and reckless behavior in 1 Samuel 13:13.

Exercise: Read 1 Samuel 13:13.

- How did Samuel describe Saul's actions?
- What was Saul accused of by Samuel?
- If Saul had acted faithfully, what would the Lord have done for him, according to Samuel?

As seen in 1 Samuel 13:14, it must have been a tough message for Samuel to deliver. It signaled the ultimate end of Saul's reign—one that looked so promising at one time. Samuel's pronouncement would have far-reaching consequences not only for Saul but for the nation of Israel as well.

"But now your kingdom shall not endure. The Lord has sought out for Himself a man after His own heart, and the Lord has appointed him as ruler over His people, because you have not kept what the Lord said" (1 Samuel 13:14).

Samuel revealed what is important to the Lord God Almighty. The Lord desires the heart of an individual above all else. The Lord saw in the new king "a man after his own heart." This had nothing to do with physical stature, family name, priestly lineage, or royal bloodlines.

Exercise: Turn and read Deuteronomy 6:5.

- What is the commandment Moses gives the Israelites in this verse?

Now turn and read Matthew 22:37.

- What does Jesus preach to those listening?
- What Scripture is he quoting?
- In Matthew 22:38, what does Jesus call this commandment?

Though the lesson may seem simple, we are careful not to carelessly skim over it. God seeks obedient hearts. It's that simple. There are consequences for our actions, regardless of who we are, what job we have, or how much money we make.

King Saul was not above accountability either, just as we are not. In fact, those with important positions of power and leadership over others are held to a higher standard.

Exercise: Read James 3:1.

- How does this verse relate to the statement above that those who hold positions of power and leadership are held to a higher standard?
- Is this a godly view of leadership?
- Where was Saul's primary error in the way he handled things?
- Do you know the identity of the "man after his own heart"?

King Saul had experienced a rough few days. The storm was raging all around him. Things were loud and hectic. His empire lay on the brink of destruction. His army was abandoning him. His enemies pressed in. Surely, we can understand why Saul felt such anxiety and pressure. Things appeared lost.

Exercise: Turn and read 1 Samuel 13:22.

- Who possessed weapons in Israel's Army?
- What were the main weapons the Israelites were fighting with?

The contents of 1 Samuel 13:22 loosely dates these events. According to 1 Samuel 13:22, iron was a new material in Canaan. The Philistines possessed the most knowledge and expertise on the new resource and monopolized it throughout the region. Archaeology confirms the Philistines were knowledgeable in the use of iron and possessed a lot of the resource, while the Israelites did not. The Bible mentions the iron monopoly, thus placing these events within the Iron Age.

The Iron Age followed the Bronze Age, which was the time of the Patriarchs and Judges. The Iron Age lasted from approximately 1200 to 1000 B.C. This date fits nicely within the framework of these events in 1 Samuel. Many scholars calculate Saul's reign as taking place circa 1040-1000 B.C.

Others claim his reign occurred closer to 1000-960 B.C. Unfortunately for Israel, they had not fully developed the technological expertise of manufacturing with iron. They lacked supply as well, thus they relied on Philistine supply.

In this time of war, the Philistines naturally cut off Israel's supply of iron and iron weapons. In the modern era, nations freeze the financial assets of other rogue countries or individuals, or place economic stipulations on trade and such. Oil and currency are big elements countries and global institutions manipulate to harm or benefit as suits. One example of this is the current situation between the United States and Iran (Russia, too) in which economic sanctions are always being threatened. These were the same tactics the Philistines would use on Israel's economy by manipulating its ability to obtain iron. By worldly standards, Israel should not have survived as it did, nor should it have thrived as it has.

Another character in the Bible experienced a similarly bleak situation, though of a different nature. Job experienced similar feelings of desperation and hopelessness. He had lost all of his possessions and all of his family simultaneously.

Saul would have been wise to seek out Job's counsel. That great sage of endurance and faith spoke out in Job 5:8.

"But as for me, I would seek God, and I would place my cause before God."

Job wanted answers and knew where to find them. Rather than hasten to do as he saw fit, Job turned to God instead. He sought an audience with God. When things look impossible, turn to God—fast! Unfortunately, Saul rushed into action rather than seeking God's counsel first.

Exercise: Turn and read Psalms 20:7.

- What did Saul boast in? Or, what did he put his faith in?
- Psalm 20 is a Psalm of David. Though he was far from perfect (adulterer, murderer), what are we learning about David?
- In what do you boast? In other words, in what do you put your faith? Job security? Family? Money? Marriage? Your church? Status? God?

As we move to 1 Samuel 14, pay special attention to the words of Jonathan, Saul's son and the commander of his army.

1 SAMUEL 14
(PART 1)

THE ODDS WERE SET IN 1 Samuel 13. Jonathan's initial victory over the Philistines in Geba (1 Samuel 13:3) had drawn the full wrath of the Philistines. An extremely large Philistine force gathered for revenge in Michmash, approximately two miles north of Geba. Just south of the main force, atop a high cliff called Bozez (slippery one), overlooking the valley and the two armies, the Philistines had established a garrison or manned outpost. The outpost was separated from another cliff, Senah (thorny one), to the south by a steep ravine, the Wadi es-Suwenit. The Israelite camp was to the Southwest of this second unmanned cliff.

In 1 Samuel 14, the passage opens with Jonathan giving instructions to his armor-bearer that they were going to "cross over to the Philistine garrison." Saul, camped nearby in Migron, was unaware of Jonathan's actions. His army had dwindled to six hundred men. Many of the Israelites had fled into the hills, hiding in caves rather than facing the mighty Philistine Army. Some Hebrews, as Scripture later indicates, even joined forces with the Philistines. Jonathan's courage is not foolhearted courage but rather anchored in godly faith.

Exercise: Read his words in 1 Samuel 14:6.

- What does Jonathan call the Philistines?
- Why does Jonathan give himself and his armor-bearer, two people only, a chance?

Jonathan was taking action; he was stepping out in faith that God could handle the situation. Jonathan even planned his course of action on what words the Lord would put into the mouths of the Philistines stationed at the garrison.

"If they say to us, 'Wait until we come to you'; then we will stand in our place and not go up to them. But if they say, 'Come up to us,' then we will go up, for the Lord has given them into our hands; and this shall be the sign to us" (1 Samuel 14:9-10).

Jonathan allowed for God's leadership, unlike his father Saul in the previous chapter. God doesn't seem to like big numbers, or better odds, or the odds-on favorite. He seems to prefer long shots, underdogs, and impossibilities. Jonathan and his armor-bearer were long-shot underdogs. They acted knowing God would provide. This happens when you have a strong, unshakable faith in God and his provision; especially when you are most distressed, hopeless, and see no promise.

GOD'S UPSETS

Exercise:

Take time to read these passages focusing on God's words, but also on the response of the men to whom God is talking.

Based on perceptions, take mental note of the favorite and underdog in each instance.

Exodus 7:7; Exodus 14:28-31

- Who was the favorite?
- Who was the underdog?
- Who was the winner?

Joshua 6:1-2

- Who was the favorite?
- Who was the underdog?
- Who was the winner?

Joshua 14:1-3; 15:13-14; and Numbers 13:33

- Who was the favorite?
- Who was the underdog?
- Who was the winner?

Note that Judges 7:1-7, is similar to Jonathan's situation and echoes Jonathan's words.

- Based on these passages, what enabled God's power to prevail?
- God is all-powerful and would have his will done regardless, but what was it about these men that caused God to work through them?

God seeks hearts, and it was Jonathan's heart that God loved. Consequently, God would use Jonathan mightily. The Philistines exhibited pride and ego in 1 Samuel 14:11-12. Their faith was in strength and numbers as well as false gods. Take note of the Philistines' response in 1 Samuel 14:11.

"And when both of them revealed themselves to the garrison of the Philistines, the Philistines said, 'Behold, Hebrews are coming out of the holes where they have hidden themselves.'"

The Philistines began to joke among themselves at the sudden appearance of these two little Hebrews. Scripture implies the Philistines felt no threat from Jonathan.

Exercise: Turn and read 1 Samuel 14:12.

- What did the Philistines say to Jonathan?

- According to Jonathan's earlier words, what did this response mean God intended Jonathan to do?

What remarkable faith and courage Jonathan showed in God. Jonathan had already scaled not just one cliff face but two cliff faces. The difficulty in such a task is evident in the names of these two cliffs. Bozez means "slippery one" and Senah translates as "thorny one." Jonathan scaled these two walls in faith, not knowing what God had in store for him when he reached the top.

It is important to note Jonathan's work ethic in this instance. Some expect to be given without working for it. Our culture promotes this sense of entitlement and encourages the notion of ease and comfort. How many of us are willing to work very hard for results we aren't sure of? Jonathan worked in scaling these cliffs not knowing if God would grant him battle or not. He acted in faith, out of duty and not out of expectation or entitlement. It's an act of faith to do one's best at whatever task, regardless of the outcome. God rewards those who do such.

Read Moses's words to Joshua in Deuteronomy 31:6-8. Moses encouraged Joshua to be strong and courageous. He urged Joshua not to be afraid, for the Lord God went before him. These were some of Moses's last words to Joshua, meant to strengthen the young leader and encourage him in his new task. Joshua would lead the people of Israel into the hostile land of Canaan.

Likewise, Jonathan led his armor-bearer over the cliff and into the middle of the Philistine garrison, a seemingly suicidal mission in hopes to hold on to the land Joshua and others had fought for. The two-man charge is depicted in 1 Samuel 14:13-14.

"Then Jonathan climbed up on his hands and feet, with his armor-bearer behind him; and they fell before Jonathan, and his armor-bearer put some to death after him. And that first slaughter which Jonathan and his armor-bearer made was about twenty men within about half a furrow in an acre of land."

One needs an idea of Jonathan's actual feat to appreciate fully this incredible offensive. A "furrow" was a term used to describe, in general, the amount of ground oxen could plow in a day. The original Hebrew text is very obscure in 1 Samuel 14:14 and understood in a variety of different ways. In general, a furrow is an acre of land, which is approximately 220 to 240 feet in length. Half a furrow, thus, is approximately 110 to 120 feet long, less than half the length of a football field.

JONATHAN'S VICTORY

At first glance, Jonathan and his armor-bearer's extraordinary attack seems highly colorful and unlikely. However, when one understands the geographical scenario, it is quite believable, but nonetheless remarkable.

The Philistine outpost sat high atop the cliff named Bozez, making it possible to survey the surrounding area for advancing Israelite threats and keep an eye on Saul's army in Michmash. The cliff's top was a flat, narrow strip of ground perfect for construction of an outpost. The rest of the cliff was covered, most likely, with trees, scrub brush, large boulders, and woods.

However, from below, neither army would have been able to see the outpost above. The main Philistine force would have relied on reports from runners, which regularly carried messages from the outpost above to the camp below. Smoke signals, too, were used for communication.

In 1 Samuel 14:11, Jonathan and his armor-bearer scaled to the top of the second cliff. As they pulled themselves over the top of the cliff wall, Philistine lookouts, or sentries, saw them emerge. Put yourself in place of these Philistines. As you stand watch, suddenly, two puny and annoying little Hebrews appear from the edge of the cliff! At this point you remark, "Behold, Hebrews are coming out of the holes where they have hidden themselves."

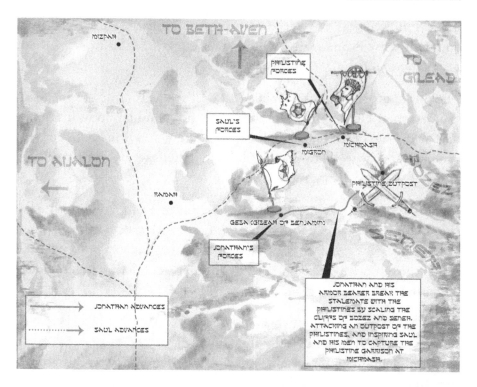

One detects the amusement and mockery of the Philistine sentries. The last thing concerning them was a Hebrew attack. The Philistines likely thought of Israel as little more than an annoyance. Many Hebrews were used as mercenaries in the Philistine Army. The Philistines had fought with these people frequently, winning many battles. In the mind of your average Philistine, it was only a matter of time before they had fully conquered Israel.

The Philistines did fear the Hebrew God. They had seen firsthand the mysterious power of this God. Though the Hebrew God was powerful, the Hebrews themselves were little threat. This attitude would explain their response to Jonathan to "come up to us." One can picture the smirk on Jonathan's face as he heard these words. He turned to his armor-bearer and in complete confidence said, "Come up after me, for the Lord has given them into the hands of Israel."

What followed was the very last thing the Philistines expected. It is common sense if one is in a fight against superior odds to swing first, fast, and not to stop.

The image we get from 1 Samuel 14:13-14 seems to indicate Jonathan did just that. He did not hesitate, but as he "climbed upon his hands and feet," he came up swinging! Scripture notes Jonathan and his armor-bearer, who followed close behind, felled twenty Philistines in a space of about one hundred to two hundred feet.

Jonathan struck in rapid, quick blows, killing a Philistine with each successive chop. His armor-bearer followed suit, and the two of them killed twenty men in a very confined space. They had exploded over the top of the cliff with lethal and deadly speed, catching the overconfident and arrogant Philistine sentries off guard.

The remaining Philistines, those not closest to the cliff face, began to flee backward, surprised by the sudden attack on their camp. Fearing a surprise Hebrew invasion, not knowing the number of troops attacking, and witnessing their fellow soldiers being slaughtered, the Philistines panicked. They fled downhill toward the main force below, away from the marauding Hebrew horde!

This is a plausible scenario. The narrowness of the Philistine outpost, surrounded by woods, ravines, and brush prevented the troops at one end from seeing clearly the troops at the other end. When Jonathan and his armor-bearer attacked suddenly and unexpectedly, they killed those in the immediate vicinity. Seeing their comrades slaughtered, troops farther from the cliff face fled, not knowing what was happening. Those even farther back in camp began to flee as they saw others fleeing, thus a chain reaction had been set in motion.

In the minds of those Philistines closest the carnage, a mere two men would not venture such an attack. Somehow, the Hebrew army had scaled the cliff walls in secret. In reality, Jonathan and his armor-bearer had scattered the Philistine outpost!

The main Philistine force camped below heard the noise from the garrison above. The outpost was under attack, though at first, perhaps, the Philistine Army simply gazed upward, wondering what in the world all the racket was about. What happened next was God delivering his people once again.

Exercise: Read 1 Samuel 14:15.

- What does 1 Samuel 14:15 seem to indicate happened?
- How is the Philistine Army pictured as reacting?
- Based on your reading of the Scripture, what happened here in 1 Samuel 14:15?
- Can God act on the earth through natural occurrences, disasters, seasons, and so on? Does a natural explanation disprove godly intervention?

God looks for the hearts of men willing to answer his call in faith, and then he delivers above and beyond what we can imagine. The obvious implication is an earthquake strikes the Philistine camp below. However, some manuscripts read the following: "So that it became a great trembling of God."

The passages listed below bear similar language, and such language may indicate something else happened that day.

Whatever God's method of deliverance was, it was effective.

Exercise:

Read the passages below and pay special attention to the language used to describe God's presence and influence.

1. Genesis 35:5
   Jacob was forced to move his family from Shechem due to the wickedness of his sons Simeon and Levi. These two sons of Jacob killed every male in Shechem, looted the city, and took the women and children as captive (see Genesis 34). As a result of Simeon and Levi's actions, and afraid that other Canaanites may attack him, Jacob moved his family to Bethel. Genesis 35:5

depicts the protection God offered Jacob as he moved through the land. Similar to the trembling among the Philistines, God placed a "great terror upon the cities which were around them." Other translations read, "A terror of God."

2. Exodus 15:16

This passage is entitled the *Song of Moses*. In Exodus 15:15, Moses spoke of "the chiefs of Edom," "the leaders of Moab," and "all the inhabitants of Canaan." In Exodus 15:16, Scripture records "terror and dread fell upon them; by the greatness of Thine arm." Once again, God provides in a dramatic way. The Hebrew word translated as "terror" is *eymah*, which means "fear." The Hebrew translated as "dread" is *pachad*, which means "a sudden alarm, feeling of dread, dreadful, awe, terror." *Pachad* comes from a word that translates as "to be startled." *Pachad* may refer to the emotion or the subject that causes the emotion (i.e., God).

3. Exodus 23:27

Once again, God is talking to Moses about the impending invasion of Canaan. He tells Moses, "I will send My terror ahead of you." This terror will throw into confusion the people Israel comes into contact with. We do not know the nature of this terror, or the confusion created by it. We can only compare passages such as these to other passages that depict God acting in a similar way. By the context of this passage, Israel was venturing into a foreign and hostile land. Israelites were to conquer the land and settle in it, something the local Canaanites would not have been eager to allow. In fact, resistance was to be stiff and fierce. The Israelites' only chance was to put their faith in God Almighty.

4. Deuteronomy 2:25

"This day I will begin to put the dread and fear of you in front of the peoples under all the heavens."

God spoke these words to Moses before Israel's campaign against the brother kings, Og and Sihon, kings of the Amorites east of the Jordan River. Sihon is believed to have possibly been warlord over all of Canaan.

His brother Og was a giant king, the last of the Rephaim. Og's bed was "9 cubits in length," which is approximately 13.5 feet long. It was also 4 cubits, or 3 feet, wide and made of iron. The Rephaim are connected with the wicked Nephilim mentioned in Genesis 6 and Numbers. The Israelites were engaging Og at his capital in Edrei. This mysterious ancient city is made completely of rock, making it a rock fortress that still stands today.

However, it is what lies beneath the city that has fascinated archaeologists and historians. Beneath Edrei is a mysterious underground city of the Amorites. The purpose of this underground city remains a mystery.

Israel stood little chance against these mighty people—who were capable of carving a city out of rock and building a mirror city underground—much as they would stand little chance against iron-wielding giant Philistines centuries later. The word translated as "dread" here is the same *pachad* from Exodus 15:16. The Hebrew word translated as "fear" in Deuteronomy 2:25 is *yir'ah*. This word translates as "fear, reverence, dreadful, or abject terror."

God is a fearful God today just as he was in antiquity. God promises us he will go in front of us throughout our lives if we will let him. Our stubbornness is much the same as the stubbornness of the Israelites throughout the Bible.

However, as in this passage, God continually promises he will go in front of us and help us tackle our problems.

5. Deuteronomy 11:25

In Deuteronomy 11:25, God reassured the Israelites he would guide and protect them by giving them strength. Still under the leadership of Moses, Israel had yet to enter into the promised land. God assured them if they stayed in line with his commands, he would empower them before their enemies. The word translated as "fear" in Deuteronomy 11:25 is the Hebrew word *pachad* from Exodus 15:16 and Deuteronomy 2:25, not the

Hebrew *yi'rah,* which was translated as "fear" in Deuteronomy 2:25.

The word translated as "dread" in Deuteronomy 11:25 is the Hebrew word *morah,* not the Hebrew *pachad. Morah* translates as "a fearful thing" or "dread." One can be easily confused as it becomes clear that multiple Hebrew words may be used with the same English word—with slight nuances lost in the English translation. *Morah* is also used in Psalms 9:20.

"Put them *in fear,* O Lord; Let the nations know that they are but men" (emphasis added).

6. Joshua 2:9

    These are the words Rahab the harlot in Jericho spoke to the Israelite spies sent by Joshua prior to their invasion. Rahab informs the spies, "the terror of you has fallen on us." The Hebrew word translated in this instance as "terror" is the same word, *eymah,* used in Exodus 15:16 above. Joshua experienced a divine visitor as well, before the battle of Jericho in Joshua 5:13-15.

7. Matthew 27:51-54

    This passage takes place immediately after Jesus "yielded up his spirit." The Gospel of Luke adds the detail that it was very dark outside despite the hour of the day. This was a supernatural occurrence that accompanied the death of Jesus. An earthquake seemed to have occurred almost simultaneously with the last breath of Jesus. The temple veil was torn from top to bottom. The "earth shook; and the rocks were split," and "the tombs were opened" (Matthew 27:51-52). The natural disaster, an earthquake, was also accompanied with various other supernatural signs and happenings.

    The point in highlighting these passages is to indicate an earthquake may well have been what took place in 1 Samuel 14. However, it cannot be ruled out that something far more mysterious took place as well. In these ancient times, man's faith in God, as well as the other gods of the foreign nations, expected divine intervention and supernatural signs and omens. The gods were sought for everywhere. As Jonathan and his armor-bearer exploded over the ledge, God and his army went before them.

A chain reaction was set off, and in 1 Samuel 14:16, Saul's watchmen see the Philistine Army in complete chaos; "and behold, the multitude melted away; and they went here and there." Saul recognized an attack had been carried out against the Philistines, and he wished to know who had initiated it. Upon learning it was Jonathan, Saul sent immediately for his priest, Ahijah, and feigned to seek God's will. It is interesting to take note of the company Saul keeps, namely his priest, Ahijah.

As Saul's primary priest, Ahijah would have advised Saul as to God's word regarding whatever situation arose. He was the king's closest advisor. Ahijah was descended from Ahitub. Ahitub, according to Scripture, was Ichabod's brother and son to Phineas. This was the same Phineas that Samuel would have grown up around in the temple. It was also the same Phineas that Scripture recorded was wicked, one of the two wicked sons of Eli. Phineas's death is recorded in 1 Samuel 4:19-25.

Given Samuel's absence from Saul and Saul's behavior, it would seem Ahijah was more concerned with pleasing the king than he was in the Word of God. His priestly ancestors proved to be weak and immoral priests, and Ahijah did not impress, either. We must take this time to learn from King Saul's mistakes—be careful who you surround yourself with.

"A man who loves wisdom makes his father glad, but he who keeps company with harlots wastes his wealth" (Proverbs 29:3).

"For the company of the godless is barren, and fire consumes the tents of the corrupt" (Job 15:34).

"Do not be deceived: Bad company corrupts good morals" (1 Corinthians 15:33).

These verses begin to manifest themselves in Saul's behavior, which becomes progressively worse. As the confusion among the Philistine camp increased, Saul cut the priest short and rallied his army.

Thus, Saul and his six hundred men rushed upon the main Philistine force from Gibeah. We also learn in 1 Samuel 14:21 that certain Hebrews had actually deserted Saul and joined the Philistine Army. We see this with David later on in the narrative.

Apparently these Israelites were "all around in the camp" (1 Samuel 14:21) of the main Philistine force in Michmash. Upon seeing their countrymen rally against the Philistines, these fair-weather Hebrews "turned to be with the Israelites who were with Saul and Jonathan" (1 Samuel 14:21). Also, the men who had fled and "hidden themselves in the hill country of Ephraim" (1 Samuel 14:22) were inspired and rallied to Saul's side. Thus, the Hebrews literally sprang up from within and around the Philistines, cutting down the shocked, panicked, and overwhelmed Philistine warriors.

Hebrews emerged from holes, crooks, cracks, and tents and rallied to pursue the confused Philistine Army. What was not visible to the naked eye was the heavenly host that went before Israel. God sent his army into the Philistine camp, as he had sent his warrior, called "the LORD" in Joshua 6:2, to Joshua decades prior (Joshua 5:13-15), and achieved victory for his people. The timeless message is clear; God delivers his people.

"So the Lord delivered Israel that day, and the battle spread beyond Beth-aven" (1 Samuel 14:23).

1 SAMUEL 14
(PART 2)

SAUL SHOWS A TENDENCY TO rush into action, as he did when he offered the sacrifices rather than being patient and allowing Samuel to offer them as he had been instructed in 1 Samuel 13:9. Saul acts equally impatient again in 1 Samuel 14, indicative that he did not learn any lessons from his previous actions.

Through the heroic act of Jonathan and his armor-bearer, and the intervention of God, the Philistine Army is in flight. It was not an easy battle, however, as Scripture indicates the men of Israel were extremely worn out, exhausted to the point of collapse. In 1 Samuel 13:24, we learn the Israelites were "hard pressed on that day," and in 1 Samuel 13:28, we learn "the people were weary."

To continue the pursuit and defeat of the fleeing Philistines, the Israelite Army needed sustenance, which often took place when victorious armies raided and plundered their defeated enemies. Saul, however, in a misguided attempt to speed up the pursuit of the Philistines, ordered that no man shall eat, "until I have avenged myself on my enemies." Saul's only concern was his victory—thus, with this order, we see both Saul's selfishness and his reckless impatience.

Such an order for the people to press on in pursuit without stopping to strengthen themselves seemed like an appropriate order to Saul. His plans, often, were not well thought out.

This order was not made with the best intentions of the people in mind, but rather with his own intentions and selfish needs placed first. Notice, too, nowhere do we see Saul consult God about his course of action. Only after he issued the order to not eat does Saul inquire of God. Saul's request is pictured in 1 Samuel 14:37.

"And Saul inquired of God, 'Shall I go down after the Philistines? Wilt Thou give them into the hand of Israel?' But He did not answer him on that day."

With 1 Samuel 14:37, we begin to witness the slow decline of Saul. God was an afterthought. He seemed to have removed Himself from Saul, his foolish council, and his cabinet. If Saul had sought God first, he would've seen the foolishness of his order. Scripture makes it plain that the Israelite Army needed rest and recovery. God had granted them a great victory and the chance to further defeat their enemies. Saul, however, had neglected God and sought to do things his own way. His hasty and reckless order would have dire consequences.

Exercise: Read 1 Samuel 14:27.

- How often do you rush into action headfirst without consulting God? Describe a time you were guilty of this.
- What lesson do you learn from watching Saul in 1 Samuel 14:37?
- Who was unaware of Saul's order? What did he do?
- What was the result of his actions?

Jonathan had not heard the order his father issued. Thus, he took time to eat and strengthen himself. Consequently Scripture records he was re-energized as "his eyes brightened." Nearby, soldiers witnessed his act and informed him he had transgressed his father's order. Jonathan's remark to them may indicate that a rift had developed between father and son.

"Then Jonathan said, 'My father has troubled the land. See now, how my eyes brightened because I tasted a little of this honey. How much more, if only the people had eaten freely today of the spoil of their enemies which they found! For now the slaughter among the Philistines has not been great'" (1 Samuel 14:29-30).

Jonathan's words indicate Israel could have inflicted far more damage to the Philistines. All of Saul's preparations and actions in 1 Samuel 14 seem hasty, rushed, and executed with little organization or planning. How often do we miss out on what God fully wants for us because of similar attitudes? How often do we forget to thank God for the victories he gives us? How often do we plunge ahead with our own agenda without stopping first to ask of God?

Exercise: Look at Saul in 1 Samuel 14:35.

- What does the Bible depict Saul doing in 1 Samuel 14:35?
- Scripture goes out of its way to give further detail concerning Saul's act. What other detail do we learn in this passage?

Read the following passages from Scripture and compare them to Saul's altar in 1 Samuel 14:35:

1. Genesis 8:18-20
   In Genesis 8:16-17, God instructed Noah that it was now okay to leave the ark. In Genesis 8:18-20, we see Noah's actions upon leaving the ark. The first thing Noah did was build an altar to the Lord and sacrifice "every clean animal and of every clean bird" (Genesis 8:20) to the Lord.

2. Genesis 12:6-7
   These verses record Abraham's first footsteps in the land of Canaan. His entrance into the promised land is in Genesis 12:6. Take notice of Abraham's actions upon entering this strange and foreign land.

3. Exodus 17:15
   In Exodus 17:14, Moses and the Israelites defeated the Amalekites at Rephidim in the wilderness. This verse records Moses's

deeds immediately following the victory. Moses, like Noah above, built an altar and dedicated it to the Lord.

4.   Joshua 8:30-31
     The Israelites are preparing to enter Canaan under the leadership of Joshua. The Battle of Jericho opened the door to the interior of the highlands. In Joshua 8:28-29, Joshua defeats the Canaanites at Ai, giving Israel a foothold in the western mountains.
     From here, the Israelites will carry out their southern campaign to conquer Canaan. Joshua, however, stops in Joshua 8:30 and builds an altar to the Lord. Notice his attitude toward the Lord is similar to that of Moses and Noah.

- In your own words, describe what you notice in these passages.
- How do Saul's actions compare to the actions of those mentioned above?
- What lesson do you take from studying Saul's actions in relation to those of the other leaders mentioned above?
- What message is God sending us?

The act of building the altar meant taking time out of the task at hand and devoting that time to God. God instructed mankind from the beginning to set aside time devoted to him. Sacrifices and thanks would be offered to God glorifying and honoring him. The sacrifice itself was important, but more so the spirit in which it was offered.

We see this principle in action with the sacrifices of Cain and Abel. Each offered sacrifices to God, yet only one was acceptable. From the beginning, the spirit of worship was crucial to our relationship with YHWH. The men of God mentioned above stopped their tasks immediately, and without hesitation, offered sacrifices and thanks to God.

Sacrifices were meant to accompany both triumphs and defeats, celebrations and hard times. They were a sign of thankfulness, as well as an offering for forgiveness of sins and transgressions. Saul did build an altar to the Lord; however, Scripture does not mention the sacrifices made upon the altar. Not only is Scripture silent as to Saul's sacrifice, but in 1 Samuel 14:37 God does not answer Saul's inquiry. God turns a deaf ear to Saul and his request, much as he looked with disdain upon Cain's sacrifice.

THE SIN OF JONATHAN

In 1 Samuel 14:38, Saul identifies "sin" as the reason God had not answered him. Sin is the one thing that separates us from God. That's why so many sacrifices were required in the Old Testament and upon the altar of the temple in the New Testament. The sacrifice reconciled man to God. The life and blood of the animal atoned for the sin of man. Sin caused death, and to seek forgiveness and restoration to God, a life was required. In the first century A.D., Jesus Christ made the ultimate sacrifice for all of mankind. His sacrifice is what the New Testament is about. His Spirit permeates all of the Bible—from creation in Genesis, to apocalypse in Revelation.

The books of Moses lay forth detailed and specific instructions from God on how to atone for sin through sacrifices (Exodus 29; Leviticus 4). Since the days of Eden, sin has sought out mankind and eagerly seeks to separate us from God.

"If you do well, will not your countenance be lifted up? And if you do not do well, sin is crouching at the door; and its desire is for you, but you must master it" (Genesis 4:7).

These are God's words to Cain after his unacceptable offering. In Genesis 4:8, Cain murders his brother. Sin was indeed crouching at the door.

"No one born of God practices sin, because His seed abides in him; and he cannot sin, because he is born of God" (1 John 3:9).

In 1 John 3:8, the devil is credited with sin and practicing sin from the beginning. God, however, will one day destroy the devil and sin. His son Jesus Christ conquered death, taking the sting out of sin for those who believe and follow. Jesus's life took the place of the blood sacrifice God demanded in the Old Testament.

"But your iniquities have made a separation between you and your God, and your sins have hidden His face from you, so that He does not hear" (Isaiah 59:2).

Isaiah spoke these words to Israel in the eighth century when Assyria threatened both Israel and Judah. Though spoken during the reigns of the Kings Ahaz, Uzziah, and Jotham, these words could have easily been spoken to Saul as well.

Exercise: Open your Bible and read Ezekiel 14:7-8.

- How serious is God about sin?
- How do you separate yourself from God?
- Who does the sinner answer to?
- What is the final result of sin?

Saul understood the seriousness of sin, which is why he set out in 1 Samuel 14:37-39 to find the sinner. The people knew Jonathan had transgressed, yet they didn't respond to Saul's inquiries. This may indicate that some of the men maintained a deeper sense of loyalty to Jonathan than the king. This, too, would have contributed to Saul's instability and insecurity (1 Samuel 14:39). Saul then seeks the Lord through the casting of lots, a common practice in the early Old Testament. The Urim and Thummim would be used for this purpose.

THE URIM AND THUMMIM

The exact nature of these items is unknown. The way in which they were used is unknown as well. The Urim and Thummim are, for the most part, a total mystery to us today. However, Scripture does give us clues.

Exercise:

Read the following passages and answer the questions to gain a better understanding of these mysterious instruments of God:

1. Exodus 28:30

    o   Where do these objects belong and who uses them?

2. Leviticus 8:8

    o   Who is wearing them in this verse?

3. Numbers 27:21

    o   Who is in charge of the Urim in this passage?

    o   What is his title?

    o   What is he using the Urim for?

4. Deuteronomy 33:8

    o   What is the significance of Levi, the son of Jacob (see Numbers 1:50; 3:12)?

    o   After Aaron and Eleazar, who was responsible for the Urim and Thummim?

5. 1 Samuel 28:6

    o   Why didn't the Urim work in this passage?

    o   Who is trying to use it?

6. Ezra 2:63

    o   This is centuries after Moses and Saul, yet who still stands with the Urim and Thummim?

7. Nehemiah 7:65

    o   Who is responsible for these objects? This is the last time in Scripture these objects are mentioned.

The literal meaning of "Urim" is "lights," and "Thummim" is "perfections." Thus, these two items were known in English as Lights and Perfections. They fit into the priest's breastplate and were used to decipher

God's will in certain situations. Dr. Spiros Zodhiates lists one theory as to how these objects may have worked. This theory states they were two flat objects with one side meaning Urim and the other Thummim.

When cast as dice, they would land with a particular side up or down. If both sides showed Urim, God's answer was no. If both sides came up Thummim, the answer was yes. If one of each came up, then God was not answering.

Perhaps this would explain Saul's inability to decipher God's response, as one of each side continued to appear when he cast them. God was remaining silent on the issue at hand.

Thus, Saul inquires of the sin in 1 Samuel 14:40-46. As the lots were cast, Jonathan was chosen as the guilty party. Once again, we see weakness in Saul's leadership ability. In 1 Samuel 14:39, Saul issues another irrational command in relation to the person found guilty of the sin.

"'For as the Lord lives, who delivers Israel, though it is in Jonathan my son, he shall surely die.' But not one of all the people answered him" (1 Samuel 14:39).

The people knew Jonathan had committed the sin. However, as previously mentioned, nobody said a word. Jonathan was eventually pegged as the guilty party, and according to the words of Saul, Jonathan had to die. King Saul plans on executing his own son!

Exercise: Turn and read 1 Samuel 14:45.

- How was Jonathan's life spared?

Anybody who has held a position of leadership over people understands Saul's mistake here. When a leader or boss declares something, then goes back on his or her word or fails to follow through, he or she loses respect among his or her subordinates.

Saul's irrational order to not eat in the first place was followed by an equally irrational order that the guilty party must die. When the guilty turned out to be his son Jonathan, Saul failed to execute him, not because he hesitated but because the people interceded on Jonathan's behalf. Nowhere do we see Saul fully seeking God's counsel and guidance in the matter. In 1 Samuel 14:19, Saul went through the motions but cut it short to join the battle.

There can be little doubt Saul was a capable and brave warrior. He was also a brave king, at times. In 1 Samuel 14:48, the Bible states Saul "acted valiantly" against Israel's enemies. Yet Saul lacked a heart focused on God.

Saul's strengths as a king began to dwindle and his flaws began to emerge in 1 Samuel 14. The early signs of self-reliance, hasty judgment, and empty ritualism began to manifest themselves in this chapter. These symptoms would combine to signal the beginning of Saul's tragic downfall in 1 Samuel 14. The sad story of Saul, the first King of Israel, begins.

1 SAMUEL 15

THE HISTORICAL CONTEXT OF THIS chapter begins hundreds of years earlier in Exodus 17, during Israel's exodus out of Egypt. We also find a precedent for these events in a similar story from Joshua 7. The verse 1 Samuel 15:1 opens with the mentor giving instructions to the pupil.

"Then Samuel said to Saul, 'The Lord sent me to anoint you as king over His people, over Israel, now therefore, listen to the words of the Lord.'"

Samuel reminded Saul of his divine appointment. Notice Samuel's humility in this instance. He had access to the king; he had the ear of the most powerful man in Israel and carried significant influence with him. Samuel, however, reflected everything back to God. It was all according to the "words of the Lord," not the words of Samuel. Samuel made it clear to Saul he was answering to God, not Samuel or any other man, but to God Almighty—El Shaddai, the glory of Israel.

Samuel wanted Saul to understand God required complete and total obedience to his instructions. Samuel, thus, established the Lord as the sole authority. In 1 Samuel 15:2–3, Samuel gives Saul God's orders to Israel.

Exercise: Turn and read 1 Samuel 15:2-3.

- What were God's instructions to Saul?
- Who was he to let live?
- What was he to take from the Amalekites?

God appeared harsh and severe with the people of Amalek at first glance. One must keep in mind the Bronze Age was a violent time, full of war and uncertainty. Many nations were very hostile toward Israel, as they are today. These orders were made to fulfill a prophecy made hundreds of years earlier. Turn to Exodus 17:8-16 and read about the incident that motivated God's command here in 1 Samuel 15:2.

THE AMALEKITES

Under the leadership of Moses, the Israelites were marching through the wilderness on their way to the promised land. Egypt was to their rear, Canaan lay before them, desert lay all around, and enemies lurked in the periphery. As is typical for the nation of Israel, these were precarious times. Moses had just struck the rock at Horeb, producing drinking water for the weary and thirsty Israelites. In Exodus 17:9, we are introduced to a new figure in the Old Testament, one who was to take on prominence in the upcoming events. For the first time we meet Joshua, son of Nun.

Amalek had come and fought against Israel in Rephidim. The exact location is unknown for certain, but some believe it to be in the southernmost parts of the Sinai.

Regardless, these people were nomads, wandering from one spot to the next, living off the land and following the seasons with their migrations. For the most part, they inhabited the desert region between Egypt and Canaan and occupied land in the Negev region. David fought against them at Ziklag, located just north of the Sinai peninsula in the Negev—Canaan's southern desert region.

In Exodus 17:8, they are in the Sinai. Moses instructed Joshua to lead the men against these wicked people. The Amalekites had attacked vulnerable and unprotected Israelites wandering in the desert. They attacked Israel's rear column consisting of the elderly, those sick or maimed, the weakest of the Israelites, young children, and others vulnerable to the harsh elements. The details concerning this unprovoked and cruel attack can be found in Deuteronomy 25:17-19. This passage in Deuteronomy is part of Moses's last sermon to Israel, delivered approximately forty years after the incident with Amalek in Exodus. The elderly, young, weak, those "stragglers at your rear when you were faint and weary," were the victims of this cruel and ruthless attack found in Exodus 17:8.

The Amalekites had butchered the defenseless among Israel. God viewed this as a wicked and cowardly attack by the descendants of Esau, the brother of Jacob/Israel. This slaughter provoked the Lord to extreme anger, and in Exodus 17, Joshua led the Israelite Army in battle against these people. Moses, Aaron, and Hur looked on at the battle from a nearby hilltop. As long as Moses held up his hands with his staff toward God Almighty, the Israelites prevailed.

However, as his arms grew tired and dropped, the battle turned against Israel. The battle raged on all day, and Moses became so exhausted, he was forced to sit upon a stone while Aaron and Hur each held up one of his arms.

Eventually the Israelites prevailed over the wicked and cowardly Amalekites, yet the future would hold many more battles between these two enemy nations. In Exodus 17, the passage ends with the Lord declaring he will "have war against Amalek from generation to generation." Moses, in Deuteronomy 25, also urged Israel to not forget God's orders to utterly destroy the Amalekites. Fast forward nearly four centuries into the future to 1 Samuel 15 and it is to be King Saul who executes God's divine judgment on Amalek.

Through a little biblical research, we learn God's orders to Saul are part of his divine plan stretching back to a time long before Saul. Yet, we also learn in Psalms 90:4 that "a thousand years in Thy sight are like yesterday when it passes by." YHWH does not forget the suffering of his people.

Samuel made it clear King Saul was the divine instrument of God toward the Amalekites in 1 Samuel 15:1-3. This was yet another test for King Saul. Would he fully obey God? What does obedience to God mean? What type of obedience does God want from us?

Exercise: Read the following passages:

1. "Through whom we have received grace and apostleship to bring about the obedience of faith among all the Gentiles, for His name's sake" (Romans 1:5).

2. "Then he took the book of the covenant and read it in the hearing of the people; and they said, 'All that he Lord has spoken we will do, and we will be obedient'" (Exodus 24:7).

3. "If only you listen obediently to the voice of the Lord your God, to observe carefully all this commandment which I am commanding you" (Deuteronomy 15:5).

4. "But Peter and the apostles answered and said, 'We must obey God rather than men'" (Acts 5:29).

5. "And the people said to Joshua; 'We will serve the Lord our God and we will obey His voice'" (Joshua 24:24).

6. "And having been made perfect, He became to all those who obey Him the source of salvation" (Hebrews 5:9).

•   How does obedience take place?
•   What can we do to become more obedient to God?

It is interesting to take note of the word translated as "obedient" in Exodus 24:7, "listen obediently" in Deuteronomy 15:5, and "obey" in Joshua 24:24. All three of these verses contain the same Hebrew word, *shama*, pronounced *shaw-mah*. This word literally means "to hear intelligently."

113

It is often used with the implication of attention and obedience. Zodhiates's *Lexical Aides to the Old Testament* in his *NASB Hebrew-Greek Key Study Bible* illuminates the fact that this verb occurs 1,160 times in the Hebrew Old Testament.

This makes it one of the most important words in all of the Bible. The principle meaning of the word is "to perceive a message or sense a sound." It is listening, to hear, to give heed, to obey. Thus, obedience in the Old Testament is unquestionably linked to listening, to giving one's undivided attention to a particular message or messenger.

The Greeks, likewise, took their cue from the Hebrew word in Romans 1:15 and Hebrews 5:9. The words translated as "obedience" in Romans and "obey" in Hebrews is the Greek *hupakouo.*

This Greek word means "attentive harkening; to hear under as a subordinate; to listen attentively." By implication, it means to heed or conform to a command or authority, compliance or submission. Obedience in the New Testament rests on listening to the words of Jesus and becoming submissive to his teachings and commands.

It was the submissive and compliant part that King Saul, like so many of us, struggled with. We must ultimately listen to God, through his Word, our studies, our time with him, pastors, priests, friends, and day-to-day living. A major part of listening is being still long enough to actually hear what is being said. Perhaps that was a problem of Saul's.

Scripture does portray him seeking a priest, then in the middle of inquiring, he asked the priest to withdraw his hand, as if Saul was not patient enough to wait for an answer. Saul built an altar, then Scripture remained silent about the altar, as if Saul had not used it. Many altars had previously been mentioned as being built and then used, dedicated in honor of the Lord. Not so with Saul.

Saul may have been too busy pursuing his own agenda, or he may not have taken the time to incorporate God into his daily affairs. Oftentimes, we get caught up in the business of our life. Day-to-day living is often chaotic, and it is easy to lose track of our time with God. Saul may have fallen into such a trap. We must seek out time to be with God. It must be a conscientious decision and effort. Read what Scripture has to say about spending time with God on a day-to-day basis.

"Cease striving and know that I am God; I will be exalted among the nations, I will be exalted in the earth" (Psalms 46:10).

"Be still, and know that I am God; I will be exalted among the nations, I will be exalted in the earth" (Psalms 46:10 NIV).

The central message is to be still! Stop running from appointment to appointment like a madman or madwoman, and take some time. Get up earlier, go to bed earlier, buy a pocket Bible, or in today's world of technology, a Bible app for your phone. Be still. Stop striving by occupying every waking moment in the pursuit of that which will rot and decay.

In 1 Samuel 15:3-9, King Saul leads Israel's Army in the desert region to the south of Jerusalem. Scripture indicates he might even have been east of the Arabah Valley, south of the Dead Sea. Israel defeats the Amalekites under Saul's leadership.

Exercise: Read carefully 1 Samuel 15:8-9.

- Does it appear as if Saul listened to God in this instance?
- What were Saul's initial instructions regarding the treatment of the Amalekites (see 1 Samuel 15:3)?
- Did he carry out these orders precisely?
- How did Saul disobey God's orders?

JOSHUA 7: THE SIN OF ACHAN

A similar situation occurred during the time of Joshua and the conquest. Open your Bible to Joshua 7. This chapter deals with Joshua's first defeat as a general at Ai. The Israelites' defeat took place on the heels of their victory over Jericho. Before Israel conquered Jericho, God had told Joshua that "the city shall be under the ban, it and all that is in it belongs to the Lord" (Joshua 6:17). However, as they set out in the second battle against Ai, they suffered a terrible defeat.

Exercise: Turn and read Joshua 7:16-26.

- What was Achan's sin?
- What was the result of his sin?
- Once the punishment was meted out, what was the result of the next battle? (Joshua 8:16-21)

The stoning of Achan's entire family may seem harsh and unnecessary to us. But we must keep in mind that God sees what we don't. Achan's sin put everybody at risk. One man's careless attitude toward God cost lives. The sin must be dealt with before God can work. The same holds true for the sin in our lives. Like Achan, we can try to hide it. We may even be able to hide it from man. We cannot hide it, however, from God. Nothing can separate us from God's eyes; nothing shields us from his penetrating gaze.

Our souls always lay bare and exposed before God: every thought, every intention, every motive is as plain to God as the sun in our sky.

ROMANS 8:38-39

"For I am convinced that neither death, nor life, nor angels, nor principalities, nor things present, nor things to come, nor powers, nor height, nor depth, nor any other created thing shall be able to separate us from the love of God, which is in Christ Jesus our Lord."

Exercise:

- What do you take from this verse? How does it (if it does) apply to your current life situation?

GOD'S REJECTION OF SAUL: 1 SAMUEL 15:10

These verses give us the events preceding the establishment of the Davidic throne through David. In order for David to be made king, however, Saul had to give up the throne. Saul's rejection by God as king over Israel was a direct result of the events in 1 Samuel 15. King Saul's mental and spiritual state quickly descended into madness and paranoia. In 1 Samuel 15:10-11, God reveals his anger toward Saul. In 1 Samuel 15:11, we hear God's words to Samuel.

"'I regret that I have made Saul king, for he has turned back from following after Me, and has not carried out My commands.' And Samuel was distressed and cried out to the Lord all night."

Samuel was greatly disturbed by God's decision regarding Saul. The Hebrew word for "cried" literally translates to "shriek." Samuel spent all night on his knees, fervently praying for Saul to the point of shrieking to the Lord. This is something we see the great men of the Bible doing: begging on their knees on behalf of man to God Almighty, even those men who are wicked and evil.

Exercise: Turn and read Genesis 18:20-33.

- Who is involved in this passage?
- What is the identity of the man Abraham interacts with, to the best of your knowledge?
- What does Abraham plea to the man for?
- Are his pleas effective? What was the final outcome?

Turn and read Exodus 32:11-13.

- Who is involved in this passage?
- What sin is committed, and by whom?
- What does Moses do for the people of Israel?
- Is Moses successful?

Turn and read 1 Samuel 15:11.

- Who is involved in this passage?

- Who pleas to God on Saul's behalf?
- In your own opinion, why does Samuel stand up for Saul before God?

Turn and read Luke 23:34.

- Who is involved in this passage?
- What is happening in this verse?
- Who does Jesus plea for?
- What was the final result of this passage?

Samuel, like the men in these passages, spent the night on his knees earnestly praying and begging for mercy from God on behalf of the wayward king Saul. Inevitably, the sun rose, and with the morning Samuel set out to find Saul and reveal the message to him. Samuel learned Saul had been spotted as he passed through Carmel, which lay on the way back from the battle with the Amalekites.

In 1 Samuel 15:12, we catch a glimpse of Saul's mind-set after the battle. An unidentified man reports to Samuel, "Saul came to Carmel, and behold, he set up a monument for himself." He did not build an altar and offer sacrifices to God. He did not give glory and thanks to God for the victory. The Bible tells us he set up a monument to honor himself. This action falls in line with Saul's previous actions, motivated by concern for his own plan and desires and not God's. Samuel finds Saul and confronts him.

Exercise: Read 1 Samuel 15:13-19.

- In Saul's mind, is he guilty of transgressing the Lord's commands?
- What do you think about Saul? Is he just lying? Does he not get it? Or, is he just more concerned about himself? What is your opinion?
- Based on 1 Samuel 15:17, why did God originally choose Saul as king of Israel? (Further study: Numbers 12:3; Psalms 10:17; Psalms 25:9; Proverbs 16:18-19; Matthew 11:29; James 4:10)

Upon Samuel's rebuke, Saul responds in 1 Samuel 15:20 by laying the blame on the people. A good leader does not seek to escape punishment by throwing his people to the wolves. Saul claimed he did obey God, but it was the people who disobeyed, not him. Saul exhibited a politician's mind-set and rationale. Too many of our current "leaders" use similar logic and arguments to justify their lies and deceptions and corruptions. They, like Saul, claim "It wasn't me!"

In 1 Samuel 15:24, Saul admits he "feared the people, and listened to their voice." When we listen to man, or society, we cannot obey God because we don't hear him. We listen to Hollywood, politicians, the rich, special interest groups, musicians, magazines, TV, and so on. All of the noise is really a distraction that prevents us from hearing God's voice. Why?

Exercise:

- Who do you listen to?

Samuel states what God really wants in 1 Samuel 15:22. His statement resounds throughout the entire Bible and is the very basis of why Jesus died on the cross.

"And Samuel said, 'Has the Lord as much delight in burnt offerings and sacrifices as in obeying the voice of the Lord? Behold, to obey is better than sacrifice, and to heed than the fat of rams'" (1 Samuel 15:22).

Exercise:

Now turn to the gospels and read Matthew 26:36-46 and Luke 22:41-44.

- Based on these passages, does it seem that Jesus, in his fleshly nature, wanted to undergo his crucifixion?
- Why did he go through with it?

Jesus had a strong willingness to obey God, his Father, rather than his earthly body and desires.

OBEDIENCE

As Samuel turns to leave Saul, Saul grabs his cloak and rips a piece of the fabric. Samuel turns and looks at Saul, saying, "The Lord has torn the kingdom of Israel from you today." Then Samuel fulfills God's orders in a very graphic and descriptive way. It is hard to imagine this man of God carrying out the following act. Agag, the Amalekite king, is brought before Samuel: "and Samuel hewed Agag to pieces." Scripture tells us Samuel never saw Saul again until "the day of his death"(1 Samuel 15:35).

However, Scripture also indicates that Samuel never ceased grieving over Saul, who once showed such promise. God, though, had already chosen his next king.

1 SAMUEL 16:1-13

THE EVENTS IN 1 SAMUEL 16 are some of the most important events in all of the Bible. This chapter records the calling and anointing of King David—from whom the promised Messiah would descend. To the Christian, the Messiah is Jesus Christ. To the Jew, the promised Messiah has yet to come. Jesus refers to Himself, or is referred to by others, as the son of David on numerous occasions in the New Testament (see Matthew 12:23; Mark 10:47; Luke 2:4; Luke 18:38; John 7:42).

"He also chose David His servant, and took him from the sheep folds: From the care of the ewes with suckling lambs He brought him to shepherd His people, and Israel His inheritance" (Psalms 78:70-71).

"And after He had removed him, He raised up David to be their king, concerning whom He also testified and said, 'I have found David the son of Jesse, a man after my heart, who will do all My will. From the offspring of this man, according to promise, God has brought to Israel a Savior, Jesus" (Acts 13:22-23).

God doesn't allow Samuel to spend long mourning Saul, for in 1 Samuel 16:1, he tells Samuel he had already selected another. Saul, however, would maintain his throne and power for the time being. He had loyal followers and controlled the army; thus, Saul's physical removal from the crown would have to wait. God had already removed him spiritually, but the next king needed time for God to groom him and prepare him for the task ahead.

"Now the Lord said to Samuel, 'How long will you grieve over Saul since I have rejected him from being king over Israel? Fill your horn with oil, and go; I will send you to Jesse the Bethlehemite, for I have selected a king for Myself among his sons" (1 Samuel 16:1).

Samuel, however, feared Saul's reaction and complained to God that Saul would take his life. Thus, God devised a scheme for Samuel. He was to take a heifer with him and offer it as a sacrifice to God on behalf of the city. By doing this, Samuel's pretense for visiting the city would not draw suspicion. As usual, the Lord provided a way around a difficult situation. Notice that Samuel simply told God his concerns, and the Lord provided.

Exercise:

- What are some difficult situations you are currently facing?
- Have you told God specifically of your difficulties? Do you believe he can provide for you, as he did for Samuel?

"Then you will call upon Me and come and pray to Me and I will listen to you" (Jeremiah 29:12).

"But when you pray, go into your inner room, and when you have shut your door, pray to your Father who is in secret, and your Father who sees in secret will repay you" (Matthew 6:6).

"Be anxious for nothing, but in everything with prayer and supplication with thanksgiving let your requests be made known to God" (Philippians 4:6).

Once again, God only revealed part of his plan to Samuel. First, he was to go. Then he would find out more later. In 1 Samuel 16:4, Scripture states the primary difference between Samuel and Saul: "So Samuel did what the Lord said." Samuel trusted God, had faith in his promises, listened intently to his voice, and obeyed God's commands—none of which King Saul did consistently.

Exercise:

- How are you going to deal with difficult times and situations in your life?

- How are you going to respond to uncomfortable tasks God requires of you?

Samuel was not comfortable going to Bethlehem. He feared for his life and told God so. God, as he is prone to do, provided a pretense for Samuel's trip. He did not leave his servants to perish. Moses complained about his lack of speaking ability, thus God gave him Aaron (Exodus 4:11-14). How must Abraham have felt when told to sacrifice his only son Isaac? That surely was an excruciating ordeal for father and son. Abraham did not waver in his obedience and faith in God's provision.

"And Abraham said; 'God will provide for Himself the lamb for the burnt offering, my son.' So the two of them walked on together" (Genesis 22:8).

Samuel lost Saul. What started so promising had soured quickly. It would seem power became Saul's god. This felt like failure in Samuel's eyes. He had anointed Saul, per God's instruction, and had tried to mentor and instruct the young Saul to become a godly king. Now, Saul had been rejected by God. Scripture implied Samuel mourned a long time for Saul, his former pupil. Finally, God nudged him from his state of mourning and urged Samuel to get on with life.

In the end, we must act as Samuel acted and do what the Lord requires. Therefore, in 1 Samuel 16:4, Samuel travels to Bethlehem in search for a new king of Israel. Recall 1 Samuel 15:33 when Samuel "hewed Agag to pieces," literally cutting him up in a gruesome act of obedience. Samuel had likely earned a fierce reputation as a powerful and mysterious man of God. The people likely whispered tales of the old prophet. They feared and respected his relationship with YHWH. He was the first prophet to appear in Israel in quite some time. His presence carried with it God's message.

As Samuel enters the city in 1 Samuel 16:4 "the elders of the city came trembling to meet him and asked, 'Do you come in peace?'"

Samuel was the man of God, the Seer, the one who dared to defy the king and get away with it. He had previously slain the Amalekite king. Samuel was not your kindhearted old grandfather in a Santa suit, but a tough and fearful prophet. He had God's Spirit upon him.

Exercise: Read the following passages and compare them to Samuel:

1. "For God has not given us a spirit of timidity, but of power and love and discipline" (2 Timothy 1:7).

2. "Have I not commanded you? Be strong and courageous! Do not tremble or be dismayed, for the Lord your God is with you wherever you go" (Joshua 1:9).

•   How did Samuel live out these verses in his life in 1 Samuel 15 and 16?

Samuel had confidence, faith, and trust in God. He knew God Almighty was who he said he was and meant what he said. Samuel acted boldly in faith, not wavering from his duty as God's man. As tough as it was for Samuel to let Saul go, God instructed him to do so.

Exercise:

•   What are some tough decisions and actions you have made and taken—perhaps letting go of a loved one, spouse, or friend?

•   Did you act boldly in faith?

•   Did you call on God for guidance and help?

Once in Bethlehem, Samuel invites Jesse and his sons to the sacrifice. It was to Jesse's house God had ordered Samuel. God gave Samuel no indication of who he was to choose, only that it would be a son of Jesse. As Samuel entered Jesse's house, the sons of Jesse were brought before him. In 1 Samuel 16:6, Jesse's son Eliab passes before Samuel.

Exercise: Read 1 Samuel 16:6.

- What did Samuel think to himself when Eliab presented himself?

- Who does this remind us of, in terms of physical appearance?

Samuel had previously consecrated Jesse's household in preparation for the sacrifices. This notion of consecration played a key role in the anointing of a king. The word translated as "consecrate" means "to be, make, pronounce, or observe as clean." It conveys the idea of holy preparation, the shedding of past sins and guilt to meet with God. Consecration is becoming holy, clean, and prepared to meet God.

Leviticus 11:44 gives a clear picture of consecration: "For I am the Lord your God. Consecrate yourselves therefore and be holy; for I am holy. And you shall not make yourselves unclean with any of the swarming things that swarm on earth."

"Speak to all the congregation of the sons of Israel and say to them; 'You shall be holy, for I the Lord your God am holy'" (Leviticus 19:2).

Peter quoted Leviticus 11:44 in 1 Peter 1:16. "Consecrated" also takes on the concept of being separated. It refers to people or things being set aside for use by God, for worship of God. Consecrated means being made holy and sacred exclusively for God. Israel was consecrated among the nations. Samuel was consecrated by his mother even before his birth.

The king of Israel was to be consecrated, or anointed, to lead God's people. Jesus Christ consecrated mankind, enabling us to stand before God blameless without sin. God consecrated Jesus for his death and resurrection. God requires us to believe in his life and death and to be obedient by abstaining from the unclean thoughts and actions of the flesh. This is considered righteousness—to believe and obey Jesus Christ.

- Do you need to consecrate yourself? If so, Jesus provides us with the forgiveness we need to achieve holiness.

- What are some things you need to separate yourself from? God may be leading you toward consecrating your heart through confession.

Samuel thought Eliab had been set aside by God based on his physical appearance. He thought God's anointing must surely be on this son of Jesse. However, 1 Samuel 16:7 indicates otherwise.

"But the Lord said to Samuel, 'Do not look at his appearance or at the height of his stature, because I have rejected him: for God sees not as man sees, for man looks at the outward appearance, but the Lord looks at the heart."

What a beautiful verse, harkening back to Saul's selection as king. Eliab, like Saul, had an impressive physical stature and look. Samuel was slow to learn that appearance doesn't matter. Scripture reveals Saul was head and shoulders above anyone else in Israel, yet, Saul failed miserably before God.

Exercise: Read 1 Kings 8:39 and 1 Chronicles 28:9.

- According to these verses, what part of a man does God look at?
- What does David tell his son Solomon in 1 Chronicles 28?
- What does David say will happen if he forsakes God? What experience could David have been drawing from in offering these words of wisdom?

Each of Jesse's sons pass by Samuel in 1 Samuel 16:8-10. In 1 Samuel 16:11, we're introduced to the future king.

"And Samuel said to Jesse, 'Are these all the children?' And he said, 'There remains yet the youngest, and behold, he is tending the sheep.' Then Samuel said to Jesse, 'Send and bring him; for we will not sit down until he comes here.'"

- What two facts do we learn about David from this verse?
- What does the fact that Jesse didn't even think to bring him before Samuel indicate about David's standing in his family?

Scripture seems to imply that David was a mere afterthought in his family. Jesse had to be prodded to even mention his youngest son David. David hadn't been present at the sacrifice because he was tending his father's sheep in the field. This is a remarkably humble and insignificant introduction to the greatest king in Israel's history. He was a young shepherd boy, the runt of the family.

Shepherds spent days and months alone with their sheep. They had to constantly monitor them and watch over them, much like an infant's parents. Hours were passed in silence, or in David's case, oftentimes with music, as David was a skilled musician. David was also protective of his sheep. Wolves, bears, and other wild beasts threatened the safety of the fold daily, and the shepherd was responsible for warding off these dangers.

It was now clear to Samuel the future king of Israel was the youngest sibling who had been consigned to tending his father's sheep. Samuel had David sent for at once. God had not spoken concerning the other sons of Jesse, so this boy had to be the one—despite his current lowly station in life. To show the sense of urgency with God's mission, Samuel instructed nobody was to sit down until David had arrived and was seated first before them. Scripture does not indicate how long they waited, yet it likely would have been at least a few hours.

Anytime God gives us a message, it is urgent. When we have a task to do, it is very urgent. Samuel possessed that sense of urgency, that sense to do God's bidding at once, no matter the circumstance. Samuel could have left Jesse's house, or come back after lunch, or he could have left a message. However, he knew the importance of fulfilling God's command immediately. In 1 Samuel 16:12, David is brought before Samuel.

Exercise: Read 1 Samuel 16:12.

- How is David described physically?
- What does God tell Samuel to do?

Though David was not as big as Eliab or Saul, he was handsome in appearance. He was ruddy, or rosy, reddish, flushed, healthy looking. He was a lad, a young boy, perhaps a teenager. He was not kingly or presidential. Notice Samuel's reaction in 1 Samuel 16:13 to God's instruction. He wastes no time.

"Then Samuel took the horn of oil and anointed him in the midst of his brothers; and the Spirit of the Lord came mightily upon David from that day forward. And Samuel arose and went to Ramah" (1 Samuel 16:13).

This is a familiar scene, one which played out nearly step-by-step in 1 Samuel 10. Imagine the look on the faces of David's brothers. Scripture mentioned he was anointed "in the midst of his brothers." The runt, little brother was anointed as the next leader of God's people. It is very likely nobody believed it to be true, not even David. The Bible is vague as to the ceremony and reactions of those present. Perhaps they misunderstood what was happening. Perhaps David's brothers became jealous. As soon as David had been anointed, the Spirit of the Lord "came mightily" upon him.

The descending of God's Spirit was a regular occurrence in this chapter of Israel's history. One harkens back to 1 Samuel 3:1 when "word from the Lord was rare." Then God called Samuel in 1 Samuel 3:4-14, saying in 1 Samuel 3:11, "I am about to do a thing in Israel at which both ears... will tingle." God spoke frequently to his people in the era of Samuel and David.

The Spirit had come upon Saul as he prophesied in 1 Samuel 10. In Numbers 27:18, the Spirit is upon Joshua.

Exercise: Read the following passages from your Bible.

1. Genesis 1:2
2. Exodus 35:31
3. Judges 3:10
4. Judges 6:34
5. Judges 11:29

6. Judges 13:25

7. Judges 15:14

8. 1 Chronicles 12:18

9. 2 Chronicles 15:1

10. Nehemiah 9:20

11. Isaiah 11:2

- What is the one constant presence in each of these verses?

- What is the driving, or motivating, force behind these brave and fearless individuals?

- Does God change over time? (See Jeremiah 4:28; Malachi 3:6; Numbers 23:19; Hebrews 7:21; James 1:17.)

- If God does not change, then his Spirit does not change. Do you know what happened at Pentecost?

- Read Acts 2 and describe, in your own words, what took place.

The Spirit of God is the Holy Spirit. He empowers us, corrects us, brings us before God in a way not previously possible for man. He was our gift from Jesus Christ upon his resurrection and ascension. This is the same Spirit of God we see rushing upon Saul and David, the Judges, Prophets, and other heroes of faith in the Old Testament. Jesus called him a counselor and a helper. It was this Spirit that filled David upon Samuel's anointing.

God's Spirit empowers inanimate objects, as we see him hovering over the waters before creation. This same Spirit is in me and you if we believe in Christ's words! We have the same Spirit that hovered over the earth prior to creation. We have the same Spirit that led Gideon, Samson, and the other great Judges to overcome impossible odds. We have the same Spirit given to Saul, David, and Solomon, Israel's first three kings. We even have the same Spirit given to Jesus to overcome death!

No wonder Paul tells us in 2 Timothy 1:7, "For God has not given us a spirit of timidity, but of power and love and discipline." The scene in 1 Samuel 16:13 is crucial to understanding the role of Jesus Christ in the New Testament. David's kingship was established forever by God in Psalms 89:4. In Micah 5:2 the birthplace of the Messiah is given.

Though many differing opinions existed among the Jews of Jesus's day as to where the Messiah would come from, Herod the Great's religious officials quoted Micah 5:2 to him, prompting the mad King Herod to slaughter hundreds, perhaps thousands of newborns in Jerusalem and Bethlehem. This cruel, heartless, and barbarous act was referred to as the "Slaughter of the Innocents."

In John 7:41-42, Scripture depicts the controversy over Jesus's origins and identity in relation to King David.

"Others were saying, 'This is the Christ.' Still others were saying, 'Surely the Christ is not going to come from the Galilee is He? Has not the Scripture said that the Christ comes from the offspring of David, and from Bethlehem, the village where David was?'"

Christ's connection to David was a hotly debated topic of the early first century A.D. It all started with this scene at young David's house. The old, mysterious prophet anointed the young, vibrant shepherd boy. The fact that David was a shepherd is by no means a coincidence. God taught David the importance of wielding power on behalf of others through his task of caring for his flock. David learned of tenderness, compassion, and love during his lone solitary stretches in the wilderness with his sheep. He learned courage and bravery from defending his flock from wild beasts and predators in the field. We can draw significant parallels between David and Jesus from this passage.

First, back up to 1 Samuel 2:10 and reread that verse. This is Hannah, Samuel's mother, praying before God, giving him thanks for her newborn baby boy, Samuel.

"Those who contend with the Lord will be shattered; Against them He will thunder in the heavens. The Lord will judge the ends of the earth; And He will give strength to His king, and He will exult the horn of His anointed" (1 Samuel 2:10).

Hannah's song of Thanksgiving proved to be a prophetic utterance of Samuel's future role anointing kings. Just as the word "Christ" means "anointed," so David was also anointed by God.

The passage in Psalms 89:20-21 further establishes David in God's eyes: "I have found David My servant; with My holy oil I have anointed him, with whom My hand will be established; My arm also will strengthen him."

David, though far from perfect, proved to be a man after God's own heart (despite his many frailties). David was his king.

Exercise: Read the following verses from the New Testament about Jesus:

1. "And seeing the multitudes, He felt compassion for them, because they were distressed and downcast like sheep without a shepherd" (Matthew 9:36).

2. "And all the nations will be gathered before Him; and He will separate them from one another, as the shepherd separates the sheep from the goats" (Matthew 25:32).

3. "I am the good shepherd; the good shepherd lays down his life for the sheep" (John 10:11).

4. "I am the good shepherd; and I know My own, and My own know Me" (John 10:14).

5. "And I have other sheep, which are not of this fold; I must bring them also, and they shall hear My voice; and they shall become one flock with one shepherd" (John 10:16).

6. "He said to him again a second time, 'Simon, son of John do you love Me?' He said to Him, 'Yes, Lord; You know that I love You.' He said to him, 'Shepherd My sheep'" (John 21:16).

The parallels between the shepherd-king David and the Messiah are striking. As David was a shepherd to his father's sheep, so too was Jesus a shepherd to his Father's sheep. Jesus called himself a "son of David," yet reminded the people though the Messiah descended from David, he was greater than David (Mark 12:35-37).

Christ's relation to King David and the references Jesus makes to David serve to highlight the fact that the origins and beginnings of Christianity are inextricably linked with the ancient past of the Jewish nation today. Though Christians and Jews may be sheep of different folds, that was not always the case, and a time is coming when yet again we will be "one flock with one shepherd."

Exercise:

- Write down parallels and similarities between King David and Jesus Christ.

- How does this—if at all—improve your understanding of God's Word?

- Are the Old Testament and New Testament part of the same story? Or, are they two different books with different meanings? In other words, are both sections of the Bible relevant today?

- Read Acts 2:29-36. How does David's rise to become king of Israel compare to Jesus's life, death, and resurrection? Think of the origins of both, their early childhood, struggles, triumphs, and so on. How are the two different?

- How can we, today, become God's anointed ones? If you're not sure, pray and seek God's Word.

1 SAMUEL 16:14-23

THE SECOND HALF OF 1 SAMUEL 16 is a troubling passage. God had already rejected Saul as king, though Saul still retained his throne. God had already chosen his next king, young David son of Jesse. The troubling part of this section of Scripture begins in 1 Samuel 16:14: "Now the Spirit of the Lord departed from Saul, and an evil spirit from the Lord terrorized him."

The troubling implication is obvious—God sent an evil spirit to terrorize King Saul. This seems quite against God's nature and what he tells us throughout his Word. Turn and read James 1:13. This verse seems to state God will not send evil temptations upon us. True, Saul was not being tempted by this evil spirit. However, if God will not tempt us himself, it would seem to follow that he would not afflict us, either. However, 1 Samuel 16:14 seems to imply just that—God afflicted Saul.

Anytime one has questions about Scripture, one should research similar instances in the Bible and compare them. A number of similar passages appear throughout Scripture; thus, we will turn to those and God's Spirit for understanding. Scripture gives us a glimpse into the inner workings of God's heavenly kingdom. Interestingly enough, periodically, God meets with his angels in heaven. We gather this from visions and passages found scattered throughout the Bible.

An example of such a passage occurs in Job 1:6:

"Now there was a day when the sons of God came to present themselves before the Lord, and Satan also came among them."

What a remarkable image! We catch a rare glimpse of how God's kingdom operates in this verse. The sons of God, or angels, present themselves before God in what would seem to be a mandatory meeting in heaven. What this meeting was for is a mystery, yet the scene in Job 1 resembles one of a king on his throne holding court. Satan showed up with the other angels, his former colleagues, for a very specific purpose.

Though God did not send Satan out to afflict Job, He did allow Job to undergo serious trials at the hand of Satan. The point being, God does not hide his people from the evil on earth, from injury, harm, or misfortune. We are, after all, part of this world of decay and corruption. Satan, thus, showers Job with a number of unfortunate and painful crises and trials. God allowed this to prove Job's faith. The importance of this passage is to show that God allows evil in this life, though he also empowers us to overcome it.

In the case of Job, Satan presented his plan to God in heaven, and God allowed Satan to go through with it, having full confidence in his servant Job's faith. Another similar scene is given in 1 Kings 22. The prophet, Micaiah, is confronting Ahab the king of Israel and Jehoshaphat the king of Judah. He related his vision, found in 1 Kings 22:19-24, to the two kings. In 1 Kings 22:19, the Scripture describes Micaiah's vision of heaven.

"And Micaiah said, 'Therefore, hear the word of the Lord, I saw the Lord sitting on His throne and all the host of Heaven standing by Him on His right and on His left.'"

Once again we see God in his royal role as King of Heaven. He is on his throne surrounded by his subjects in a scene very similar to the one in Job 1. Without being too presumptuous, it would seem God holds these meetings in heaven to discuss, among other things, what is taking place on earth. In this instance from 1 Kings, Israel and Judah are discussing plans to go to war with Aram. Ahab, in all of his ungodliness and idolatry, has asked his false priests to inquire of God. All of them tell Ahab what he wants to hear.

Micaiah continues to relate his vision to the two kings.

"And the Lord said, 'Who will entice Ahab to go up and fall at Ramoth-gilead?' And one said this while another said that. Then a spirit came forward and stood before the Lord and said, 'I will go out and be a deceiving spirit in the mouth of all his prophets.' Then He said, 'You are to entice him and also prevail. Go and do so'" (1 Kings 22:20–22).

What an amazing scene! God has convened His court in Heaven in order to formulate a plan for how to intervene on earth. This situation is very similar to 1 Samuel 16:14. One must keep in mind God had blessed Ahab. Ahab, however, pursued Jezebel and her Phoenician gods. He forsook the ways of the Lord for the ways of foreign gods and idolatrous practices. He was an evil king and his day of reckoning had arrived.

What is interesting to note is God does not choose the method of enticement. He allows the volunteering spirit to choose. God lays forth the order. "Who will entice Ahab?" His court, those holy ones gathered before him, then talk it over. "And one said this while another said that." One of God's soldiers spoke up and volunteered, "Then a spirit came forward and stood before the Lord."

Finally, the order was given and carried out. Ahab's priests wrongfully advised him, and he refused to listen to the true prophet of God, Micaiah. God ordained the spirit to entice Ahab, then the spirit decided the exact means. We also see God's justification for such an order (not that he needs such) in Ahab's stubborn and hardened heart. Ahab was an evil king. He was leading Israel into apostasy. His death and defeat were the results of his refusal to follow God, thus God ordered his punishment.

Even more intriguing is the picture of a democratic process in heaven. Though God alone rules, he does so as a benevolent king. His subjects are seen in discussion among one another in his presence, and he allows a certain measure of freedom in how they carry out his orders—though nothing is done without his order and without his knowledge. Everything originates and ends with God, let us make no mistake. Lucifer abused God's benevolence and was cast out of heaven to the earth below.

Saul's "evil spirit from God" may have been something similar to that which happened to King Ahab in 1 Kings 22. In 1 Kings 22:18-23, a scene in heaven is portrayed in which "a spirit came forward" and volunteered to "entice Ahab" at the request of God Almighty. The Lord, thus, "put a deceiving spirit" in the mouth of Ahab's prophets to deceive Ahab, which ultimately led to Ahab's death.

Two passages from Judges can shed light on Saul's spirit. The first is from Judges 9:23-24. In this particular passage, God deals with Abimelech, the son of Gideon through a Canaanite woman. Abimelech, with the help of men from Shechem, killed his seventy half-brothers from Gideon. Thus, in Judges 9:23, God is shown intervening.

"Then God sent an evil spirit between Abimelech and the men of Shechem; and the men of Shechem dealt treacherously with Abimelech, in order that the violence done to the sons of Jerubbaal might come, and their blood might be laid on Abimelech their brother."

The second passage deals with Samson in Judges 16:20. Samson's strength came from his hair. He, like Samuel, was a Nazirite. Samson, though, possessed a far different spirit than Samuel—for he was a playboy of sorts. His primary weakness was found in Philistine women. He, thus, took a Philistine wife named Delilah. Samson's secret was for him and God alone to know, however, his fleshly desires led him to divulge his secret to his Philistine wife, Delilah.

Delilah, in turn, betrayed him to her countrymen, "the Philistine lords." Hence, in Judges 16:20, we see a helpless Samson.

"And she said, 'The Philistines are upon you Samson!' And he awoke from his sleep and said, 'I will go out as at other times and shake myself free.' But he did not know that the Lord had departed from him."

Though an evil spirit was not sent upon Samson, God did withdraw himself from Samson. Nations, too, are subject to evil spirits. In Isaiah 19:2 and 14, we learn of Egypt, a country in turmoil and revolution in modern times. We see God exerting his divine influence against Egypt.

"So I will incite Egyptians against Egyptians; And they will each fight against his brother, and each against his neighbor. City against city and kingdom against kingdom." Then again he speaks of Egypt in Isaiah 19:14.

"The Lord has mixed within her a spirit of distortion. They have led Egypt astray in all that it does, as a drunken man staggers in his vomit."

Egypt, of course, enslaved Israel and fought against her for much of the Old Testament. Though each passage referenced above is different and unique, the main idea is that of divine punishment for repeated transgressions. Egypt, Abimelech, and Samson were each repeatedly hostile and disobedient, either to God in the case of Samson or his people Israel as in the cases of Abimelech and Egypt. Consequently each was punished accordingly. Accountability demands such.

In Romans 1:28, Scripture speaks of disobedience to God.

"And just as they did not see fit to acknowledge God any longer, God gave them over to a depraved mind, to do those things which are not proper."

This verse pegs Saul. He repeatedly ignored God and disobeyed him on several occasions. Thus, we see Saul's mental state gradually decline throughout the book of 1 Samuel, beginning in this passage.

A similar future decline of society as a whole is predicted to accompany the end times when "the man of lawlessness is revealed." In 2 Thessalonians 2:11, we see this future decline.

"And for this reason God will send upon them a deluding influence so that they might believe what is false."

God departed from Saul, who repeatedly chose not to acknowledge and obey God's commands. God's withdrawal from Saul made King Saul vulnerable to the enemy's advances, which engulfed Saul and tormented him. Saul's state was such that only music from a harp would soothe him. As luck had it, one of Saul's servants happened to know a young man who was a skilled harpist.

Saul immediately sent for the harpist. This musician was none other than David, the king in waiting, though this fact was hidden from King Saul. Thus, 1 Samuel 16:21 begins the relationship between Saul and David.

"Then David came to Saul and attended him, and Saul loved him greatly; and he became his armor-bearer."

We gain insight into young David through this passage. David had already been anointed as the next king by Samuel. In 1 Samuel 16:19, Saul sends for David at Jesse's house. It is possible that David and Jesse thought Saul knew of David's anointing and was sending for young David to imprison him or perhaps even kill him. David, likely nervous at the timing of Saul's summons on the heels of his anointing, nonetheless faithfully leaves his father's house for the King's palace. Once there, he faithfully performs the tasks Saul asks of him, despite Samuel's past promise he would be the next king. David was neither impatient nor ambitious. He faithfully serves Saul, leaving it to God's timing as to when he would be crowned king of Israel. David performed the task at hand without looking for the next "gig," or manipulating the situation to accelerate his coronation. David was a patient and faithful servant to both Saul and God.

"And loving-kindness is Thine, O Lord, for Thou doest recompense a man according to his work" (Psalms 62:12).

"So it came about whenever the evil spirit from God came to Saul, David would take the harp and play it with his hand; and Saul would be refreshed and well, and the evil spirit would depart from him" (1 Samuel 16:23).

1 SAMUEL 17:1-20
(PART 2)

IN 1 SAMUEL 17, WE FIND Israel and the Philistines squared for battle once again. The Philistines marched east from their coastal region and encamped between Socah and Azekah. The Israelites had marched south and west from their hill country and encamped in the Valley of Elah. The area where the two armies encamped is a crossroads, with roads leading north–south and east–west intersecting.

Each army was camped on a mountain hillside, looking at the other from across the Valley of Elah, which separated the two mountain camps. The two camps stared each other in the face. Approximately two hundred years before, Joshua took this area from the Canaanite kings. Another battle against mighty Philistines would be fought near the two towns. In 1 Samuel 17:4, we are introduced to one of the most famous characters in the entire Bible—an imposing and deadly Philistine warrior, the giant champion Goliath.

"Then a champion came out from the armies of the Philistines named Goliath, from Gath whose height was six cubits and a span."

Each morning, this champion would descend from the Philistine camp and stand in the Valley of Elah, staring down the Israelite Army. Goliath would shout taunts at the Israelites and chastise them and the Israelite God. Scripture tells us that Goliath was a champion and stood at approximately 9 feet and 9 inches tall. This is roughly the height of a basketball goal. He was also covered in armor.

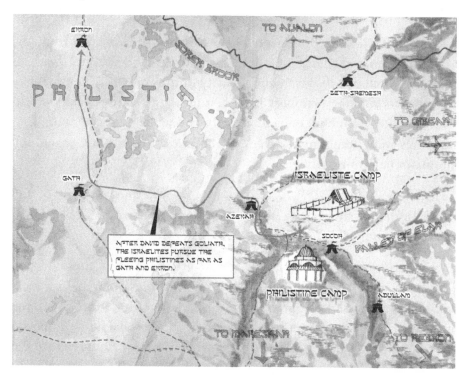

His helmet was bronze, and he wore scale armor. This armor likely weighed between 130 and 170 pounds. He also wore bronze greaves around his legs and carried a javelin "slung between his shoulders." His spear was massive, and Goliath's shield bearer walked in front of him. He was an iron death machine glistening in the sunlight from the valley floor. The Israelite Army, from their camp above, gazed down on Goliath in sheer terror.

Goliath was from Gath, an interesting and mysterious city. Gath lay undiscovered for thousands of years, leading skeptics to claim the Philistines were made up. However, archaeology unearthed its many layers of occupation. Gath was a real city, and one of the five Philistine strongholds, or the Philistine Pentapolis, just as the Bible states. The other cities were Gaza, Ekron, Ashkelon, and Ashdod. The Biblical city of Gath, modern Tell es-Safi, has produced remarkable archaeological finds. One find in particular raised eyebrows. A small shard was unearthed, which bore two non-Semitic names, possibly relating to Goliath!

In Joshua 11:22, the Bible states Joshua drove the Anakim from the land and confined them to Gath, Gaza, and Ashdod. Joshua's feat was startling when one discovers the identity of the Anakim. Their identity is first mentioned in Numbers 13:33. Moses sent spies to search out Canaan from the Israelite encampment in the wilderness of Paran. The Israelites were preparing for their conquest of the land of Canaan, the promised land of Abraham.

"There also we saw the Nephilim (the sons of Anak are part of the Nephilim); and we became like grasshoppers in our own sight, and so we were in their sight" (Numbers 13:33).

In Deuteronomy 9:1-2, Scripture sheds further light on these people. "Hear, O Israel! You are crossing the Jordan today to go in to dispossess nations greater and mightier than you, great cities fortified to the heaven; a people great and tall, the sons of the Anakim, whom you know of and whom you have heard it said, 'Who can stand before the sons of Anak?'"

One must turn all the way back to Genesis 6:2-4 to learn the identity of the Nephilim. These are a controversial and mysterious people, yet their descendants remained in the land during the time of Moses. They, too, were giants and mighty warriors. Joshua, however, with divine assistance, confined them to Gath, Gaza, and Ashdod. Notice he could not extinguish them altogether, only limit their settlement. In essence, Joshua subjugated them to Israel. These three cities would become three of the cities that the Philistines ruled from. Thus, it is likely the Anakim and the Philistines had intermarried and merged cultures.

This, however, must remain purely theoretical, as no evidence other than the textual implication exists that places these two cultures together. The Bible, however, implies they coexisted in at least three cities. It is interesting that Goliath was mentioned as a giant and champion and hailed from one of these three shared cities the Anakim were confined to in the time of Joshua. The time of Saul, in the present narrative, was approximately two to three hundred years removed from Joshua and the conquest. This is plenty of time for one society to comingle and intermarry with another.

The spies feared the Anakim and trembled before them. Likewise, the Israelite Army feared the Philistine champion Goliath and trembled before his taunts. Goliath, fully armed and wearing full body armor *with* a shield bearer walking in front of him, would strut into the Valley of Elah and shout his taunts at the cowering Hebrews. His taunts are recorded in 1 Samuel 17:8-10. Israel's response is found in 1 Samuel 17:11.

Exercise:

- How did King Saul and Israel respond to Goliath's challenge?

It is interesting to place oneself in the ranks of Israel's Army. What must the men have been thinking? What were they saying to one another? It is ironic there was only one man in all of Israel who could physically stand a chance against Goliath. There was only one man among the Israelite army with enough size to even be considered a threat to the giant champion. That man was King Saul. Yet he shrank from the challenge. With great challenges and difficult tasks come great opportunities... for those willing to rise up and meet them.

- What are some "giants" you are currently facing?

Whether spiritual, social, or emotional, in work, home, marriage, or a limitless number of other possibilities, life is full of Goliaths and challenges that seem overwhelming and impossible to defeat.

- Where is your focus: on the challenge, or on the opportunity?
- Have you asked God for help?

Read these passages about trials, tribulations, and mighty challenges:

1. "Or has a god tried to go take for himself a nation from within another nation by trials, by signs, and wonders and by war and

143

by a mighty hand and by an outstretched arm and by great terrors, as the Lord your God did for you in Egypt before your eyes?" (Deuteronomy 4:34).

2. "Consider it all joy, my brethren, when you encounter various trials, knowing that the testing of your faith produces endurance. And let endurance have its perfect result, so that you may be perfect and complete, lacking in the nothing" (James 1:2-4).

3. "And Moses summoned all Israel and said, 'You have seen all that the Lord did before your eyes in the land of Egypt to Pharaoh and all his servants, and all his land; the great trials which your eyes have seen, those great signs and wonders'" (Deuteronomy 29:2-3).

4. "In this you greatly rejoice, even though now for a little while, if necessary you have been distressed by various trials, that the proof of your faith, being more precious than gold which is perishable, even though tested by fire, may be found to result in praise and glory and honor at the revelation of Jesus Christ" (1 Peter 1:6-7).

5. "Strengthening the souls of the disciples, encouraging them to continue in the faith, and saying, 'Through many tribulations we must enter the kingdom of God'" (Acts 14:22).

6. "Have I not commanded you? Be strong and courageous! Do not tremble or be dismayed, for the Lord your God is with you wherever you go" (Joshua 1:9).

7. "Blessed is a man who perseveres under trial; for once he has been approved, he will receive the crown of life, which the Lord has promised to those who love Him" (James 1:12).

•   What do you think God wants for us to do when we encounter tests and challenges?

•   Why do you think it's necessary we encounter trials, hard times, depression, pain, and tribulation?

Read Matthew 11:28-30 and apply it to the above questions and passages. What are your thoughts for God? Let him know what you're thinking, and ask him any questions you may have.

As Saul was cowering in fear, young David was making his way to the front lines on an errand for his father. In verse 13, we learn that David's three older brothers are fighting in Saul's army. David, too young to fight, stayed behind to help his father run the house, keep the herds, and so on. Jesse, according to Scripture, "was old in the days of Saul, advanced in years among men."

Young David must have surely wanted to fight in the army, yet he faithfully served his father Jesse instead.

In 1 Samuel 17:15, David goes back and forth from Saul's presence to his father's flocks. It is likely this episode takes place several years after David had served as Saul's musician.

In 1 Samuel 17:17, Jesse instructs his youngest son to take some food, an *ephah* (approximately twenty-two liters) of roasted grain, and ten loaves to Eliab, Abinadab, and Shammah, his older brothers. Jesse also gave him ten cuts of cheese to give to their commander and then asked David to check on his brothers.

Jesse showed the same concern and love for his sons in this passage that parents, at least good ones, from all generations and ages share. Jesse wanted to show his boys he was thinking of them and loved them. Jesse wanted to provide for them, show his love for them in their absence. He is being a good father and role model for his sons in this passage. David, the secretly anointed king-in-waiting, was sent by his father from their home in Bethlehem to deliver the gifts and check on his brothers.

Exercise:

Take time right now and read 1 Samuel 17:20-58, the story of David and Goliath.

"You come to me with a sword, a spear, and a javelin, but I come to you in the name of the Lord of hosts."

1 SAMUEL 17:20-58
(PART 2)

In 1 Samuel 17:20, we see a faithful and diligent David making his way to the Israelites' base camp.

"So David arose early in the morning and left the flock with a keeper and took the supplies and went as Jesse had commanded him. And he came to the circle of the camp while the army was going out in battle array shouting the war cry."

On display from the start is David's diligence. He rose early in the morning to leave, rather than sleeping in and taking his time. He had already arranged for another to keep his flock of sheep. David had already laid out and organized the supplies he needed for the long trip. David had everything packed and ready to go. David was a loyal and obedient son to his father.

Exercise: Look up and read the verses on diligence listed below.

1. Deuteronomy 4:9
   Deuteronomy 4 is part of a longer speech given by Moses to Israel in the wilderness. In Deuteronomy 1, Moses recounted Israel's history after the Exodus from Egypt. In Deuteronomy 2, he specifically addressed the wilderness wandering. In Deuteronomy 3, Moses recounted how they "turned and went up the road" (Deuteronomy 3:1) and defeated Og and Sihon on

the eastern banks of the Jordan River, both miraculous victories against all odds. In Deuteronomy 4, Moses got to the heart of things and urged the people to obey God's law. This would certainly require diligence, as did their survival up to that point.

2. Deuteronomy 6:5-8
   In this passage, the Hebrew word *shanan* is translated as "teach them diligently." It literally means "to point, to pierce through, to sharpen, to enforce, to inculcate, to teach diligently."

3. Deuteronomy 6:17
   In this verse the Hebrew word *shamar* is translated as "diligently keep." This word is used over four hundred times in the Hebrew Old Testament. The first occurrence is in Genesis 2:15, in which man exercises great care for the garden of Eden. It literally translates as "to hedge around something, to keep, to guard, to beware." Religiously speaking, it conveys the idea of careful attention to the obligations of a covenant. In Genesis 18:19, God uses this word in talking about Abraham and how he and his descendants will "keep the way of the Lord."

4. Joshua 23:11

5. Proverbs 4:23

6. Proverbs 12:27

7. Proverbs 8:17

8. Proverbs 21:5

9. Romans 12:6,8

10. Ephesians 4:1,3

11. 2 Timothy 2:15

12. 2 Peter 1:10

David showed diligence, a sense of urgency, and obligation to duty in following his father's orders. When he arrived at the Israelite camp, the army was marching out in battle array. Troops were bustling back and forth, the sun glistening off of the metal swords, men yelling amid the clanging of metal. Dust and noise defined the camp as the army let loose its war cry. David arrived in the middle of all the action, and in 1 Samuel 17:21–22, we get a sense of a youth's excitement and curiosity with the sights and sounds of battle.

"And Israel and the Philistines drew up in battle array, army against army. Then David left his baggage in the care of the baggage keeper, and ran to the battle line and entered in order to greet his brothers" (1 Samuel 17:21-22).

The restless young David could not wait to meet his brothers on the front lines and catch a glimpse of the mighty and feared Philistines. The lesson we can take from David in this instance is to get involved! Do not be afraid to get involved in your life. David took advantage of an opportunity to see something that excited him. He had an eager and adventurous nature and was not afraid to act on it.

God wants people who run to the front lines and are not afraid to mix it up in life. God wants people open to being uncomfortable, those not afraid to abandon the false comfort and security our society has built up.

Many put hopes in retirement plans, paychecks, air conditioner, television, and so on. We need the attitude young David displayed in this instance. He was always ready! David could not wait to see what was happening. He possessed a spirit of boldness, of adventure.

The biblical narrative continues as David visits with his brothers. In 1 Samuel 17:23, the Philistine champion Goliath emerges from the opposite mountainside into the Valley of Elah below, as he had done numerous times previously.

This was the fortieth consecutive day Goliath had stood in the valley and issued his challenge to Israel. For thirty-nine days, the Israelites failed to produce an opponent, the army and their king cowering in fear.

Scripture tells us the Israelites "fled from him and were greatly afraid." How many times have we run from the Goliaths of life? How many times have we shied away from seemingly impossible and ludicrous tasks for fear of failure? The Bible calls David a man after God's own heart. David's response to Goliath is a demonstration of his faith in YHWH.

"Then David spoke to the men who were standing by him, saying, 'What will be done for the man who kills this Philistine, and takes away the reproach of Israel? For who is this uncircumcised Philistine, that he should taunt the armies of the living God?'" (1 Samuel 17:26).

David showed no fear, only outrage and anger at the insult cast at his God by this "uncircumcised Philistine." Whereas everyone else saw a ten-foot giant covered in metal and huge weapons, David was insulted and offended. David had already fought and defeated wild predators, including at least one bear. He had been trained in the fields with his sheep to trust God. With this Philistine, David saw another opportunity for God to work.

The men told David the king would give his daughter to the man responsible for Goliath's death, along with riches and exemption for that man's household from the kingdom's taxes.

Exercise: Take a minute to reread David's response in 1 Samuel 17:26.

- What makes David so confident when everybody else, including King Saul, shrank back in fear?
- The men of Israel knew God, too, yet they failed to act in faith. David was simply a ruddy, young shepherd boy on an errand for his father. In your opinion, what did David possess that made him act in faith that these other men did not have?

In 1 Samuel 17:28, there seems to be some sibling animosity between David and his brothers. In fact, throughout David's life he seemed to have problems within his family, and 1 Samuel 17:28 makes it clear Eliab, his oldest brother, thoroughly disliked him. This likely was a case of sibling jealousy, as David had been anointed king in front of his older brothers previously. Years later, David's own son Absalom would rebel against him, driving David from Jerusalem and threatening to usurp the throne. In the present narrative, Eliab overhears David talking about Goliath and confronts his youngest brother in 1 Samuel 17:28:

"Now Eliab his oldest brother heard when he spoke to the men; and Eliab's anger burned against David and he said, 'Why have you come down? And with whom have you left those few sheep in the wilderness? I know your insolence and the wickedness of your heart; for you have come down in order to see the battle.'"

Eliab made a point of putting David in his place by asking him about "those few sheep," and asking who he left the sheep with. Eliab's question was not out of curiosity, but to show the men standing nearby this young loudmouth was really just a simple little shepherd boy and not to be taken seriously. Eliab's comments were extremely provocative and accusatory. He mocked David, accusing David of being insolent, refused to thank him for the provisions, and claimed he only came to see the battle.

Turn back to 1 Samuel 16:6-7. Eliab was the first of the sons of Jesse to pass before Samuel. Eliab was the impressive looking firstborn son of Jesse. The firstborn son received the double portion of the family's inheritance. If any of Jesse's sons would be anointed king, surely it would've been Eliab. The old prophet Samuel thought so. God, however, had rejected Eliab "for God sees not as man sees, for man looks at the outward appearance, but the Lord looks at the heart."

In this exchange, we can see what God saw inside of Eliab's heart: bitterness, envy, jealousy. The lesson here is that somebody will always try to keep you from attempting great things. Don't be discouraged by the Eliabs of this world and their condescending words. Take note of David's reaction.

Exercise: Turn and read 1 Samuel 17:29-30.

• How does the Bible depict David as responding to Eliab's hurtful comments?

He simply turned from Eliab without any response and continued his inquiry into Goliath. David completely ignored Eliab's comments, for he was forming a plan in his mind and would not be deterred. Rather than argue and attempt to justify his presence, David moved forward, leaving Eliab behind with his own jealousies.

Interestingly, if we venture to look back at Genesis 37, a similar passage can be found dealing with sibling jealousies. The brothers of Joseph had similar feelings toward Joseph that Eliab displayed toward David. Most know the story of how Joseph's brothers sold him into slavery to a passing band of Ishmaelites (a people descended from Ishmael, another example of sibling jealousy).

Exercise: Turn to Genesis 37:4 and read of Joseph's plight.

It was situations like these that led the author of Proverbs 18:19 to write, "A brother offended is harder to be won than a strong city, and contentions are like the bars of a castle." David, however, rose like Joseph above these petty jealousies. He refused to be sucked into meaningless arguments fueled by jealous accusations.

Word of David's questions reached King Saul. Saul knew he was the only one that could really challenge Goliath. Yet, he also knew that he would die doing so. Goliath, thus, had issued his challenge to Israel for thirty-nine consecutive days without anyone accepting the challenge. Saul must have been desperate. Word reached the king that there may be a man willing to fight Goliath in the Israelite camp!

Saul would've been off the hook, thus he immediately sent for this daring man. In 1 Samuel 17:31, David comes before King Saul once again. Saul, however, does not recognize David (or at least pretended not to). This can be explained, scholars argue, by the fact that a number of years may have passed since David served as Saul's musician. David had changed from what Saul remembered.

Exercise: Turn and read David's first words to the king in 1 Samuel 17:32.

- What does David tell Saul?

- Reread 1 Samuel 16:13. How might this explain David's willingness to put himself in harm's way?

David made it clear to Saul he had no qualms about fighting Goliath. This is a prime example of putting one's faith into action.

Exercise: Read the exchange between Saul and David in 1 Samuel 17:32-40.

- How does David respond to Saul's criticism and doubt?

- What does David cite as training for his fight against Goliath?

- What is the underlying source of David's confidence?

- Why is he certain he will defeat the Philistine giant?

- How is the choice of weapons, first chosen by Saul, then by David, indicative and symbolic of the condition of each man's heart toward God?

Oh, the wonder of God! How majestic is that Divine Hand that moves unseen, yet felt, over the fabric of time, weaving together individuals and events to further his plan of Redemption! David trained all of his life for this precise moment in time, unknown to him, yet known all along by God Almighty.

David's training ground was his father's flock and the field. David listened to God during those long solitary stretches. He played his harp to his sheep, keeping a constant eye on them and their safety. He fought off predators, pursued them when necessary, and rescued his sheep from untold dangers. It is also quite natural to assume he had lost many of his sheep to death, whether through disease, predators, and other accidents.

David had learned of loss as well. God used all of this to teach David a very important lesson: wield power on behalf of others. God saw his king in the ruddy-faced shepherd boy. He taught David how to rule by first giving him a flock of sheep to protect and look after. It was from these humble beginnings that David practiced and prepared for what God had in store.

- What is your training ground? It may be work, school, marriage, kids, and so on.
- How is God training and preparing you for what he has in store?

God is fathering us and preparing us each and every day of our life journey. Everything we do has a purpose, though we often fail to see it due to our limited perspective. During those long, lonely stretches in the wilderness, or during those adrenaline-filled moments fighting off wild beasts, David did not foresee a ten-foot giant stalking his life. However, David did see God in each of those moments. God builds us up one block at a time, so that when those ten-foot giants do appear we are ready to rely on him.

Exercise: Flip your Bible back to Joshua 1:5-9.

- How many times do you read the words "strong and courageous?"
- Why should Israel have such confidence?

Now turn and read 1 Samuel 17:37 again.

- Is David unsure about the outcome?
- Who is fighting for David? Ultimately, who or what does David rely on?
- What quality does David exhibit in this instance? In other words, what specific principle does he put into action?

David's faith in God provided him with the strength and courage to encounter the unexpected. He arrived in camp per his father's orders, with food and provisions for his older brothers. He was readying himself to fight the Philistine champion Goliath, a feared and mighty warrior twice the size of David. It was moments like these David would later write about, as he did in Psalms 7:1.

"O Lord my God, in Thee I have taken refuge. Save me from all those who pursue me, and deliver me."

David was completely confident in God's sovereignty. In 1 Samuel 17:37, he tells Saul, "He will deliver me from the hand of this Philistine." He says this with confidence, as if it were a matter of fact, and without the slightest sign of doubt. David prayed to the Lord for strength and he knew God heard that prayer and would deliver his servant. Centuries later, James would echo the faithfulness of David's prayer in James 1:6:

"But let him ask in faith without doubting, for the one who doubts is like the surf of the sea, driven and tossed by the wind."

So confident was David that he saw no need for Saul's armor; it only hindered his movement. God was the real protection, not Saul's armor. We oftentimes set up false securities for ourselves, too.

Exercise: Turn and read 1 Samuel 17:39-40.

- What did David wear into the battle with Goliath? What weapons did he carry with him?

Anthropologists say the average height of the Hebrews in antiquity was probably 5 feet 5 inches to 5 feet 7 inches. Goliath was 9 feet 9 inches tall! His armor and weapons combined weighed over three hundred pounds! David had a slingshot, five stones, and a stick. Goliath approached David with a human shield bearer (probably close to David's height) walking in front of him. David approached Goliath with a shepherd's leather pouch full of stones.

It is worth a moment to pause right here and let the scene soak in. Both armies prepared for battle, camped on opposite mountain sides, staring across the valley at each other. From among the Philistines emerged their champion. A bronze-clad Philistine giant strode arrogantly across the valley floor. Heavily armed, and in full body armor, the sun glinted off of him like a golden statue. His brilliance was awe inspiring. A human shield bearer, likely David's size, walked in front of him holding a massive shield. Goliath was a living and breathing killing machine. He arrogantly taunted the cowering Israelites, as he had done the forty days prior.

This time, surprisingly, the Israelite ranks broke file and a figure emerged in response. Goliath looked on amused. A small Hebrew, what appeared to be a boy, wearing no armor and having no shield bearer—in fact carrying no weapons at all—emerged from the Hebrew camp and walked toward the Philistine giant. All the lad carried was a leather pouch at his side and a slingshot. Goliath rolled his eyes in disgust. Both armies looked on in disbelief. Smirks, laughs, and taunts from both armies surely followed David across that valley floor. Goliath himself looked at David "with disdain." Scripture tells us Goliath became angry at David's challenge. He was beneath the challenge of a ruddy-faced boy who didn't even have proper weapons to fight with. This was beneath him.

Exercise: Turn and read 1 Samuel 17:43-44.

- What was Goliath's response to David?
- Who did Goliath specifically curse in these verses?

David stopped a small distance from Goliath, listening to his taunts and curses, unwavering in his faith. Then, without flinching, David delivered one of the most beautiful passages in all of the Bible, recorded in 1 Samuel 17:45-47.

"Then David said to the Philistine, 'You come to me with a sword, a spear, and a javelin, but I come to you in the name of the Lord of hosts, the God of the armies of Israel, whom you have taunted. This day the Lord will deliver you up into my hands and I will strike you down, and remove your head from you. And I will give the dead bodies of the army of the Philistines this day to the birds of the sky and the wild beasts of the earth that all the earth may know that there is a God in Israel, and that all this assembly may know that the Lord does not deliver by sword or by spear; for the battle is the Lord's and He will give you into our hands.'"

- Before the battle began, who did David credit with the victory?
- The battle between Israel and Philistia was really whose battle?

Read Joshua 6:16 concerning the Battle of Jericho.

- Write down the similarities in the two battles.

David's approach to this showdown was one we should stop and consider. One, he stuck with what he knew. Saul wanted to suit him up in the king's armor with the king's weapons. David knew this armor was not going to win the fight for him. It was heavy, cumbersome, awkward, and foreign to David, for he had likely never donned armor before. David had been trained by God in the fields and pastures with his flock. He stuck with that training. He trusted his past experiences with God. All he needed was his slingshot, a weapon he had used countless times before. The Hebrews had a strong history with the slingshot (see Judges 20:16).

Two, he did not let the taunts from his own people or the enemy deter him. He knew where his strength lay (Psalms 18:39). David understood things were not always as they appeared.

Three, Goliath's pride was countered by David's humility. Goliath fought for his own personal glory and gain. David fought to defend the name of God, giving all glory to the Lord of hosts (Isaiah 2:17). Goliath took pride in his weapons, his size, strength, and fierceness. David took pride only in his God.

As the battle began, Goliath drew his sword and approached David for the quick and easy kill. David wasted no time, for Scripture tells us the fearless shepherd "ran quickly toward the battle line to meet the Philistine." Wow! David did not shrink back, look around hoping for an interruption, or even hesitate. Rather, he engaged! When the going got real, David got going. The faith he displayed in this battle is a tremendous encouragement, for as previously stated, David was not without his own human frailties and inadequacies. He acted in faith by engaging the Philistine against overwhelming odds.

"And David put his hand into his bag and took from it a stone and slung it, and struck the Philistine on his forehead. And the stone sank into his forehead, so that he fell on his face to the ground."

Exercise: Read 1 Samuel 17:50-54.

- What did David not possess during the battle?
- What did he do to Goliath's dead body? Whose sword did he use?
- How did David's victory over Goliath affect the Israelite Army? The Philistine Army?

The God of Israel, Elohim, the Most High, had delivered his people through the faith of a little shepherd boy with a bag full of rocks. David's victory inspired the Israelite Army to pursue the Philistines. Goliath's shield bearer fled as soon as David's stone sunk into the dead champion's head, and now the Philistine Army followed suit. The Israelites, a moment before cowering in their camp, scared of the mighty Philistines, now pursued without fear.

The Israelite Army shot forward from its ranks across the valley floor in blood-thirsty pursuit of the Philistines. Inspired by David's victory, the nation of Israel experienced a great victory as well over the Philistines that day in the Valley of Elah. God's victories can arise anywhere faith is practiced. It is truly amazing what the faith of one man can accomplish.

Exercise: Read the following passages and answer the question regarding it:

1. Matthew 17:20

   o What does this verse tell us is possible with faith?

2. Habakkuk 2:4

   o What do the righteous live by?

3. Matthew 21:21-22

- o   What does Jesus tell us we will receive if we live and pray by faith?

4.   Psalms 31:24

- o   How are we to live our lives if we hope in the Lord?

David put all of these principles into action with his battle against Goliath. On the fortieth day of Goliath's prideful challenge, Goliath encountered a little man with big faith, a faithful servant of the Most High. David must have appeared as little as a mustard seed when standing in front of Goliath. Yet, within that little man we find the fulfillment of 1 Corinthians 1:27-29.

Exercise:

Take a moment to read 1 Corinthians 1:27-29, highlight it, and put it to memory.

- •   How can David inspire you to rise up against your giants?
- •   What strength can you draw from when confronting your Goliaths?

Next time you face an impossible task, a daunting challenge, extreme adversity, or a ten-foot giant, remember the young shepherd who defeated a Philistine champion and recall how he did it. Remember his words, "But I come to you in the name of the Lord of hosts, the God of the armies of Israel." Confront your giants with faith as your sling, and the words of Jesus in Matthew 17:20 as your stones, "and nothing shall be impossible for you."

1 SAMUEL 18

THE END OF 1 SAMUEL 17 has Saul interrogating David, asking him to reveal his identity and family so that the king may reward him for slaying Goliath. This seems strange given the two men's past relationship. David had served previously as Saul's musician, yet, as stated earlier, that was likely years ago and it was possible Saul did not recognize David. Perhaps Saul had completely forgotten about the young harp player, or perhaps Saul simply pretended not to remember David. A study of Saul clearly shows him to be a man of confused and paranoid thoughts and actions. Saul's state of mind was anybody's guess! Regardless, in 1 Samuel 18:1, David meets a man who would become like a brother to him and save his life more than once.

"Now it came about when he had finished speaking to Saul that the soul of Jonathan was knit to the soul of David, and Jonathan loved him as himself."

Jonathan was King Saul's son and held an important position in the kingdom and army. He was likely in the presence of the king as David came and went during the battle with Goliath. Scripture makes it plainly clear Jonathan heard David's words to King Saul after the battle, at the close of 1 Samuel 17. Perhaps Jonathan's eyebrows raised in 1 Samuel 17:32 when young David first revealed to Saul he would fight the Philistine. Jonathan, too, was a man of action and possessed much courage.

Exercise: Turn back to 1 Samuel 14 and read of Jonathan's exploits against the Philistines.

As David talked to the king about killing Goliath, Jonathan surely took notice and was impressed by David's courage. He, too, had tackled impossible odds when he scaled two cliffs with his bare hands and launched a two-man attack on the Philistine outpost. Jonathan had spoken similar words in 1 Samuel 14:6, when he said to his armor-bearer, "Perhaps the Lord will work for us, for the Lord is not restrained to save by many or by few."

Jonathan recognized a godly warrior when he saw one, as he too was a warrior for the Lord. He liked long shots. He liked men of action, courage, and faith. Both men had won great victories for Israel due to their faith and confidence in the Almighty Lord of Hosts. Thus, as David slew Goliath, then met with Saul, Jonathan couldn't help but feel a certain kinship with David that went far deeper than mere glory in battle.

These two men were bound together by their faith and love in God. Scripture relates, in 1 Samuel 18:1, "the soul of Jonathan was knit to the soul of David." Similar language is used in Genesis 44:30 to express Jacob's love for his youngest son Benjamin, the brother of Joseph and child of Jacob's most loved wife, Rachel. We can learn an important lesson here: godly friendship is vital to the growth and development of faith.

As will be seen, this friendship formed an important part of David's growth and development as a leader.

Exercise: Read the following passages:

1. "A friend loves at all times, and a brother is born for adversity" (Proverbs 17:17).

2. "A man of many friends comes to ruin, but there is a friend who sticks closer than a brother" (Proverbs 18:24).

3. "For where two or three have gathered together in My name, there I am in their midst" (Matthew 18:20).

Humans were not designed to live and work alone. We are social be-
ings, and godly friendship is a divine gift from God. Jonathan and
David discovered each other through God's workings, and they in-
stantly became like brothers. We also see God working in his kingdom.
Though Saul was still king, the throne of Israel had already been torn
from him by Samuel in 1 Samuel 15:28-29 and given to David. Saul
likely was not aware the next king would be David, though he eventually became very jealous and suspicious of David and grew to perceive
David as a threat.

However, the moment was not according to God's timing for David to
become king. Instead, God trained David to be better prepared for
when his timing was right by placing him as a commander in Saul's
army. Military knowledge and ability would be vital for Israel's survival
in its infancy—just as it is today in the twenty-first century C.E.

God frequently moves in seasons, and he uses the different seasons in a
man or woman's life to prepare his servants for their work in his plans.
David left one season behind, that of a shepherd boy, and now would be
trained as a commander in the army. God would use this time to further prepare David for what lay ahead, which only God could see. Thus,
our present training must be viewed as being perfectly aligned with
what God sees as best for our future, if we accept him and his sovereignty over our life. David, it seemed, reached that important place in
his relationship with God and accepted God's sovereignty over his life.
In this respect, David was very much a man after God's own heart.

Exercise: Read 1 Samuel 18:5.

- What position did Saul give David?
- How might God use this position to further train and prepare
  David?
- How did the people of Israel receive David?

Scripture reveals that David "prospered." Another translation reads he
"acted wisely." How many of our current leaders act wisely? David's assignment and service was "pleasing" to the people, and he grew in

popularity and fame among Israel. Those in power who act wisely gain instant popularity among the people they represent. In the pitiful condition of our current political system, those people are few and far between.

We see this principle in action in the fact that Israelites had grown tired of Saul's mood swings and impulsive decisions. In 1 Samuel 17:7, it seems the people elevated David above Saul, at least militarily.

Exercise: Turn and read 1 Samuel 18:7-9.

- What was being said of David?
- What was Saul's reaction?
- How did Saul look at David afterward?

These verses record the beginning of a saga that would dominate the remainder of 1 Samuel. Saul's suspicion, which was really envy and jealousy, led him to pursue David's life without rest for the remainder of his days as king. In fact, the very next day, David was again playing the harp for Saul, when "an evil spirit from God came mightily upon Saul." We have already discussed the possible nature of such a spirit, and why God issued such an order against Saul. The word used in this instance for evil is the same as in 1 Samuel 16:14. This time, however, Saul is driven to make an attempt at David's life.

Exercise: Turn and read 1 Samuel 18:10-11.

- In what manner does the "evil spirit" come upon Saul?
- What was going on when this happened?
- How was Saul acting?
- What did Saul try to do to David?

The picture of Saul here was one of a man possessed. He "raved" about the palace while David played the harp. Scripture records a spear was in Saul's hand, which as will be seen, he frequently carried with him. Saul was in such a frenzy, he tried to kill the very man who delivered his kingdom to him from Goliath and the Philistines. Saul's real motivation, however, was fear. Pay close attention to 1 Samuel 18:12.

"Now Saul was afraid of David, for the Lord was with him, but had departed from Saul."

In this passage, Saul begins his descent into madness. Meanwhile, David begins his rise to Israel's throne. Why? Because the Lord was with David, and he departed from Saul. We must understand the final outcome of faith to see faith's true power.

Exercise: Read the following verses:

1. "'Woe to the rebellious children,' declares the Lord, 'Who execute a plan, but not Mine, and make an alliance, but not of My Spirit, in order to add sin to sin'" (Isaiah 30:1).

2. "And so in the present case, I say to you, stay away from these men and let them alone, for if this plan or action should be of men, it will be overthrown; but if it is of God, you will not be able to overthrow them; or else you may even be found fighting against God" (Acts 5:38-39).

3. "Have you not heard? Long ago I did it; from ancient times I planned it. Now I have brought it to pass, that you should turn fortified cities into ruinous heaps" (2 Kings 19:25).

4. "And it happened when our enemies heard that it was known to us, and that God had frustrated their plan, then all of us returned to the wall, each one to his work" (Nehemiah 4:15).

5. "For the Lord of hosts has planned, and who can frustrate it? And as for His stretched out hand, who can turn it back?" (Isaiah 14:27).

6. "Declaring the end from the beginning and from ancient times things which have not been done, saying; 'My purpose will be established, and I will accomplish all My good pleasure... Truly I have spoken; truly I will bring it to pass. I have planned it, surely I will do it'" (Isaiah 4:10-11).

7. "The Lord nullifies the counsel of the nations; He frustrates the plans of the peoples. The counsel of the Lord stands forever, the

plans of His heart from generation to generation" (Psalms 33:10-11).

8. "Evil plans are an abomination to the Lord, but pleasant words are pure" (Proverbs 15:26).

9. "'For I know the plans I have for you,' declares the Lord, 'plans for welfare and not for calamity, to give you a future and a hope'" (Jeremiah 29:11).

Though these verses deal with different time periods and events throughout all of the Bible, from the reign of Hezekiah to the acts of the apostles, one message remains the same.

* What is the central message of these verses?
* How does this message apply to the situation between King Saul and David?

Saul's next attempt to thwart the chosen one of God is recorded in 1 Samuel 18:17-30. Take time to read these verses for background information. His plan involved getting David to marry one of his daughters, thus making him his son-in-law. Saul knew he could not kill David, yet he planned on David meeting his death in battle with the Philistines, who plagued Saul and threatened Israel throughout his entire reign. The war with the Philistines was a long, drawn-out affair between the two nations.

The entire forty-plus-year reign of Saul was occupied with this war. Even before Saul's reign began, the Israelites and Philistines were fighting. In fact, it was because of the organized military nature of the Philistine Pentapolis that the Israelites felt the need for a similar earthly structure represented by a king.

During the reign of the Judges, such as Samson, the two sides fought. It is likely the two nations fought for nearly a century. The Philistines arrived in Canaan circa 1200 B.C. Israel had already existed in the region since the conquest, circa 1400–1300 B.C. Both dates, of course, are debated. Many thousands of men on both sides had died over the course of the decades of fighting. Saul was hoping David would become a casualty as well.

In 1 Samuel 18:17, Saul crosses a dangerous line. He uses God as a pawn for his schemes against David. He tells David to take Merab, his oldest daughter as wife. The only requirement made by Saul was that David "only be a valiant man for me and fight the Lord's battles." Saul used God as pretense for David to fight the Philistines. Saul showed his lack of fear and reverence for God Almighty. The Bible has much to say in regard to individuals who do not fear the Lord:

"And it came about at the beginning of their living there, that they did not fear the Lord; therefore the Lord sent lions among them which killed some of them" (2 King 17:25).

"Transgression speaks to the ungodly within his heart; there is no fear of God before his eyes" (Psalms 36:1).

Saul lost all fear of the Lord, though he would fear David's rise to king. In humility, David refused Saul's first offer to marry his daughter and thus become his son-in-law. David's reasoning was he could not afford the dowry. He was a poor man and "lightly esteemed." Saul countered, however, with yet another scheme.

Merab, Saul's oldest daughter, had already been given away after David's initial refusal. Another of Saul's daughters, Michal, was in love with David. Scripture records that this was agreeable to Saul, thus he arranged for Michal and David to be married. Rather than require a dowry, Saul required one hundred Philistine foreskins. This required David to first kill one hundred Philistines and then circumcise their dead bodies.

Saul's gruesome and disturbing request was made with the intention of getting David killed "by the hand of the Philistine." One hundred Philistine foreskins was an impossible task. It echoed of Samson-like exploits.

Later, ironically, King David would use a similar tactic toward Uriah the Hittite—placing him in the deadliest part of the battle in hopes he would die. David's plot was successful, as Uriah fell in battle—and David married his wife, Bathsheba.

Exercise:

Before reading any further, turn and read Matthew 19:26. David's response to Saul's challenge is recorded in 1 Samuel 18:27.

- Who accompanied David on his task?
- Did these men have a personal stake in the matter? Why would they risk themselves for David's sake?
- What was the outcome? Did David accomplish his task?

Imagine the look on Saul's face when David walked in with twice the number required! Perhaps David knew Saul had intended for his demise, perhaps he did not, Scripture is silent. Regardless, Saul's schemes had once again been foiled by the power of God that rested upon David. Not only that, but his daughter was passionately in love with David. Scripture makes it plain in 1 Samuel 18:28–29 that Saul greatly feared and resented David's rise to prominence and fame.

"When Saul saw and knew that the Lord was with David, and that Michal, Saul's daughter, loved him, then Saul was even more afraid of David. Thus Saul was David's enemy continually."

Remember these passages as we continue to follow Saul and David. Despite Saul's fervent efforts, 1 Samuel 18:14–16 makes it plain that David continued "prospering in all his ways." Saul grew to dread, despise, and fear David. However, the people, Saul's subjects, loved David and hailed him as a great warrior and leader. David's men loved him as well—as did Saul's daughter. David was the favored son of Israel.

We should all be weary of the Sauls in our lives—the bosses who inflict misery intentionally at work, those out to hurt us, the lying politician, and so on. Their plans will ultimately fail, and their power over individuals exists only to the extent that each individual allows. The sovereign plan of God cannot be thwarted by any man, angel, or the adversary himself.

Exercise:

- Think and identify the Sauls of your life.

- Do they bring you down?

- David continually met and overcame Saul's efforts. What can we learn from David and Saul?

- Write down one verse from 1 Samuel 18, or today's lesson, that you can cling to.

1 SAMUEL 19

IN 1 SAMUEL 19, KING SAUL openly declares to his son and his servants a command "to put David to death." Saul failed in his first attempt. This time, he decides on a frontal attack. He declared openly, thus making it policy that David was to be killed. Fortunately for David, his close friend Jonathan, the King's son, heard Saul's declaration. Jonathan remains loyal to David, betraying his own father in 1 Samuel 19:2–3.

Exercise: Turn and read 1 Samuel 19:4-7.

- How does Jonathan defend David?
- What does he say to Saul?
- What is Saul's initial reaction?
- Do you trust Saul's words? Why, or why not?

Despite David's many great victories on behalf of King Saul and Israel, Saul still wanted David dead. In 1 Samuel 19:5, Jonathan reminds his father of one such victory—David's defeat of Goliath—in hopes Saul would retract his order to kill David. What must David have been thinking? How was he able to cope with the emotional turmoil and the unjust physical danger he dealt with daily? David also wrote poetry, which he used to express his state of mind during these dark times. In Psalms 18:1-6, we see David's thoughts during this episode in 1 Samuel 19.

Exercise: Turn and read Psalms 18:1-6 and 1 Samuel 19:5.

- What do you think David's mind was always aware of?
- What did that state of mind provide him with?
- What lesson can we take from David's example?

David's life was a continual lesson on God's provision.

God provided Saul with a great victory, too, in 1 Samuel 11. He provided Jonathan with a great victory in 1 Samuel 14. He provided David with victory over Goliath. Our God is a victorious God. He also provided for David's protection, as he will do for those faithful to him.

Exercise: Turn and read 1 Chronicles 11:10-15.

- What else did God provide David with?

Even in dark times, God provided for David with "a great victory." God also provided David with a faithful friend in Jonathan. Jonathan shared important information with David regarding Saul's mad plans. He even goes as far as to confront his father on behalf of David's cause in 1 Samuel 19:5: "Why then will you sin against innocent blood, by putting David to death without cause?"

Saul had fallen so far from God that he didn't need cause to kill David. He was mad with jealousy. He was infected with an evil spirit. He fell in love with his throne and the power that came with it. Saul forgot how he had arrived at the throne—he forgot God's provision for him. Through Moses, God established laws regarding the shedding of innocent blood.

Exercise: Turn and read Deuteronomy 19:10-13.

- What must happen to the one who sheds innocent blood?

In this light, read Psalms 69:4. David continually cried out to God. He understood where his salvation and strength was, and disregarded the impossibility of his situation. The situation often looked as if he would die, yet his faith never faltered. In 1 Samuel 19, Saul relents at Jonathan's request, and "Jonathan brought David to Saul." In the end, David continued to faithfully see to both Saul and Israel. In 1 Samuel 19:8, we learn more of David's military prowess.

"When there was war again, David went out and fought with the Philistines, and defeated them with great slaughter so that they fled before him."

Scripture reveals the identity of David's mighty men—exceedingly great warriors who personally accompanied David wherever he went. These men functioned as David's secret service. It was quite possible many of his mighty men served under him during these battles. David gathered a core group of men who continually and faithfully fought with him and served under him. These men were vital to David's survival, and God began forming this group during this time. We see these same men with David thirty years later, still serving their leader during Absalom's rebellion in 2 Samuel 15-17.

YHWH was building David's future kingdom through these present challenges in ways David could neither see nor fathom in his wildest dreams. God had already covered David with his foresight and protection. Whereas we only see the here and now, God sees the big picture. Where David saw a wolf threatening his sheep, God saw Goliath threatening his people.

He provides for our future needs during our present triumphs, struggles, and failures. Our present state is preparation. Our faith is manifested in our lives to the degree in which we *really* believe God has our best interests in mind.

Exercise: Read 1 Samuel 19:9-11.

- How did Saul try to kill David?
- Why?
- In 1 Samuel 19:11, who emerged from the background to protect David?

David wrote Psalm 59 during these events. Turn and read Psalms 59:3, 16-17.

We get a sense of Saul's irrational desire to kill David when Scripture tells us Saul's own household risked their lives to save David. First, Saul's son and then his daughter saved David's life. Saul's own family realized his behavior had become erratic and dangerous. David had a madman after him, and a powerful one at that; but he had help from the mad king's own family.

In 1 Samuel 19:12, Michal, Saul's daughter and David's wife, saves David by lowering him out of a window. Perhaps Saul's men had arrived at the door, or were stationed outside awaiting Saul's orders. David's escape brings to mind the daring efforts of Rahab the harlot saving the Hebrew spies by aiding their escape from Jericho prior to the Israelite invasion.

Exercise:

Read the two accounts, Joshua 2:3-13 (*The Spies in Jericho*) and 1 Samuel 19:11-17.

- List some similarities between the two narratives.
- Who was searching for the spies in Jericho? Who was searching for David?
- Who was responsible for the deliverance of both?

God's deliverance will often come from unexpected places. Read the words of Mordecai, uncle to the Jewish queen of Persia, Esther, in Esther 4:14:

"For if you remain silent at this time, relief and deliverance will arise for the Jews from another place and you and your father's house will perish. And who knows whether you have not attained royalty for such a time as this?"

Mordecai understood God's deliverance as well as his sovereign plan. God is in control of *everything*. He rescued David through Saul's own household. Saul's daughter Michal is depicted "using the household idol" to feign David's appearance. This tidbit of information also sheds light on the state of Saul's household. He failed to bring his children up to forsake idols and other gods.

Idolatry was openly practiced in Israel, as it was throughout much of the Old Testament. David's involvement in this worship was not stated; however, it was clear his wife, Saul's daughter, practiced idolatry and kept this idol readily available.

Exercise: Turn and read Genesis 31:22-35.

- What did Rachel hide that Laban searched for?
- What does this tell us about God's people throughout the Old Testament?
- What is the common denominator between Genesis 31:35 and 1 Samuel 19:13, though separated by hundreds of years?

Now read these verses: Psalms 103:17; Isaiah 63:8-14; Luke 17:13-14; Romans 9:16.

- What is the common denominator in these verses, though generations and centuries separate them?

God's deliverance in times of need and trouble is a direct result of his mercy, grace, and love toward all of mankind. He created man, and as he knew how to care for Adam, so did he care and provide for David, and so does he know how to provide and care for us today, thousands of years later in the twenty-first century C.E.

"As the mountains surround Jerusalem, so the Lord surrounds His people, from this time forth and forever." (Psalms 125:2).

"For I, the Lord, do not change; therefore you, O sons of Jacob, are not consumed" (Malachi 3:6).

1 SAMUEL 20

AFTER BEING LOWERED THROUGH HIS window by his wife, David fled to the seer Samuel's house in Ramah. God's glory repeatedly encircled David, protecting him from Saul, keeping him one step ahead of the bloodthirsty king. At the close of 1 Samuel 19, Saul was in pursuit of David. Saul and his men marched to Naioth, Samuel's hometown. However, despite his deadly intentions, Saul was overcome by the mighty presence of God. In 1 Samuel 19:24, we learn how Saul stripped naked and prophesied before Samuel all day and night. God's presence easily defeats the wickedness of man and the presence of evil. Even the demons shrieked at his name (Matthew 8:29; James 2:19).

It was in Naioth that many biblical scholars believe Samuel founded a school of prophets. The Bible hints at such an institution, or institutions, throughout the Old Testament. The prophets taught these schools, and the students at such schools were called "the sons of prophets." The earliest references to such a school is in 1 Samuel 10:10 and 1 Samuel 19:20. One school was in Gibeah and the other in Naioth, near Ramah. Samuel taught at both schools, and it was at the school in Naioth that King Saul arrived with murderous intent. The Lord then essentially possessed Saul, making him strip naked and prophesy in front of Samuel rather than hunt down and kill David. This allowed David to disappear into the night unnoticed.

"Then David fled from Naioth in Ramah and came and said to Jonathan, 'What have I done? What is my iniquity? And what is my sin before your father, that he is seeking my life?'" (1 Samuel 20:1).

David immediately sought out his closest friend Jonathan. He wanted to know why Saul wished him dead, and who better to ask than Jonathan? Jonathan was effectively caught in the middle of a struggle between his best friend and his father. One can imagine the conflicting feelings and emotions Jonathan experienced. He had to choose his words extremely carefully and thoughtfully gauge his every move.

In 1 Samuel 20:2, Jonathan informs David he is his father's right-hand man and advises him on all matters. Jonathan insists Saul had not made mention of plans to kill David. At this point, one must appreciate the extremely tough situation in which Jonathan found himself. Does he remain loyal to the king, his father, even though he seeks innocent blood? Or, does he remain loyal to his best friend, and thus betray his father? It was clear Saul's anger toward David was motivated by jealousy and fear. Jonathan knew David had done nothing wrong—he had pointed that fact out to his father previously.

Exercise: Turn and read 1 Samuel 18:3-4.

- Who is this passage talking about?
- How does it say Jonathan felt about David?

Now read Jonathan's response to David in 1 Samuel 20:4.

- How did Jonathan react to David?
- Should he turn his back on his father, King Saul?

David and Jonathan had made a covenant, an ancient and solemn ritual dating back to God's covenant with Noah. Another covenant is discussed in Genesis 15:1-21.

Exercise: Turn and read about this covenant.

- Who is involved in this covenant in Genesis 15:1?
- What actions were taken in Genesis 15:9–10?

- Who oversaw and made the terms of this covenant?
- What was involved in Genesis 15:4—18?

Covenants among the ancient Hebrews were serious and grave matters. In today's culture, we have lost the sense of importance for such rituals and what they represented. The marriage covenant no longer holds firm as it once did, indeed the very definition of marriage is being changed in the modern era. Divorce runs rampant. A person's word, especially that of politicians and "leaders," means less and less.

This was not the case with Jonathan and David. Their covenant was to the point of death. In a world absent of a legal system and documents as today, one's word was all one had to verify trustworthiness. Making a covenant meant placing one's word on the line. One was binding one-self to the other half of the covenant. Jonathan had already made up his mind to risk his life for David. Jonathan painfully recognized he was on the side of righteousness by going against his father, Saul. All indications in Scripture point to Jonathan being a righteous and godly man, thus it was highly likely this matter had been taken up in prayer numerous times. Jonathan had decided, presumably through prayer, on the right thing to do.

Exercise: Read John 15:13.

- How does Jonathan live out this verse?

When we know we are doing the right thing, tough decisions are easier to make. Godly choices carry God's blessing, and though all choices carry consequences, we can rest in the peace of God's grace when doing his will.

Exercise: Turn and read Philippians 4:6-7.

- When in a tough spot like Jonathan, what does this passage say to do?

Turn and read, also, Luke 11:9.

- How does this verse apply to Jonathan's situation?

Jonathan presumably asked for godly wisdom from the Lord. It is also likely he prayed for his father, King Saul. Jonathan found himself caught between his family and his friends. Jonathan found himself in a situation where his father had strayed far from the truth, and Jonathan had a choice to make. Would Jonathan follow God's way, or Saul's way? How many reading this have been in a similar situation?

It is a difficult one to be in.

Jonathan's situation was heightened by the fact that if he sided with David, he was guilty of sedition against the king and could be killed by his emotionally unstable father. It is in times such as these, when things seem most helpless, that godly wisdom prevails.

Exercise: Read Exodus 31:3.

- Who gives wisdom?

Read Job 12:13 and 16.

- Who did Job credit as being wise?

The book of Psalms has much to say about wisdom. It is, perhaps, the centerpiece of what is known as the Biblical Wisdom Literature.

Exercise: Read Psalms 51:6; 90:12; 111:10.

- What is the beginning of wisdom?
- In your own words, what does "the beginning of wisdom" mean?

Read Proverbs 1:7.

- What is the beginning of knowledge?
- Did Jonathan fear the Lord?

Read Proverbs 2:3-7.

- Who dispenses wisdom?
- Is it just handed out? How do we find wisdom (Proverbs 3–4)?

Read James 1:5-8.

- How do we gain wisdom?
- What are the conditions in asking for it?

Unquestionably, Jonathan felt torn. Yet, he had right on his side, for David had done no wrong. Justice was on Jonathan's side, and this knowledge must have given him a sense of peace in what many would view as betrayal of the king and his father.

Exercise: Turn in your bible and read Luke 12:53.

- In your own words relate that verse to the situation in 1 Samuel 20.

Perhaps Jesus had Jonathan in mind when he said those words in Luke. Jonathan's covenant to help David was sedition against the king, thus father was set against son. In fact, as if Jonathan realizes such in 1 Samuel 20:11, he takes David to the fields outside of the palace to escape the eavesdropping walls.

It is outside, away from Saul's loyal subjects, that Jonathan declares his intent to keep his end of the covenant. Their plan revolves around the Festival of the New Moon.

Exercise:

Turn and read Numbers 10:10 and Numbers 28:11-15 for information on the Festival of the New Moon.

- When did this festival take place (Numbers 10:10; 28:11)?
- What was done during the duration of the festival (Numbers 28:12-15)?
- What was the purpose of this festival (Numbers 10:10)?

The New Moon was a time to inquire of the Lord and worship at his temple or tabernacle. It was one of the festivals Israel was ordered to observe; thus, all work was to cease and business was put on hold. It was a time of great reverence, according to Dr. Spiros Zodhiates, and a time of fellowship. The king would hold a great banquet for his loyal subjects; thus, David's presence would be expected.

David and Jonathan devised a plan to feel out what Saul intended to do. In 1 Samuel 20:8, David reminds Jonathan that "you have brought your servant into a covenant of the Lord," thus he was required to be completely faithful and truthful with David. One can sense David's unease.

Exercise: Read 1 Samuel 20:9-29.

- How would Jonathan communicate Saul's intentions to David?
- What was the covenant Jonathan had made with David (1 Samuel 20:14-16)?
- Describe the relationship between David and Jonathan.

Jonathan makes an interesting comment in 1 Samuel 20:13: "And may the Lord be with you as He has been with my father." Oftentimes, people invoke God's name as someone who is with them, for them, or on their side. Scripture tells us God had departed from Saul by this time. Jonathan, like most sons, was sure to have idealized his father, though at one point it would seem reality set in. Perhaps Jonathan still thought the Lord was with Saul, or perhaps he was referring to the early periods of Saul's life when God still favored Saul.

Regardless, there was a time when Saul was looked upon with favor by God Almighty. It is often difficult to decipher the false hypocrites from the authentic people of faith. Saul was at one point authentic; however, he had strayed far since that time and lost God's favor.

Exercise: Turn and read Joshua 1:5.

- Based on this verse, how can we tell who God favored in Scripture?
- Pay special attention to David's plight as the narrative continues. Take note of how David honored God in relation to how Saul reacted.

The first day of the New Moon is recorded in 1 Samuel 20:25. King Saul, Jonathan, and Abner, the king's commander, are all present at the banquet, "but David's place was empty."

Exercise: Now read 1 Samuel 20:27-31.

- What was Saul's reaction to Jonathan's explanation of why David was not present?
- What did Saul call his son in 1 Samuel 20:30?
- What did Saul accuse him of?
- What was King Saul's vow in 1 Samuel 20:31?

Saul exploded on Jonathan. He even vowed to find another heir to his throne, "as long as the son of Jesse lives on the earth." Saul was mad, he had lost and the situation was rapidly deteriorating further. Saul ordered for David to be brought before him, "for he must surely die."

At this moment, Jonathan had two options. One, obey his father, also his king, even though Jonathan knew he was wrong and it would lead to David's execution. Or, his second option was to risk his life by keeping his end of the covenant with David.

Jonathan attempts to bring rational thinking into the situation by asking Saul what David had done to deserve death. He asks the simple and innocent question in 1 Samuel 20:31:

"What has he done?"

Madness possesses no logic and has no answers. In Proverbs 27:4, Scripture states, "Wrath is fierce and anger is a flood, but who can stand before jealousy?"

The jealousy within Saul was so intense that upon Jonathan's simple question King Saul attempted to kill his own son.

Exercise: Read 1 Samuel 20:33-34.

- How did Saul attempt to kill Jonathan?
- How did Jonathan react?

Such outbursts were not uncommon with King Saul. He is often depicted with his spear in hand or laying nearby—a dangerous prop considering his twisted mind-set and fits of rage. This is the third time in Scripture Saul is shown trying to murder someone with his spear. He failed in all three attempts, bringing into question his prowess in battle. Twice Saul sought David's life, and now he sought the life of his own son Jonathan.

Scripture notes that Jonathan arose "in fierce anger" from the table, likely shocked and deeply hurt, and left the banquet. One can imagine the reactions of Saul's other servants. If Saul was willing to kill his own son, then surely he would not think twice about killing them. Saul had become a tyrant, leading through fear of execution. Obedience to his irrational and unpredictable behavior was required at the expense of death. David was not safe, and Saul made it clear he would stop at nothing—not even the execution of his own flesh and blood son—to kill the hated "son of Jesse."

The next day, Jonathan arose and fulfilled his end of the covenant, shooting an arrow past David's secret hiding place. The signal was clear: Saul intended to kill David. The passage at 1 Samuel 20:20 closes with an incredibly moving scene between two men willing to risk it all for each other. Two friends depart, possibly never to see each other again.

Exercise: Turn and read 1 Samuel 20:41-42.

- In your own words, describe the scene. What was David's bow to Jonathan symbolic of?
- What did Jonathan state would always be between David and him, even their offspring and descendants?

"Be gracious to me, O Lord, for I am in distress; My eye is wasted away from grief, my soul and my body also. For my life is spent with sorrow, and my years with sighing" (*A Psalm of David*, Psalms 31:9-10).

1 SAMUEL 21
(PART 1)

SCRIPTURE IS SILENT AS TO the preparations David took before Jonathan's signal and blurry as to whether David fled alone or had men with him. In 1 Samuel 21, David appears to be alone and on the run, with no food, nor any weapons, and King Saul wants him dead.

Exactly where David stayed is not clearly stated. Saul ruled from Gibeah, thus David would have spent much time there in the king's service. It is from Gibeah that David fled after Jonathan's warning.

In 1 Samuel 21, we come to an interesting chapter in this Old Testament book. We have plenty of evidence as to what David was thinking and feeling during these times, as he wrote three Psalms: Psalm 34, Psalm 52, and Psalm 56, during the course of these events.

After an emotional departure from Jonathan, an exhausted and tense David arrived in Nob to see Ahimelech the priest. Earlier in the narrative, David sought refuge with the old prophet Samuel at Ramah, which was north of Gibeah. He fled to the southeast of Gibeah. Nob was just north of Jerusalem, or Jebus as it was known at this point in history, and was under Jebusite control, not Israelite control. Ramah was five miles north of Jebus, with Gibeah and Nob lying in between the two cities. Perhaps because he first fled north to Naioth, David decided it was safest to go south this time to Nob. David's presence in the city would prove fatal to its inhabitants.

It is interesting to note that in the two instances that David fled Saul's presence, he fled to a man of God; first to Samuel and now to Abimelech. Who do you turn to in times of trouble and adversity? Even modern society, so quick to eliminate God from every aspect of life, will turn to him in prayer when adversity strikes.

David arrived tired, hungry, emotionally spent, and on edge, not to mention without weapons or food. Notice Abimelech's reaction in 1 Samuel 21:1:

"And Ahimelech came trembling to meet David, and said to him, 'Why are you alone, and no one with you?'"

Exercise:

- Why do you think Ahimelech "came trembling" to David?

David's humanity is seen in his "white lie" to the priest. Up to this point in the narrative, David had remained spotless, perfect in obedience and achievement, innocent though wrongly pursued. David, though, was far from a saint. He was, first, a survivalist—and he did what he needed to do to survive.

Exercise: Read 1 Samuel 21:2.

- What was David's response?
- Was it a truthful response?

David's lie was his first impropriety during this incident.

Now read the remainder of the episode in 1 Samuel 21:3-6.

David's hunger led him to a serious violation of the Mosaic law. The Mosaic law dictated that the "bread of the presence," or the loaves of bread in the temple, also called the "shewbread," could only be eaten by the priests.

This bread was placed on the table within the tabernacle as a reminder of God's provision to the Israelites in the wilderness. Thus, in a way, though David was sinning against the law, for the bread was only to be eaten by the priests; the bread was serving its function in regards to David's situation: God was providing for him as he had provided for the wandering Israelites.

Exercise:

The following verses give more insight into the bread of the presence:

1. Exodus 25:30

    o   Where was the bread of the presence to be placed?

2. Exodus 40:23

    o   Who was the bread for?

3. Leviticus 24:5-9

    o   How many cakes were to be made?

    o   What is the significance of this number?

    o   What was the purpose of the shewbread?

    o   How often was the bread of the presence set out before the Lord?

    o   What does Leviticus 24:8 say the bread stands for?

    o   Who was allowed to eat the bread when it was replaced on the Sabbath?

The shewbread, or bread of the presence, was a sacred demonstration of Israel's everlasting covenant with the Lord. Twelve loaves, one for each of the twelve tribes of Israel, was to be set on the table each Sabbath and left there until the next. Each loaf was a sacrifice to God as a reminder of the everlasting covenant between God and Israel. Only the priests were allowed to eat the bread, and only after it was replaced by fresh loaves.

In 1 Samuel 21:6, Scripture tells us the bread "was removed from before the Lord," meaning it had been set aside and was ready for Ahimelech and the other priests to eat. David blatantly disregarded this stipulation and consumed the bread himself, willfully violating the law.

Jesus himself used this very incident to teach an important lesson in Matthew 12:1-7; Mark 2:23-28; and Luke 6:1-5. Read each passage carefully.

David's lie to the priest was certainly wrong. His eating of the bread was in direct violation of Mosaic law. However, Jesus used this incident to cut to the heart of the matter when confronted by the Pharisees. They were quick to condemn Jesus for allowing his disciples to gather food on the Sabbath, which was also strictly prohibited by the Mosaic law.

These same Pharisees also held King David in the highest esteem, as he was considered their greatest king. King David was placed on a pedestal perhaps more than any of the other significant figures in the Old Testament. Christ immediately shed light on their hypocrisy by referring to this incident, and bringing to attention the fact that their beloved and honored king also violated the law in similar fashion.

Dr. Spiros Zodhiates had this to say about Jesus's encounter with the Pharisees: "He reminded them that the king whom they held in such high regard had patently broken the law. Apparently they did not point out this fact in their teaching."

The Pharisees picked out the parts they wanted and preached on those, and Jesus was quick to confront them about it. The main point is that David, though a man after God's own heart and Israel's greatest king, was still a man and subject to human frailties and weaknesses. The hypocrisy of the Pharisees was plainly obvious, and Jesus was quick to hold them accountable for it. Jesus, according to Matthew 1, was a descendant of David through his earthly father, Joseph. David was the first of the royal house of Judah and went on to be considered Israel's greatest king.

Yet, what we gather from this incident and Jesus's reference to it is that we should not be afraid to look upon those we hold in high regard with subjective eyes. For all have sinned and fallen short of the glory of God. We are not to build false idols through false hopes in fallen men as the Pharisees did with the memory of King David. Nobody is free from sin, though we are often too quick to pounce on those in positions of authority when they fall. We should always keep in mind the fallibility of man and look with open eyes at the motives of man.

Jesus tells us to be honest and forthright. In the life of King David, we see even the highest and noblest can fall. And while many seek to condemn and are perhaps quick to point out the wrongs of others, Jesus spoke concerning this in Matthew 7:2, "For in the way you judge, you will be judged; and by your standard of measure, it will be measured to you."

Exercise:

- Can you think of a time you were quick to judge somebody because of a shortcoming?
- What should we do rather than jump to judgment?

The moral is that we should be careful not to put the wisdom and words of others—such as King David, a fallen man—over those of God's Word. God is the final authority, and we should always be reminded of this. Our focus should be on the Father and Son, and not on the politicians, rich, and famous of this world.

Exercise: Read Hebrews 12:1-3.

- Relate this passage to what we have discussed thus far about David's actions and Jesus's words to the Pharisees.

Jesus points out another lesson we can learn from David's actions. Re-read Matthew 12:6-7; Mark 2:27-28; and Luke 6:5. Jesus pointed out David's sin, yet he also showed compassion by highlighting the fine line between strict legalism and human need. In the passage from Matthew 12, Jesus quotes from the prophet Hosea.

Exercise: Read Hosea 6:6.

- What are your first impressions about this verse?
- What was Jesus's point in quoting this verse?

This is a tremendously important Old Testament passage. The Old Testament is laden with sacrifices and regulations. Yet God still desired the heart of man above all else. In fact, the sacrifices and the law were designed to keep God in the hearts of men. King Saul was caught up in legalism, where the sacrifice or offering itself was more important than the faith and obedience behind it. Scripture records multiple instances of Saul halting a priest in the middle of an offering or sacrifice to pursue his agenda. He was not *really* interested in God's way.

By quoting Hosea 6:6, Jesus announces the priority given the human heart and soul over strict observance of the law. David's actions of eating the shewbread went against the law, yet there is no doubt his heart was inclined toward God. David remained loyal and faithful to God, consistently trusting in his provision, despite breaking the Mosaic law by eating the bread of the presence.

William Barclay phrased it best in his commentary on this passage in Matthew concerning David: "Jesus insisted that the greatest actual service is the service of human need." David's need took precedence over strict legalism in this case. To help your fellow man is to worship God.

Man's motives and intentions dictate his behavior. David was certainly in need. He was very hungry and on the run; his actions were to sustain his life, not flout God's law. Proverbs 16:2 best summarizes this incident.

Exercise:

- How can you ensure your motives are right before the Lord?

After David secured sustenance from Abimelech, he turned his attention to obtaining weaponry. Scripture seems to insert an innocent detail in 1 Samuel 21:7.

Exercise: Read 1 Samuel 21:7-9.

- Who was also present at the tabernacle?
- What was his job, and why was he there?
- Was his presence good or bad for David?

Doeg's full role manifests itself later in the narrative, but he was not a righteous man. We know this because the Bible plainly states he was "detained before the Lord." We do not know why Doeg was under arrest of some sort, only that the implication of detaining somebody is for a violation of the law in some way.

Exercise:

Turn and read Psalm 52. David wrote this psalm about Doeg the Edomite, though this Psalm speaks of Doeg's future actions.

- What are your impressions of Doeg based on Psalm 52?
- What do you think Doeg will do now that he has seen David being helped by Abimelech?

When David fled to the tabernacle, he was obviously unaware Doeg was there. Perhaps this lends insight into David's words in Psalms 54:3:

"For strangers have risen against me, and violent men have sought my life; they have not set God before them."

David's own country was now against him. He could not reasonably expect another Israelite to hide him. Saul would execute anybody accused of aiding David. The king had nearly killed his own son for simply speaking up on David's behalf. Ahimelech not only fed David but also gave him Goliath's sword, which seemed to be stored in the tent. Scripture is not specific regarding the reason Goliath's sword was at this location or how long it had been there.

Desperate, with little provisions and no allies, David's course of action was indeed bold and daring. He defected to the enemy's camp—the very enemy whose champion he had once slain. David fled to the Philistine city of Gath, Goliath's home, ironically, and one of the chief cities in the Philistine Pentapolis. Achish was king of Gath, which was one of the five Philistine strongholds in the region known as the Pentapolis.

The Bible does not state how much time had passed between David's victory over Goliath and his defection to Gath, yet Israel was still at war with the Philistines. David sought protection from his own country in the hands of the enemy.

Exercise: Reflect on the previous reading and answer the following questions.

- What was David's intent when he ate the showbread?
- Was this a sin against God's law?
- What were the points Jesus made to the Pharisees?
- Why should we leave judgment to God?
- When you encounter legalism and mere observance, keep in mind Hosea 6:6.
- How would you complete the following thought: Above all else, God desires my _____.

1 SAMUEL 21

(PART 2)

THE PHILISTINES WOULD EVENTUALLY BECOME uneasy allies with David. Their relationship was always on edge, as war was frequent. In David, the Philistines likely saw a way to get at Saul and tear apart Israel—rather than an actual ally that could provide them with any assistance. The Philistine model was divide and conquer, and through accepting David, they could further divide Israel and eventually conquer the annoying little nation.

Little did the Philistines know David would eventually destroy them and reduce them to insignificance. In 1 Samuel 21, the Philistines are extremely suspicious toward David. It must be remembered David had already killed many Philistines in numerous battles the Bible briefly touches on. What kinds of battles must these have been? For the Philistines, they had giant Philistine warriors, equipped with the finest weaponry in Canaan, clad in bronze body armor, and oftentimes in chariots when the terrain was favorable for such.

For the Israelites, they possessed little to no armor, slingshots, stolen weapons, and swords of likely far inferior quality. At one point, the only Israelites with swords were Jonathan and Saul. In 1 Samuel 21, we see that iron was monopolized by the Philistines. By all indications, these battles should have been short and one-sided massacres. Yet, somehow David and his men wrought havoc on the Philistines.

David must have been at wits' end. He fled Gibeah to Nob, where he unluckily encountered a servant of King Saul. He received minimal sustenance in Nob, though he had secured Goliath's sword. Then he fled to the one place Saul would never think to look—the Philistine camp. The Bible relates very little about this encounter. The text reads as if he were alone. He likely was taken into custody upon approaching the city gates.

Perhaps they recognized his sword as the former sword of their slain champion. The two nations were in open war, and had been for decades, thus a defecting Hebrew was a golden opportunity but had to be treated with suspicion.

Exercise: Read 1 Samuel 21:11-12.

- Was David able to hide his identity?
- What did the servants say to Achish in regards to David?

David's situation was bleak, to say the least. He was alone, with little to no food, loved by his countrymen though hated by his king, and surrounded by the dreaded Philistines. It would not take long for somebody to recognize him as *the* David of Israel, responsible for the deaths of their brothers—most famously that of the champion Goliath. These men likely would've remembered that fateful day—they might have even lost a comrade in the fight itself. David's life hung in the balance.

Exercise:

- How would you feel in such a situation?
- How did David feel? What did he do?

In 1 Samuel 21:11, "the servants of Achish" recognize David and say, "Is this not David the king of the land?" It seems unlikely these Philistines were aware of David's anointing by Samuel. It seems most fitting they referred to David as "king of the land" due to his popularity with fellow Israelite countrymen. David's feats and exploits became legendary in his own lifetime. Even in these early years, he was known and loved by his people.

This would fit with 1 Samuel 18:5, which states that wherever Saul sent David he "prospered." Again in 1 Samuel 18:4, Scripture relates David "was prospering in all his ways." David was a fierce warrior and had a fierce reputation. He was feared and hated by the Philistines; loved and hated by Israel. Despite his past exploits and fearless mentality, David now feared for his life. Upon being discovered in 1 Samuel 21:11, verse twelve reveals, "David took these words to heart and greatly feared Achish king of Gath."

Other versions read "David put these words in his heart," with the implication being he took them very seriously. He was "afraid" of what the Philistine king would do. David's preparations before defecting were not recorded by Scripture, thus we do not know if his actions were preplanned or spontaneous. However, his response in 1 Samuel 21:13 shows incredible impromptu acting.

David would later write about his experiences in the Philistine camp in Psalm 34 and Psalm 56. We can glimpse into the heart and mind of David during these difficult times and discover why God called him a man after his own heart.

It is quite remarkable to observe how David talked to God in Psalm 56. David was brutally honest with God. He told God exactly how he felt. David provided us with a model on how to approach God.

Exercise:

Read Psalms 56:1-13. Notice how David opened his prayer in Psalms 56:1-2:

"Be gracious to me, O God, for man has trampled upon me; fighting all day long he oppresses me. My foes have trampled upon me all day long, for they are many who fight proudly against me."

Imagine David, perhaps in a Philistine cell, certainly alone, scared, abandoned by his own country, at the mercy of his enemy, and with nothing but his thoughts and God. Psalm 56 is called *A Mikhtam of David when the Philistines Seized Him in Gath*. Two countries at war with each other were united in their pursuit of young David. The pressure was enormous. David, rather than turn to self-pity, turned to God for deliverance and protection.

It is no wonder why themes of deliverance, redemption, and rescue are quite common throughout the narrative of David, including his Psalms.

Exercise:

Compare Psalms 56:1-2 with the following Psalms: Psalms 17:8-9; Psalms 35:1; Psalms 32:25; Psalms 57:3; Psalms 59:1.

Now reread Psalms 56:3-13 and take note of any repeated thoughts or phrases.

- What did David repeatedly say?
- David stated with absolute certainty that he knew something. What did David state that he knew?

David adhered to a very important biblical principle: he asked of God with certainty. Maybe not with certainty that God would answer his prayer the way he wanted it, but with absolute certainty and faith that God heard his prayer and had his best interests in mind. We must come before God in faith as David does here. The New Testament has much to say about this.

Exercise:

Read the following verses: Matthew 14:30-31; Matthew 21:21-22; Mark 11:23-24; James 1:6-7.

- What is the main idea behind each of those verses?
- Can you think of a time you prayed and God answered? If so, jot it down. If not, ask God for an opportunity so he may show his power to you.
- How did David's prayer turn out?

Turn back to 1 Samuel 21:13-15 and read to find out.

- What did David do?

David's scheme worked perfectly. God provided David with the wits necessary to pull off such a stunt, and he guided the Philistine king to disregard David. Now turn to Psalm 34. Is there any doubt who David praised for his deliverance from Gath? Is there any question as to who David continually turned to despite his human weaknesses?

Exercise: Read Psalms 34:4.

- Who did David seek?
- Who delivered David?

When we read these Psalms in context with David's life, we get a beautiful and real-life example of God's deliverance! We see David's situation and we can read his thoughts through his writings. In Psalm 34, we can peer into David's mind as he was rejected by both the Philistines and Israel. David was truly alone, with nobody to turn to save the Lord. David told us that the righteous have a very powerful presence that "encamps around those who fear him."

- What is the identity of this presence in Psalms 34:7?

The angel of the Lord appears many times throughout the Old Testament, often in times of great need or peril.

Exercise:

Read the following passages concerning the one who "encamps around those who fear him."

1. Genesis 16:7-13
2. Genesis 21:17
3. Exodus 3:2
4. Exodus 14:19
5. Numbers 22:21-22, 31
6. Joshua 5:13-15
7. Daniel 3:25
8. Daniel 6:22
9. Revelation 22:16.

Scholars have debated the identity of the angel of the Lord. Some view him as a pre-incarnate Christ. The appearances of this angel occur at critical times throughout the Old Testament. Scripture is silent as to the precise identity and nature of this messenger. But from the times of Abraham and Hagar to Moses and Joshua—and from David to Daniel—the angel of the Lord protects and delivers the people of YHWH.

In Psalm 34, we see David's deliverance. Just as God sent David the angel of the Lord during the Iron Age, He sent Israel his son, Jesus Christ, nearly one thousand years later. In this present age we have the very Holy Spirit of God, left behind by Jesus upon his ascension. In a world of ever-increasing evil and injustice, we can be assured the Holy Spirit of the Lord watches us, encamped around us and within us, and is watching us on all sides. He always has been and always will be—from before the Iron Age to the Millennial Age and beyond.

Praise be to God, our Deliverer, our Rock, our Refuge, today, tomorrow, and until the end of time! Amen.

1 SAMUEL 22
(PART 1)

THROUGH HIS CLEVER RUSE OF being mad, David escaped the Philistines. Scripture uses the word "escapes," which in Hebrew is *malat*. This word translates literally as "to be smooth," and it implies "escaping by means of slipperiness." "Slippery" is a great word to use in describing David. He is a slippery one, as time and again he slips through the grasp of those pursuing him. David's slipperiness was a result of God's protection and deliverance.

In 1 Samuel 22, we learn David escaped to "the cave of Adullam." Adullam was a city that had been around since at least the time of Jacob (Genesis 38:1). Near the city was a cave that David fled to. The city was located in the south of Canaan, in the Negev, or desert region. It was approximately sixteen miles southeast of Gibeah, thus over a day's journey from Saul's capital. Adullam was less than ten miles from Gath and located twelve miles west of Bethlehem, David's hometown. He knew the area well.

During the time he spent in the cave, David wrote Psalm 57 and Psalm 142. We will use these to gain insight into David's frame of mind. He became a nomad, an outlaw, a hunted man. His own king had tried to take his life at least twice. Saul was determined in his quest for David's life. David had also tried to defect to the Philistines, who also rejected him.

David could not return to Bethlehem as the king's men likely lurked about keeping an eye out for him. His last attempt to reach out to the only sympathetic group he had—the priests—led to Saul slaughtering an entire village. David had nowhere to turn. Thus, David sought refuge in a cave near Adullam, perhaps one he had discovered years ago while tending his father's flock. It was not unusual for shepherds to travel a day or so from their home in search of grazing land for their flocks. They could travel several miles in one day, and Adullam was only twelve or so miles west of Bethlehem. Perhaps God led David to this cave years earlier in anticipation of this very moment.

The scenario is a plausible one to consider. David had spent years alone with his flocks, wandering for grazing pasture for days on end. He staved off predators, rescued lost sheep, and probably spent many a night in caves like this one. In his current state, he was an outlaw with nowhere to go. He searched his mind for places of solitude and naturally thought back to his days as a shepherd. God always sees our future in our present. We must learn to trust him.

Exercise: Turn and read Psalms 57:1 and Psalms 142:4-6, written during this time.

- What is your opinion on David's feelings based on these verses?
- Based on Psalms 142:4, was David alone at this time or not?
- How would you feel in David's situation?
- What does David pray for in these two Psalms?

Now read 1 Samuel 22:1.

- Who joined David?

The Bible is silent as to how long David was alone in the cave before his family showed up. Perhaps David first penned Psalm 141, and God, in answer to his prayer, sent "his brothers and all his father's household to him." Such a scenario would not be unlikely. God tends to bring us to the end of ourselves before he fully reveals his power to us. What better way to strengthen his servant David than to direct David's family to his whereabouts?

Jesse, like any good father, was not going to let his son perish alone. Notice it was not just his brothers and his father but "all his father's household" that came out to meet him. David was no longer alone and would never be alone again. However, God was not finished, as is evident in 1 Samuel 22:2.

Exercise: Read carefully 1 Samuel 22:2.

- Who does Scripture say "gathered" to David?
- How many people came out to meet him?
- Does the Bible say how they heard about David, or why exactly they came out to him?

Now, turn and read all of Psalm 142. Notice David's language: "I cry aloud," "I make supplication," "I pour out," "I cried out," "Give heed to my cry."

- David humbled himself before God. Take Psalm 142 and 1 Samuel 22:2 together. Would you say God "heeded" David's cry?

Turn to the New Testament and read Ephesians 3:20-21.

- Relate this verse to what happened with David in 1 Samuel 22:1-2.

Read Psalms 142:7.

- Did God make that happen?
- Do you think David knew four hundred people were on their way out to meet him? Did David give any indication in Psalm 57 and 142 that he expected this to happen?

We gain further insight into this situation when we look at the Hebrew word *marah*, used twice in 1 Samuel 22:2. It is translated as "distress" in the first occurrence, and "discontented" in the second. *Marah* is defined as "bitter, bitterness, bitterly, bitter in soul, angry, and chafed." These people were bitter at life, for whatever reason. They were heavily in debt to the king, wronged by other individuals or Saul's government.

Likely, many had been forced from their homes or had land and fields taken from them as a result of war and/or taxes.

Samuel warned that people would become disillusioned with the king in 1 Samuel 8:10-22. Read this passage for a better understanding of the context.

Saul himself hints at his confiscation of fields and redistribution of them to his men in 1 Samuel 22:7. He asks his servants if David will "give to all of you fields and vineyards," the insinuation being that he himself had. Perhaps some of the men flocking to David had their land confiscated by Saul.

Saul's kingdom appeared divided and in a state of unrest. The Philistines remained an ever-present threat, and Saul's policies had proven ineffective at times. Discontentment spread throughout the empire, and some found their way to David. The people praised David for slaying "ten thousand" compared to Saul's thousand in 1 Samuel 18:7. Many of these people now found themselves desperate on account of Saul.

David was well known, for he was also the king's son-in-law. It is quite possible that many of the people fleeing to David were from the tribe of Judah, David's own tribe. Many of these men would have likely known much about David's exploits, his flight from Saul, and his flight from the Philistines. These people were drawn to David because he had escaped two kings from two different nations, killed a Philistine champion, won many battles as a commander, was the king's son-in-law, and like them, was on the run after having been wronged by the authorities.

It is extraordinary to read David's thoughts during this time. He wrote many Psalms during these turbulent times, including Psalms 142:4. David's prayers in the cave of Adullam attest to his desperation.

"Look to the right and see; for there is no one who regards me; no one cares for my soul."

David thought he was alone. He cried out to God. How God works for those who love him, even when we aren't aware of it! God was gathering his people to David in the wilderness.

His anointed king was undergoing real-life training. God uses the wilderness and cave experiences of our lives to teach us as he did with David thousands of years ago.

This experience for David was his first kingship, and these were his first subjects. Though much easier said than done, we must fight to remember that God uses the trouble and affliction that befalls us for our benefit and growth. These are our training experiences, as they were for David.

Exercise: Read Matthew 4:1.

- Describe this wilderness experience—who, where, what, etc.

Read Galatians 1:17.

- Describe this wilderness experience.

Read Deuteronomy 29:5.

- Describe this wilderness experience.
- Are you currently experiencing a wilderness time in your life? If so, ask God to show you what he wants to teach you. This is a time you may learn more fully about God and experience God in a profound way. Don't let it slip by because you are focusing on the trouble. Focus on God. Keep your eyes focused upward on Christ. Write out a prayer to God about your wilderness time. Do not be afraid to be honest.

1 SAMUEL 22:6-23
(PART 2)

AFTER DAVID'S ARMY GATHERED TO him at the cave of Adullam, he secured the well-being of his parents by placing them with the king of Moab. David's parents led the initial wave of people out to meet David in the cave. In 1 Samuel 22:6, King Saul catches word of David's whereabouts.

Exercise: Read 1 Samuel 22:6.

- Where is Saul in this verse?
- What does he have in his hand?

Saul, spear in hand, was likely in a foul mood when the news of David's location arrived. Saul was prone to strike out at individuals nearby, as he had done with his own son, Jonathan, as well as David. It is easy enough to imagine Saul struck out at his servants as well. Saul, though, bribed them for their loyalty.

Exercise: Read and compare 1 Samuel 8:14 and 1 Samuel 22:7.

- Who was talking in 1 Samuel 8? In 1 Samuel 22?
- What did Saul give to those loyal to him?
- What does 1 Samuel 22:7-8 reveal about Saul's leadership methods?

In 1 Samuel 22:9, we read of a familiar figure. Doeg the Edomite, from 1 Samuel 21:7, resurfaces. We last encountered Doeg being held captive at the tabernacle for an undisclosed offense. Now, perhaps not surprisingly, he is in the company of King Saul. Saul rants and raves at his servants, accusing them of conspiring against him. One can imagine Saul waving his spear frantically and haphazardly—at any point capable of unleashing the spear toward an unlucky bystander.

Doeg knew the time had come for him to reveal the information he had. His revelation would lead to one of the most heinous acts in all of the Bible. The depth of Saul's depravity and evil were revealed, as was the void between him and God.

Exercise: Read carefully 1 Samuel 22:9-19.

- What did Saul accuse Ahimelech of?
- What was Ahimelech's response?
- King Saul ordered the death of Ahimelech in 1 Samuel 22:16–17. What was the response of "the guards who were attending him?"
- Who did the king ask to execute "the priests of the Lord?"

Read Psalms 52:1-5.

- How does this passage corollate with what we know about Doeg?
- How many men did Doeg slay?
- Not only did Saul order the death of Ahimelech, but what else was carried out by Doeg and his men? What was the extent of their second act (1 Samuel 22:19)?

The shocking and senseless murder of God's priests is a testament to how far Saul had fallen. This leads one to ask the question: How can God allow such evil to take place? Why do bad things happen to good people? Let's turn back to a psalm of David he wrote while in the cave, Psalm 57. The events of 1 Samuel 22 are happening simultaneously as David is hiding out in the cave.

Exercise: Read Psalms 57:2.

- Who does David say he will cry to?
- What does God accomplish for David?

The Hebrew word David used to address God is El Elyon, or "God Most High." Throughout the Old Testament, especially in Genesis, different names are given for God. Each of these names reveals a distinct part of his being. El Elyon is first recorded in Genesis 14:18-19. El is the Hebrew for "god" or "God." "Elyon" translates as "elevation, lofty, supreme, higher or highest, uppermost, most high."

Exercise: Turn and read these Daniel 4:17 and Psalms 21:7.

- What is God called in these verses?
- According to Daniel 4:17, who and what does God rule over?

Other names for God include El Roi, or "the God Who Sees Me" (Hagar, Genesis 16:13), and El Shaddai, or "God Almighty" (Genesis 17:1). In Exodus 6:3, God reveals himself to Moses as YHWH, the Great I Am. Each of these appellations lead to a deeper understanding of God's nature and another revelation into his character. He is the One Who Sees us, our struggles and victories; Almighty King over our lives; and Most High above all else, Creator of everything.

To answer the question "why do bad things happen to good people?" requires one to submit to God's sovereignty. "Sovereignty" is defined as "supreme excellence or an example of it, supreme power, freedom from external control, a controlling influence, one that is sovereign." Saul's actions against the priests and their city were not undertaken without God's knowledge. After all, his sovereignty reigns supreme.

The best illustration of God's sovereignty is in Psalms 115:3:

"But our God is in the heavens; He does whatever He pleases."

One of the most incredible allowances of God's sovereignty is free will. God has given humans the ability to choose actions and beliefs, even if they fly in his face. However, with free will comes responsibility and accountability. Another factor must also be kept in mind. If one believes in God, then there must also be a real belief in the enemy.

He, too, goes by many names: Satan, Lucifer, the Adversary, Beelzebub, the serpent, the Morning Star, Babylon. The Adversary seeks to thwart God's will at every turn. It was God's desire and will that Saul follow his commands (1 Samuel 10:7). Saul, however, chose not to follow God's commands. As a consequence, Saul was influenced by an evil spirit (1 Samuel 18:10). The enemy has been given authority over the earth, as Scripture plainly indicates. Thus, to a limited extent, Satan has sovereignty over the earth, as much as God allows him.

Exercise: Turn and read Job 1:6-12.

- Where did Satan tell God he had been?
- Compare this verse to Peter's warning in 1 Peter 5:8.

Also read 1 Chronicles 21:1 and Zechariah 3:1-3.

- How do these verses depict Satan? Is he a passive influence or an aggressive influence?

Read 2 Corinthians 11:14.

- What is another form Satan may take?

Let us not forget the tempter's tricks on Jesus Christ in the wilderness, which failed. Nevertheless, Satan was allowed to tempt Jesus in Matthew 4.

Read carefully Matthew 4:8-9.

- What did Satan offer Jesus?
- How did Satan have the authority to offer this?
- What does this reveal about Satan's position on earth?

Jesus rejoiced with the seventy he sent out as they reported back with joy in Luke 10:18. They had been given authority over the demons. Jesus said in response, "I was watching Satan fall from heaven like lightning." Satan's fall from heaven landed him on earth, where he was given a limited amount of authority. Satan offered Jesus the kingdoms of the earth because the kingdoms of the earth were Satan's to offer—as allowed by God. This world, this body of flesh, is ruled by the influence of Satan until the day of the Lord.

Satan is the great tempter, the deceiver, the great liar. Saul chose to slaughter Ahimelech and the other priests. God did not make him do it; Saul chose. Satan certainly had a hand in Saul's decision, and looked on with great satisfaction. God was not the cause of this bad thing happening. God allowed Saul to choose his actions. Saul made a choice; he was the cause.

In 1 Peter 5:8, the devil is called "a roaring lion, seeking someone to devour." Saul opened the door for evil influence, and the roaring lion ate his fill of Saul's soul. It is this very ability to choose (otherwise known as free will) that places mankind right in the middle of a cosmic battle we cannot see. God wishes for his creation to choose him. When we do, God's grace and love empower us to overcome.

Lucifer tempts mankind to choose his ways, which produce war, murder, strife, and chaos. Satan then feasts on his prey's soul. In 1 Samuel 22, King Saul took his stand against YHWH—the God who anointed Saul. David, on the other hand, took in the lone surviving priest from Nob. Abiathar, a son of Ahimelech, escaped the ruthless butchering and fled to David. Humans cannot begin to grasp the depth and overall extent of God's sovereign nature and plan. Bad things happen on earth because that is the state of our fallen world. We can only look to God for truth and peace.

Exercise:

Read the following verses: Psalms 115:3; Genesis 2:7-9; 41:51-52; Deuteronomy 2:7; Psalms 18:38-39; Hebrews 13:20-21; Galatians 5:22-25.

One of the most popular verses in all of the Bible speaks of God's sovereignty. In John 3:16, God's purpose is revealed for his Son and mankind.

- What do you think God finds pleasing?
- What does he intend for his people?
- Why does God allow evil?
- Why do bad things happen to good people?
- What is your role in the battle between God and the Adversary?

Saul's ruthless actions in 1 Samuel 22 can bring us into a deeper understanding of God if we understand that consequences come about with each and every decision and choice we make. We are caught in a struggle, one that has been raging since before the days of Saul and David. God's Word is here for us to learn from. Let us learn from observing Saul's decisions and actions.

He had so much to give his nation, such promise for Israel. Yet, he gave himself up to his own lusts and desires and dismissed the words of God. Consequently, a potentially great man of God was given into the hands of the enemy. Saul's demise is painful to follow in Scripture.

1 SAMUEL 23

DAVID AND HIS MEN CONTINUED to dwell in the cave of Adullam for an extended period of time. David knew this region well. It was within the tribal territory of Judah. David was among his clansmen, tribal members sympathetic to his cause and more likely to hide his whereabouts from King Saul.

David was from Bethlehem of Judah, located approximately six miles south of Jerusalem. All of the southern wilderness region, including the wildernesses of Judah, Ziph, Maon, and the Negev were within Judah's tribal boundaries. David used this vast wilderness and his ties to the people and land to his advantage. It was during these times he established a foothold in the south, hiding and fleeing from Saul, slipping through the King's fingers time after time. This southern stronghold would ultimately lead to his kingdom being established in Hebron.

In 1 Samuel 23, the Philistines raid a nearby town, Keilah. Keilah was less than five miles south of Adullam, thus word traveled quickly to David concerning the battle. In 1 Samuel 23:1, Scripture relates the situation: "Behold, the Philistines are fighting against Keilah, and are plundering the threshing floors."

The threshing floor was where the wheat was separated from the chaff, and these were typically large, circular, flattened-out areas in or near a village. Full threshing floors meant the crop had been harvested. In essence, the Philistines were attempting to plunder the food supply of

Keilah. This likely was not a full-scale military operation on the part of the Philistines. It was, in all probability, a raid conducted by a local Philistine force, probably located near Gath. We catch a glimpse of David as commander in chief in 1 Samuel 23:2.

Exercise: Read 1 Samuel 23:2.

- What is the first course of action David took?

How many times have you seen a person in a position of leadership consult God before big decisions? What would the perception be of a CEO stopping a board meeting to "inquire of the Lord?" Prayer is being forced out of institutions and other public settings. David, in this instance, showed us what godly leaders do—they seek God. David's first thought was to ask his God if attacking the Philistines was the prudent thing to do.

He put into practice what he constantly wrote of in his Psalms—seeking God's guidance and direction (Psalms 4:1; 5:1-2; 13:3; 18:6; 143:1). These verses show David was not shy in asking for God's help. His cries were often desperate.

Exercise: Read 1 Samuel 23:3-5.

- How many times did David seek God?
- What was God's answer?
- What was the result?

David was becoming somewhat of a local celebrity. His exploits and victories against the mighty Philistines were known throughout all of Israel. By saving his fellow tribesmen at Keilah, he was gaining a reputation as an able leader. Other towns and villages in the area would eventually seek his protection as well. However, after his victory at Keilah, Saul became aware of his whereabouts and dispatched men to find David. David couldn't take a step in any direction without danger lurking close by. If it wasn't the Philistines, it was Saul.

Saul thought David was securely shut inside the city of Keilah. So, 1 Samuel 23:8 tells us Saul "summoned all the people for war, to go down to Keilah to besiege David and his men." Once again, David went to the well that is God's grace and wisdom.

Exercise: Read 1 Samuel 23:6, 10-12.

- What did Abiathar have with him (see Exodus 28:30-31)?
- What did David ask God?
- What was the Lord's answer?

Saul's power is seen here in the fact that the men of Keilah would have given David up. Even after David saved their food supply, they still remained loyal to the king. With God's forewarning, David and his men left Keilah, "and they went wherever they could go."

With Keilah's betrayal, men from David's own tribe turned against him. This puts into context David's state of mind in Psalms 31:13 when he cries, "terror is on every side of me."

David's first move was to turn to God in times like this. While most people act first and think later, David took time to pray for guidance and instruction.

Exercise: Read Psalms 63:6-7.

- When does David think of God?
- In 1 Samuel 23, is David sleeping or awake? Is he actively thinking of God, even in these chaotic moments?

Though certainly no saint, David was aware of God's presence and authority throughout most of the text. He had, and would continue to have in the narrative, his moments of human weakness and failure, but David was unquestionably a man concerned with God. David was not the gentle, clean-cut, soft-spoken Christian man held up by many today as the model of Christianity. "Turn the other cheek," they say.

Perhaps our modern-day church needs a little more Abraham and David. These guys were rough and tough. They were outdoorsmen, warriors, leaders, and survivors. They fought for justice and against oppression. They killed people in battle. David was called a man of bloodshed in 1 Chronicles 28:3. They were also deeply concerned with godly matters. David had to keep himself alive, and if that wasn't enough, he was now responsible for approximately six hundred other men and their families.

Exercise:

Read Psalms 63:1 for a description of David's wilderness. This Psalm was written by David years after these events, when he was already king and spoke of this same Judean Wilderness. Perhaps Psalm 63 was a nostalgic reflection from an elderly King David on the very times discussed here in 1 Samuel 23.

- How does David describe this large area?
- What resource was scarce?

Despite the hardships, trials, and constant hiding, David would not be discouraged. We get not only a sense of his helplessness through the various Psalms he wrote but also a sense of his utmost confidence and faith in God.

Exercise: Read Psalms 16:8-9 and Psalms 32:7.

- What do these verses say to you? What insight do you gain from them?

This is faith in action—complete helplessness coupled with complete confidence. David constantly asked God to deliver him, and he constantly had new enemies pursuing him. Yet, pay close attention to the final line of 1 Samuel 23:14.

Neither Saul nor any others would find David and his men, for "God did not deliver him" into any of their hands.

In 1 Samuel 23:15-23, Scripture depicts yet another city of Judah betraying David's whereabouts. King Saul moved out from Gibeah with an army to pursue David. In 1 Samuel 23:15, David becomes aware of Saul's movements south.

The Hebrew word translated as "became aware" also translates to "look, see, to look at, regard, perceive." It implies visual recognition.

Saul and his army continually pursue David, yet Scripture makes it plain the Lord protected David. While Saul and his men sought without success, Jonathan found David with ease. Jonathan appears at his side to strengthen and encourage him in 1 Samuel 23:16. Jonathan, remarkably, came to David, hiding at Horesh in the wilderness of Ziph. One can imagine how risky this would have been for Jonathan—the son of the very king seeking to kill David. Scripture is silent as to how Jonathan hides his mission from his father, King Saul.

Remember 1 Samuel 20:30-34 when Saul hurled his spear at his own son, in a blind fit of rage and jealousy over David? Saul's reaction would be even more cruel and brutal if he discovered Jonathan's true intentions. How Jonathan knew where to find David is not revealed by the Bible. The two were very close, and it is likely they developed a means by which to communicate in secret with each other. Read 1 Samuel 23:16.

"And Jonathan, Saul's son, arose and went to David at Horesh, and encouraged him in God."

The King James Version says Jonathan "strengthened [David's] hand in God." Jonathan brought godly friendship and encouragement at a time David needed it most. Some of his own tribe betrayed him, and the world was quickly closing in on him. God, though, always knows the precise time to send encouragement.

The Hebrew word translated as "encouraged" literally means "to fasten upon, to seize, be strong, to be attached, to gird." Godly friends should follow Jonathan's example in this passage. Once again he goes out of his way and risks his life for David. His encouragement in 1 Samuel 23:16-17 is meant to strengthen David in the Lord. The concept behind the Hebrew word is to fasten oneself to something, to gird or support oneself.

Exercise: Read 1 Samuel 23:17-18 carefully.

- What did Jonathan tell David is going to happen?
- What did the two do before parting ways?

Jonathan and David made another covenant reaffirming their friendship and bond. The two, by now, were closer than brothers. Their love superseded even life and death. God used this visit by Jonathan to strengthen and refocus David in his time of need. David would need this strength, for in the very next verse (1 Samuel 23:19), some more of his tribesmen betray him to Saul.

Exercise: Read 1 Samuel 23:19.

- Who initiated contact in this verse?
- Where were these people from, and what did they tell Saul?

After fleeing the Keilahites, David and his men moved to Horesh in the wilderness around Ziph, just south of Hebron. Horesh was a city that has not been positively identified, but is thought to exist approximately five miles southeast of Ziph. Scripture speaks of "the strongholds of Horesh," and though scholars aren't positive as to the identity of these strongholds, many believe the future Herodian fortress of Masada was one of these strongholds. Ziph is located northeast of Masada and just east of En-gedi. Ziph and En-gedi are both located near the Dead Sea.

It was here, among the rugged hills and desolate landscape, that David hid from Saul. His hiding places, though, were quickly diminishing.

Exercise:

Stop and read the list of people, groups, and nations seeking David's life:

- King Saul and his army
- The Philistines
- The men of Keilah
- The men of Ziph

He wrote Psalm 54 during this time in the wilderness of Ziph. Fortunately, we can glimpse into David's state of mind. Turn and read this short psalm.

The NASB states David wrote this psalm "when the Ziphites came and said to Saul, 'Is not David hiding himself among us?'"

- How did David begin this psalm?
- What kind of men were pursuing David?
- How did David describe God?
- List some themes from other Psalms we have read that are similar to those found in Psalm 54.

Saul gave the Ziphites clear instructions on what they were to do. He also revealed his delusion by claiming the Lord would bless Ziph. Scripture was clear that the Lord left Saul to his own devices. Saul, then, was using the Lord's name to justify his actions against David and to fool the Ziphites into thinking they were doing the right thing.

Unfortunately, it is the practice of many men, kings, and nations to use the name of God to advance their agenda, power, and influence. We must be careful about using God's name in an unholy way. In this instance, Saul used it to convince the Ziphites they were doing the right thing by betraying David's location. David, however, again learned of the betrayal and moved his men further south into the wilderness of Maon.

As Saul moved southward, David moved southward further into the wilderness. There he would hide from Saul.

In 1 Samuel 23:24-29, a principle is at work in regards to God's sovereignty. There is something unique in this verse, as there is in Isaiah 44:28; Isaiah 45:1; Daniel 2:28; and Ezekiel 30:10. Each one deals with a foreign ruler as an agent of God. This was a notion that many Jews struggled with. God was their God. He had chosen them, and though they frequently rebelled, they would eventually turn back. He used his people to accomplish his purposes. The Messiah was a Jew. God's revelation and blessing was to the Jews. This was a privilege strictly reserved for Israel and Jerusalem.

However, the Bible clearly shows God is not limited to just using the Jews. He uses what he wishes and whom he wishes to accomplish his work. God's sovereignty takes everything and everybody into account, and his dominion is not limited to one type of person, nation, or religion.

Isaiah called the Persian King Cyrus (Cyrus the Great) God's "shepherd" and "anointed"! God is not limited to only using the righteous, or only using the Jews, or only using the Christians, to accomplish his purposes and plans.

Exercise: Who is the ruler discussed in Ezekiel and Daniel?

Masada was a perfect site for one of the strongholds of Horesh. Centuries later, circa 37 B.C., Herod would fortify Masada. In 70 A.D., it was the last Jewish holdout against the Roman Empire. The rock of Masada juts out over fourteen hundred feet above the terrain to the east, and over three hundred feet in the west. This rocky mountain could've provided the backdrop for verse 26. The Bible says that "Saul went on one side of the mountain, and David and his men on the other side of the mountain."

However, Saul tightened the noose around David, who found himself in trouble, barely able to escape. Saul could smell David's sweat he was so close. The king would have to wait, for God had other plans in mind. A messenger arrived with news the dreaded Philistines raided the land. King Saul's attention was needed elsewhere. The timely Philistine raid had forced Saul to abandon his pursuit of David, thus David was delivered once again.

Exercise:

- Record an instance God delivered you from a tough situation in an unexpected way.

- List the other nations from the Old Testament discussed in chapter 26.

- Memorize Psalms 54:4. "Behold, God is my helper; The Lord is the sustainer of my soul."

1 SAMUEL 24

WHEN SAUL WAS FORCED TO abandon his pursuit of David, David was able to flee and hide "in the strongholds of En-gedi." En-gedi was approximately fifteen miles north of Masada, on the western banks of the Dead Sea. It was at this oasis, sandwiched between the sea and the desert, with cliffs rising some 650 feet to the plateau above, that David was staying in 1 Samuel 24:1.

Beyond the cliffs above En-gedi was the vast Judean wilderness. The various wildernesses of Ziph, Maon, and Judea lay to the west and southwest of En-gedi and the Dead Sea. A temple shrine was discovered near En-gedi dating back to approximately 4000 B.C. The site, thus, was ancient by the time David hid there circa 1050 B.C.

Saul resumes his pursuit of David upon learning of his whereabouts in the opening verse of 1 Samuel 24. We are told that Saul takes three thousand "chosen men from all Israel" with him in pursuit of the rebel David. He was not playing around. Saul had tired of the cat-and-mouse game he and David had been playing. He chose three thousand of the finest warriors, hunters, scouts, and killers from all of Israel and set out toward En-gedi—all to find and kill one man.

Take time to read the rest of 1 Samuel 24. This chapter will deal with the text as a whole, using various verses to emphasize certain points.

The Philistine threat, which interrupted Saul's earlier pursuit of David, had subsided. The king was able to concentrate all of his efforts on David. As Saul led his men toward En-gedi, it was likely they spread out in a search pattern as they hunted for David. Saul's group was nearing En-gedi when they encountered a cave.

Nature's call struck Saul as they passed by the cave's entrance. He called out for his squad to halt as he entered the cave to relieve himself.

Exercise: Read 1 Samuel 24:2-7.

- Who was in the cave?
- What is this other person urged to do?
- What does David call Saul in 1 Samuel 24:6?
- How did the situation end?

We learn a tremendous amount concerning David's character from this encounter with Saul. This was obviously a God-ordained coincidence. We are not told how many of David's men were in the cave with him. It is unlikely all six hundred men could escape notice, though some caves can certainly fit that many people. It seems quite possible David would've been fleeing with a smaller, more mobile group, likely his "mighty men" discussed in 1 Chronicles 11.

David's mighty men were thirty men set apart as David's personal warriors, likely functioning much the same way as bodyguards. Three men were further selected out of these to be leaders. It was possible part or all of this force was with David in the cave. These men were fiercely loyal to David and ready to kill for him at any moment.

They likely had little to no compassion for Saul, though he technically was their king. They were ready to anoint David as king. He was more their king than Saul. It seems only natural they would have urged David to kill Saul, pled with him even. Perhaps some of them begged to be the one to end Saul's life.

Yet, David refused to give in to their pleas. Instead, he crept up on King Saul and cut off a piece of his royal robe. Saul, squatting in the dark cave, was oblivious to David's presence mere feet from him. David's feat is reminiscent of a modern-day sniper, creeping through open fields, fighting impossible odds, stealthy as the wind, and finishing the job.

With one swipe, David could be free from all of his troubles. The man pursuing his life was just feet, perhaps even inches away, and yet David let him go. David's actions bring to mind the words of Jonathan from 1 Samuel 23:17. Jonathan prophetically told David that "the hand of Saul my father shall not find you."

Exercise:

- Why does David spare King Saul's life?

David's attitude and reasons for sparing Saul's life have very little to do with Saul himself. This is a remarkable demonstration of David's commitment to God. The basis of his decision can be found in the word "anointed." Saul had been anointed by God, David's same God, thus David could do nothing to him out of respect and reverence for the Lord's chosen.

ANOINTED

The Hebrew word used here is *mashiyach*. Its literal translation is "anointed" or "Messiah." The one who was anointed was also called Messiah. The word has far-reaching implications, especially when used by David. It is one of the most important words in the Hebrew Bible, and we need to look closer at it to fully understand its significance. *Mashiyach* finds its root from another word which translates as "to besmear, to rub, to anoint." *Mashiyach* signifies a consecrated individual, meaning one who has received anointing from God for a specific function. In Psalms 105:5, the patriarchs are called "anointed ones."

In 1 Kings 19:16, Elijah is told to anoint Elisha as a prophet. In 1 Samuel 10:1 and 1 Samuel 16:12-13, Samuel anointed King Saul first, and then King David. Patriarchs, priests, prophets, and kings were all anointed by God. Christ, too, was anointed by God. In fact, the Greek word for "Messiah" is "Christos," translated in the New Testament as Christ. The literal name of Jesus Christ, thus, is Jesus Messiah.

Christians view him as the Messiah spoken of by the prophets of the Old Testament, the anointed ruler of God's Kingdom, descended from King David. To the Christian, one day the Messiah will return again. To the Jew, he has yet to come the first time.

Exercise: Read Isaiah 45:1.

- Who is called the Lord's anointed?
- Who was this person?
- Who is the one that did the anointing?

Now read 2 Samuel 22:30-31 and Psalms 18:50.

- Who was the anointed in these verses?

Read 1 Samuel 2:10 and Psalms 2:2.

- Who was the anointed in these verses?

In each case, it was God who anointed his servants, whether Cyrus king of Persia or David king of Israel. The one anointed by God was set aside by him to achieve a certain function or purpose. Being anointed highlighted a special and unique relationship between YHWH and the anointed.

Exercise: Read Daniel 9:25.

- What person was mentioned in this verse?
- Who was this person being mentioned?

The phrase "anointed one" has also been translated as "Messiah" in certain instances. The two words are very closely related. In Daniel 9:25, the Messiah is a future person, manifested in Jesus Christ. Jesus was anointed by God to be mankind's Savior. He was the Messiah, the Anointed One.

The Messiah in Daniel is mentioned throughout all of the Old Testament, and spoken of by the prophets in the Old Testament. The Messiah was a central theme of the Old Testament, and the key figure in God's redemption of mankind. To the New Testament writers, Jesus Christ was the Messiah. He was the fulfillment of God's promise in the Old Testament to send a ruler to rule Israel and establish his kingdom on earth. Jesus served in this role. Jesus is the Messiah.

Exercise: Read John 1:41.

- Who is speaking in this verse? Who is he speaking to?
- Who does the speaker claim to have found?
- What is the identity of this person the speaker claimed to have found?

Andrew just found the "Messiah," also translated in some versions as the "Anointed One." The original Greek word used in the text is "Christos." From "Christos" we get Jesus Christ, the Anointed One of God the Father. David understood the significance of what being anointed by God meant. He showed his understanding in his treatment of King Saul.

Saul, whether David liked it or not, had been anointed by God, though the anointing would later be stripped from Saul by God. As God would later choose Cyrus to allow the Jews to rebuild Jerusalem and Jesus to save and redeem mankind, he would anoint Saul to lead Israel during the formative years of their United Monarchy.

Though Saul had proven unworthy, David still respected God's sovereignty over the matter. Despite Saul's repeated attempts on his life, David would not reciprocate against God's anointed. David's faith was a real-life faith, lived out in his daily life and evident in his treatment of Saul. Though David was far from perfect, he absolutely knew God was in control; and whatever God had ordained, such as Saul's anointing, David would not interfere with the Lord and his plans. Thus, he spared the life of Saul.

The verse at 1 Samuel 24:4 also sticks out in this narrative. Read carefully and notice what David's men say to him. They urge him to take Saul's life by saying, "Behold, this is the day of which the Lord said to you." The question arises, how do David's men know what the Lord has said to him?

It is clear that many of these men were Israelites, thus knew of God. Other of David's men were likely foreigners, perhaps unfamiliar with the God of Abraham, Isaac, and Jacob. However, neither group would have known of David's belief unless he had told them prior. It seems obvious David had been talking to his men about God. David's men were rough, tough—likely crude and vulgar—warriors and killers, yet David took the time to talk with them about his God.

These men would witness firsthand God's miraculous deliverance of David time and again. David, in this respect, was a warrior-missionary type! He was not just leading men, but teaching them as well. Whether they believed or not, God would provide numerous demonstrations of his might and power over the course of their time with the shepherd-king.

The second part of 1 Samuel 24:4 is just as revealing. The Lord said to David he would give "your enemy into your hand and you shall do to him as it seems good to you." Make no mistake about it; this was a test for David. God gave him Saul on a platter. David's men knew their trouble was over and their master would become king. Everything could be set right, and all David had to do was kill an unarmed and vulnerable man.

The natural thing to do was kill Saul. God, however, wanted to see David's heart. All of David's men must have thought he was crazy. God, however, rejoiced at his servant's decision. David showed mercy and forgiveness in the toughest situation to be forgiving—when you are betrayed by the one you must forgive. Saul betrayed David, yet David showed forgiveness through mercy to Saul.

Exercise: Read and compare 1 Samuel 24:13 to Matthew 7:16-20.

- In your own words, discuss what these two passages are saying.
- How do these two passages relate to Saul and David?

David did not spare Saul for Saul's sake, or for his own sake, but for the sake of God; for what, God anointed, David would not harm. David sought God's glory above his own life and safety, and he clearly demonstrated this inside the cave. In 1 Samuel 24:7, we see David's leadership and charisma as he was able to keep his men at bay.

David's mighty men, as stated above, were restless warriors. They lived life by the sword. They lived life on the run for their safety. They lived each day looking over their shoulders for the next enemy. In their world, mercy and forgiveness got you killed. Life in their world was reserved for the valiant and skillful in battle. Each of David's men desired to be the one who killed Saul.

Thus, when the chance came to take Saul's life, they pressed David to act upon it. This was the moment they had all waited for: the death of their enemy, the vanquishing of King Saul, the victory of their king, David. Yet they respected and obeyed their leader even when his orders did not make sense to them.

We, too, in this modern era are anointed, just as Saul and David were, and just as King Cyrus was, and all of the other prophets and mighty men of the Bible who were anointed by God.

Exercise: Read carefully the following verses: 2 Corinthians 1:21; 1 John 2:20, 27.

- Who was the anointed in these verses?
- Who was the one who did the anointing?

The God of Abraham, Isaac, and Jacob—the Almighty Lord of Hosts—has anointed you through the blood of Christ. It is important to remember that being anointed means you have been set aside for a specific purpose. You have been consecrated to act in a certain way.

Learn from David and take that anointing to heart. Seek not your desires, but those of the one who anointed you. He set you aside for a special purpose, and to perform a special function.

Exercise:

- What is your purpose and function in relation to God's anointing of you?

"Thou didst go forth for the salvation of Thy people, for the salvation of Thine anointed. Thou didst strike the head of the house of evil. To lay him open from thigh to neck" (Habakkuk 3:13).

1 SAMUEL 25

IN THE OPENING VERSES OF 1 Samuel 25, Samuel the Seer passes away. Dedicated to God before his birth by his mother Hannah, Samuel toiled his entire life for the Lord. He rejoiced over God's selection of Saul, taking the young king under his wing. Saul, however, had been a major disappointment. Samuel probably spent many sleepless nights praying for King Saul, all to no avail.

God used Samuel to anoint David as next in line, and the old man again became a mentor, this time to a young shepherd-king. Conceivably, David was very fond of Samuel as well. Scripture tells us David sought his protection and advice often in the struggle against Saul. Samuel was a well-known, respected, and feared man of God throughout all of Israel. His influence and impact on Israel during its early years was profound and enduring. His loss was a major blow to the young monarchy, as well as to David and Saul personally.

Samuel's funeral must have been quite an event. For decades Samuel settled the people's disputes, counseled them in their daily lives, prayed for them to God, guided them, and taught them in the Scriptures. Samuel was the mouthpiece of YHWH to Israel. The people grew accustomed to Samuel's leadership, and then he was gone. The Bible says, "All Israel gathered together and mourned for him." King Saul certainly would have been present as well.

Saul may have even led the service, held in Samuel's hometown of Ramah. David, though, was unable to attend due to Saul's murderous intent. Instead, Scripture tells us, "David arose and went down to the wilderness of Paran." This was not a convenient trip for David to make. Paran was located in the extreme south of Israel, outside the boundaries of the land of Canaan. Paran was considered a part of the Sinai, as it lay south of the Arabah Valley, which itself was south of the Dead Sea. Paran was to the north of the Gulf of Aqaba and southeast of Kadeshbarnea.

Moses and the Israelites encamped in the wilderness of Paran for an extended period of time in the wanderings. The *Septuagint* calls it the wilderness of Maon. It was a several days' journey from En-Gedi, on the banks of the Dead Sea and the wilderness David hid in. David was deeply grieved by the death of Samuel, his mentor.

He journeyed to Paran in the far south to be alone with his grief and God. There are times when we simply need to get away and be alone, and such was this time in David's life. The death of Samuel weighed heavily on the young fugitive's mind and heart. Samuel provided David the guidance and leadership he needed on earth. Now, God alone would lead David.

Exercises: Turn and read 1 Samuel 25:2-8.

- What was the rich man's name? What are we told about him?
- Who was his wife, and what do we know about her?

Take time to read the remainder of 1 Samuel 25. David's men were providing protection for the local residents in the region. Prior to the reign of David, seminomadic people from the desert, such as the Amalekites, would sweep into the Negev and southern Judah, raiding the towns and villages. These desert invaders plundered and terrorized the locals. At one point, these desert nomads threatened to cut off all of Israel's food supply by raiding the crop field at harvest time (see Judges 6). These people were a constant menace to the south. Couple this threat of invasion with that of the Philistines in the west, and times were indeed precarious for the fledgling nation.

David and his six hundred men patrolled the south, specifically the southern portions of the tribe of Judah, the areas we have been discussing. His forces protected the towns and villages from the Geshurites, Girzites, and the feared Amalekites. David's men also functioned as bodyguards, escorting shepherds and their flocks as they grazed and moved from one pasture land to another. Traveling parties would also move alongside David and his men for protection when the opportunity afforded itself. They were the guardians of the Negev. This obviously strengthened David's popularity in the south and provided chances for him to gain loyal subjects.

David's services were not free, however. David and his men needed sustenance and would seek food, water, and other supplies from the local towns and villages they protected.

In 1 Samuel 25:9, David's men approach a wealthy businessman named Nabal, from nearby Maon, for "payment." David and his men spent much time in the wilderness of Maon (1 Samuel 23:24). While there, they escorted Nabal's shepherds and flocks for a lengthy period. This would've included guarding the flock against dangers and protecting the shepherds from death. David and his men, however, had practical needs such as food and supplies essential to survival. David felt Nabal owed them a little for their help.

Exercise: Read 1 Samuel 25:7.

- Who was the shepherd talking to?
- How did David's forces behave toward the shepherds?
- What did the shepherd compare David and his men to?

It was obvious David carefully and respectfully watched over Nabal's men. The shepherds tell Nabal's wife, Abigail, "they were a wall to us both by night and by day."

Read Nabal's response to the request of David's men in 1 Samuel 25:10-12.

- In your opinion, was David's request for provisions justified? Or, was he in the wrong for asking?

- How did Nabal respond to the request?

Scripture tells us in 1 Samuel 25:3 that Nabal "was harsh and evil in his dealings." Nabal was big business, and big business typically cares very little for anything other than profit. His response to David's request reinforced his selfish attitude.

Exercise: Read 1 Samuel 25:17.

- What was Nabal called in this verse?

- Who was speaking in this verse?

Scripture makes it clear Nabal was not a loved man. He was wealthy, rich, and powerful, and he lorded that over those around him. His heart was hardened, and he had little to no compassion save for his money. Nabal represents greed and selfishness. His haughty answer to David's men in 1 Samuel 25:10 indicates his arrogance and pride.

God hates all sin. Scripture makes that plain. Yet, it seems there is a special dislike of arrogance and pride by the Lord. Nabal's heart was full of arrogance and pride. Nabal provides a perfect example of what David means in Psalms 86:14, when he prays; "O, God, arrogant men have risen against me." Again, in Psalms 119:122, David cries, "Do not let the arrogant oppress me." Nabal was the type of man David spoke of in these verses. These were real-life pleas, and Scripture gives us both David's actions and inner thoughts.

Exercise:

Read the following verses: Isaiah 13:11; Jeremiah 50:31-32; Mark 7:22-23; James 4:16; 2 Timothy 3:2.

- What was the end result of arrogance and pride according to these verses?

The book of Proverbs has much to say about pride and arrogance as well in Proverbs 11:2; Proverbs 14:16; Proverbs 16:18; Proverbs 28:25; and Proverbs 29:23.

Like the Proverbs, David showed little patience for the arrogant and prideful. In Psalms 101:5, he states, "No one who has a haughty look and an arrogant heart will I endure." We see these words in action in 1 Samuel 25:13. After David's men report Nabal's arrogance, he wastes no time in his response.

Exercise: Read 1 Samuel 25:13.

- What was David's response? Write out his words.

David and four hundred of his men picked up their swords and prepared to march on Nabal, slaughter his household, and plunder his goods. David's men must have been giddy with anticipation, eager for a chance to plunder the rich and powerful. David states in 1 Samuel 25:22 he will slay every male in Nabal's household.

Enter Abigail, Nabal's wife mentioned earlier in 1 Samuel 25:3. In 1 Samuel 25:14, one of "the young men" informs Abigail of the situation.

Exercise: Read 1 Samuel 25:18-20.

- How did Abigail respond to the young man's report? What was her first instinct?

We see a Biblical principle at work with Abigail. She exercises keen discernment in regard to the situation at hand. Discernment is discussed frequently in the Bible, and we see an excellent example of this biblical quality in Abigail. How important was discernment to God? In Deuteronomy 1:13, he tells Moses, "Choose wise and discerning and experienced men from your tribes, and I will appoint them as your heads."

It was a required quality to be a leader of Israel under Moses. God specifically mentions people of discernment in his Word. The first person of discernment we meet is Joseph. In Genesis 41, Joseph interprets Pharaoh's dream when nobody else in the land of Egypt can.

Exercise: Read Pharaoh's words to Joseph in Genesis 41:39.

- What did he call Joseph?
- What was Joseph placed in charge of?

Joseph was famous for being the spoiled brother, sold into slavery by his conniving older brothers, imprisoned, wrongly accused, interpreter of dreams—and ultimately second-in-command to the pharaoh of Egypt. It was his discernment that elevated him to second-in-command over all of Egypt. His ability to perceive and distinguish information and to respond with intelligence and understanding impressed Pharaoh. Of course, Joseph's ability and discernment was God-given, not man-earned.

Exercise: Read the following verses: Proverbs 2:2-5; Proverbs 10:13; Proverbs 28:7.

- What was discernment associated with in these three verses?
- According to Proverbs 2, what will you discover if you seek discernment?

Now turn to 1 Kings 3:9-11.

- Who were these verses talking about?
- What was happening in these verses?
- What was God pleased with?

King Solomon was considered one of the wisest and most talented kings in Israel's history. He was the son of King David, and the architect of the first temple. Under Solomon, Jerusalem grew to be the center of a major empire. His request of God wasn't for riches, glory in battle, expansion of the empire, or even the continuance of his throne. Rather, it was for the ability to listen, discern, and rule his people with a just and upright heart.

In 1 Kings 4:29, the Bible tells that God "gave Solomon wisdom and very great discernment and breadth of mind." God was pleased that his servant "asked for yourself discernment to understand justice."

Our last example of a man of discernment is the great dream inter-preter Daniel.

Exercise: Read Daniel 2:14.

- How did Daniel respond to Arioch?

Now read Daniel 2:17-18.

- How did Daniel show discernment?
- Why was that an example of practicing discernment?

The Hebrew use a couple of different words that translate as "discern" or "discernment."

The meaning of the Hebrew words center on separating or distinguish-ing information and knowing how to proceed with wisdom. They mean intelligently listening and having understanding and perception.

Notice how quickly Abigail discerned the situation in 1 Samuel 25. Immediately after her servants related to her the situation, Scripture records in 1 Samuel 25:18, "then Abigail hurried." This indicates two things.

One, she wasted no time in approaching Nabal, for she knew he was an evil man. She also believed in the justness of David's request. Two, she knew David meant business, and she wasted no time gathering the supplies together. Not only did she hurry to prepare provisions herself, but when she encountered David in 1 Samuel 25:23, she did so cloaked in much humility, similar to David's approach to Saul in 1 Samuel 24:8.

Exercise: Read and compare 1 Samuel 24:8 and 1 Samuel 25:23.

- What was the act of bowing down symbolic of?

Abigail put herself at the mercy of David, and in 1 Samuel 25:24, she shows great accountability by taking the blame. Abigail intelligently perceived the situation. She knew in her heart Nabal was wrong. She then acted quickly, decisively, and with great wisdom.

Exercise: Read David's response to her in 1 Samuel 25:32-35.

- How did David receive Abigail?
- What did he bless?
- What were David's intentions?

David made special mention of Abigail's discernment. One could imagine he was greatly impressed with this beautiful woman. Not only was she beautiful, but she was bold to approach David, and very wise in the way she did it. David came away not only impressed but attracted to her. David possessed a flair for the opposite sex. A bold and beautiful woman would not escape his notice and go unappreciated. Abigail caught his full attention. David was so impressed with her, that after Nabal dies from a heart of stone in 1 Samuel 25:38, David proposes marriage to Abigail.

Once again, she shows great discernment by accepting without hesitation. In 1 Samuel 25:42, Abigail "quickly arose" and hurries to her new husband. Scripture makes it plain that good discernment goes a long way. Joseph, Daniel, Solomon, and Abigail all benefited from a discerning mind. The great apostle Paul also had a quick and discerning mind. His perception and judgment in stressful situations and trying times propelled the young Christian sect into the Roman Empire. He realized the importance of such a godly trait in Philippians 1:9.

"And this I pray, that your love may abound still more and more in real knowledge and all discernment."

1 SAMUEL 26

THE PASSAGE IN 1 SAMUEL 26 is almost identical to 1 Samuel 24. David once again finds himself in a position to kill King Saul. In 1 Samuel 26:1, men run to Saul to tell him where David was hiding.

Exercise: Read 1 Samuel 23:19.

- Who went to tell Saul about David's whereabouts?

It would seem David and his men were not welcome by the Ziphites, though Scripture doesn't tell why. For the second time, these men give Saul David's location. There was clearly bad blood between David and the men of Ziph. What and why is not stated, but the Ziphites gave up David to Saul not once but twice. Once again, we are reminded of David's plea in Psalms 54, written about these very Ziphites.

Exercise: Read Psalms 54:3-4.

- According to this verse, what type of men lived in Ziph?

David pled to God in Psalm 54 for deliverance. Saul, in 1 Samuel 26:1-2, moves out once more toward "the hill of Hachilah." In 1 Samuel 26:2, King Saul has three thousand "chosen men of Israel" once again in pursuit of David. This time Saul is in the wilderness of Ziph near the Dead Sea. Shedding insight on David's forces is 1 Samuel 26:4.

David is said to have "sent out spies." These spies spot and track the movements of Saul, keeping David abreast of the situation. The Lord was shaping, developing, and growing David as a leader during these wilderness experiences. David's group of six hundred organized into an army. He now had an intelligence network in full operation. The picture Scripture paints is of an evolving military force under the leadership of David.

David had been a commander under Saul and experienced great success. He was a natural warrior. He had experience as a leader both in his days of shepherding sheep as well as leading men. David followed in the line of Moses, who also sent spies into Canaan in the book of Numbers. Interestingly enough, Israeli intelligence in the modern era is as effective an agency as there is in the world. The Mossad is a lethal, deadly, and stealthy branch of the Israeli Armed Forces. Israeli spy operations date back thousands of years!

Apparently David's spies located Saul's camp and reported its location to David.

Exercise: Read 1 Samuel 26:5-6.

- What did David do?
- Who did he take with him?

David chose one man, Abishai, also his nephew (1 Chronicles 2:16), to accompany him on a stealthy night mission into Saul's camp. Abishai's brother is Joab, the future leader of King David's army. Together, Joab and Abishai would become instrumental in the future military success of David. The two brothers became David's closest men. David was a fearless and courageous ruler who stayed at the front lines. His men knew he would risk his life, thus they willingly did the same for the man they served. David's courage was a result of his faith and confidence in God's sovereignty.

Exercise: Read 1 Samuel 26:7-12 for the narrative of Abishai's night mission.

- Where, precisely, did David and Abishai find Saul within the camp?
- What was Abishai's reaction? What was David's?
- How were they able to sneak into the camp?
- What would you have done to Saul?
- What verse in 1 Samuel 25:9-12 emphasizes David's reliance on God?

David demonstrates a godly forbearance in 1 Samuel 26, a trait he displays time and again during these turbulent years fleeing the erratic and irrational King Saul. What is forbearance? The *ENCARTA Dictionary* defines it as "patience; refraining from action; refraining from legal right." In today's age, this is a lost notion.

A self-entitled sense of deserving has crept into society. People have become litigious, quick to take disputes to court in hopes of quick gain at another's expense. Society preaches self-realization, self-promotion, and self-empowerment. Scientology and other false, New Age religions preach self-awareness, self-actualization, and self-enlightenment. All of this leads to selfishness, that is, the "self-life," which can lead to narcissism and other forms of extreme selfishness and self-absorption. Fortunately, God gives us guidance and instruction on how to practice forbearance, which is a form of self-denial.

JACOB AND LABAN

In Genesis 29–31, we learn the narrative of Jacob and Laban. Laban was the son of Nahor, kin to Abraham and Jacob's father-in-law. The narrative concerning Laban and Jacob provides a perfect parallel to the situation between David and Saul and helps shed light on forbearance.

In Genesis 27, Jacob steals (with the help of his mother) the birthright from his brother Esau. Jacob, in turn, flees Canaan to escape Esau's anger.

He is also seeking a wife from among his father's kin, a common practice within certain ancient cultures. Jacob flees to Paddan-aram, in the vicinity of Haran, the city named after Abraham's brother. Israel had ancient ties to the land of Mesopotamia. His ultimate destination is the house of Laban, who is his mother Rebekah's brother. It would be at his uncle Laban's house that Jacob would find a wife—two actually. The history of the twelve tribes of Israel, in essence, begins with Jacob at Laban's house.

Exercise: Read Genesis 29:16-18.

- How many daughters did Laban have?
- What were their names?
- Who did Jacob love?
- How long did he serve Laban for her hand in marriage?

Talk about forbearance! Jacob would wait seven years to obtain Rachel as his wife.

Read Genesis 29:25.

- After Jacob's seven years of service, what did Laban do?
- Did Jacob get what was rightfully his?

Laban's wickedness and dishonesty is evident in his deception of Jacob. Jacob had every right to grab Rachel and run. He had every right to flee.

Exercise: Read Genesis 29:27.

- What type of agreement did the two reach? How much longer would Jacob serve Laban?

Jacob already practiced forbearance by not striking out at Laban, which he had the right to do. Rather, God had another plan in mind, and Jacob stayed behind to obtain the woman he loved. Thus, he served another seven years with Laban.

Exercise: Read Genesis 31:38-41.

- How long in total did Jacob serve Laban?
- Was Laban fair in his business dealings with Jacob?
- Do you get the sense these were enjoyable years for Jacob (Genesis 31:42)?

For twenty years, Jacob toiled for Laban! What started out as a forty-day journey for a wife turned out to be a twenty-year sojourn in a foreign land. Twenty years passed since Jacob saw his family. He was lied to and deceived. He spent his own money on Laban's losses over the years (Genesis 31:39).

Despite all of the wrong Jacob experienced, he remained a faithful husband, worker, and son-in-law. Jacob was loyal though Laban was not. Laban changed Jacob's wages ten times. Laban deceitfully gave Jacob the wrong daughter in marriage. Laban manipulated and deceived him into service, then charged him for business-related expenses! Laban, unfortunately, represents all too many bosses in today's world. How many of you can relate to Jacob's situation? How many have suffered at the hands of a petty, selfish, lying, manipulative boss?

Exercise:

- What was Jacob's reaction to all of this? Did he strike out at Laban, or did he faithfully toil under adverse circumstances?
- How do you think Jacob was able to persevere so long under such stressful circumstances?

In Genesis 31:42, Jacob tells Laban, "God has seen my affliction and the toil of my hands, so He rendered judgment last night." Jacob lived a life of godly forbearance. He refrained from taking action against Laban, even though he had every right to do so. Jacob refused to look at his plight through the eyes of the world—as a victim and deserving of revenge.

Instead, he took a godly stance and turned his eyes upward. Godly forbearance is having patience with God. Read Proverbs 25:15. In this verse, the Hebrew word translated as "forbearance" literally means "length of anger."

The New Testament gives us insight as well. Of course, the life of Jesus Christ is the ultimate depiction of godly forbearance. Any page of the Gospels is sure to illustrate this word by the actions and words of Jesus. Jesus is still showing forbearance now, refraining from ultimate victory until the appointed time, which only the Father knows. Jesus's patience defines the very essence of forbearance.

Exercise: Read Romans 3:25.

- According to Paul, how did God exhibit forbearance?

The Greek word translated as "forbearance" in Romans 3:25 is *anoche*. This word literally means "a delaying, tolerance, forbearing." *Anoche* stems from *anecho*, and it means "to hold up, bear with, to endure." In the case of Romans 3:25, Dr. Spiros Zodhiates indicates it can also translate as "to overlook." In essence, God overlooked Israel's previous sin.

Exercise:

- How does the Greek word relate to the narrative of David and Saul in 1 Samuel 26?

Some synonyms of the Greek word *anecho* are "tolerance," "patience," and "self-control." Forbearance is associated with self-control, especially in instances where one does not respond to provocation. David shows excellent self-control in refusing Abishai his wish to kill Saul. David's forbearance with Saul can only be explained by his deep faith in God Almighty, developed from those lonely and oftentimes frightful nights with his sheep in the field.

David waited on God. He recognized and acknowledged God's sovereignty, then actually lived his life by the principle and belief that God really is in charge. To hammer home David's forbearance, reread 1 Samuel 26:10. His refusal to kill Saul, grab the throne (which was his anyway, according to Samuel) and end the threat to his life and the lives of his men was a direct result of his faith and belief in God's plan. David lived out the words spoken centuries later by one of his relatives, James, the half-brother of Jesus, in James 1:2-3.

"Consider it all joy, my brethren, when you encounter various trials, knowing that the testing of your faith produces endurance."

Exercise:

- Earlier it was stated forbearance is a form of self-denial,
- Explain why you agree or disagree with this statement.

1 SAMUEL 27

AT THE CLOSE OF 1 SAMUEL 26, Saul confesses to David he made a mistake, admitting he "committed a serious error." David, however, does not fall for Saul's emotional instability. The first time David spared Saul in a cave, Saul said the same exact things.

Exercise: Read 1 Samuel 24:8-22 and 1 Samuel 26:13-25.

Each time, Saul meant the words he was speaking—at the time he was speaking them. As Saul proved on multiple occasions, he was prone to deceitful speeches and whimsical decisions. David proved wise in the past not to place his trust in Saul after such speeches. However, David was running out of places to hide. It was clear Saul would not stop his pursuit, and now some local townsmen, members of his own tribe (the tribe of Judah), have turned against David. David felt he had nowhere to turn. Accordingly, David forms another plan.

Exercise: Read 1 Samuel 27:1-4.

- Where did David go?
- How many men did David take with him?
- Where did he live?
- How did Saul react?
- Record any other observations you have regarding these verses.

Once again, David defects to the Philistines! He took all of his men and their families and "crossed over" to the Philistine Army in Gath. This time, King Achish gladly took him in. It was common in antiquity for armies to accept bands of what were called Habiru, or displaced people oftentimes under the leadership of a single individual.

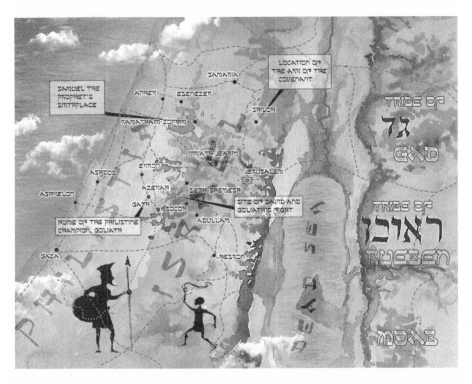

These groups of displaced peoples were not united ethnically, but rather by social circumstances. In many cases, these were mercenary groups. David and his men were biblical examples of this much-debated group of people. The Philistine king, Achish, hungry for more men, and fully convinced David was an enemy of the state of Israel, eagerly took them in and housed them and their families. Another Philistine motivation was the further division of Israel—their main foe in the area. By supporting David, they were further weakening Saul. Once they finished with Saul, they would then finish off David. Divide and conquer was their modus operandi.

Imagine, if you can, David's state of mind. He was forced to flee his homeland, friends, and perhaps some family, all by his father-in-law the king, for no reason other than jealousy. He became a fugitive, then a defector. He and his household were living in a strange land among foreigners—and Philistines, nonetheless!

Philistine religious beliefs and practices were in direct conflict with God. Recall the ark of the covenant's journey through Philistine land in the early chapters of 1 Samuel. Remember how Yahweh desecrated the idol of Dagan in Dagan's temple. The Philistines practiced human sacrifice.

Sacred prostitution was a big part of their religious system. Not only this, but they were also at war with Israel. David was surrounded by evil on every side. It would seem God had abandoned him. The Psalms lend insight into David's mind.

Exercise:

Read the following Psalms: Psalms 9:18; Psalms 11:1; Psalms 16:1; Psalms 17:8-9.

- Did David indicate he doubted God's protection?
- Based on these verses, in your own words, describe David's faith. Was it lacking? Was he confident in God?
- Can you relate to being surrounded on all sides by the enemy? Have you ever felt like God wasn't there? If so, describe the situation and outcome.

David, his men, and their families settled into Philistine life. Rather than live in the capital city of Gath, David sought another location. He, as always, had a plan of his own. David did not want to live under the watchful—and likely suspicious—eyes of the Philistines. He needed space, and thus asked the king if he could live elsewhere. Achish's response was to give David what would become his headquarters.

Exercise: Read 1 Samuel 27:6-17.

- What city was given David and his men?
- How long was David with the Philistines?

It is a well-documented fact by historians and archaeologists that the Philistines possessed a large chariot force. They were first to fully utilize iron in Canaan, and the Bible recorded they had a monopoly on the vital resource (1 Samuel 13:19). These were technologically advanced people. They were far superior to Israel in weapons and armory. Their chariot force roamed the coastal plain, confining Israel to the mountains, where the chariots were rendered less effective.

However, on the hillsides and in the valleys the Philistine chariot force plundered the Israelite towns and villages. By all reasonable assumptions, the Philistines appeared ready to take control of Canaan, including the land Israel dwelt in and claimed. Perhaps this situation was the inspiration for David's Psalm in Psalms 20:6-7.

David's plan worked beautifully under the watchful eye of God Almighty. Once again, the Lord provided David with means. It was expected by the Philistine king that David would participate in raids upon Israelite towns and villages. David would then give Achish a portion of his plunder, and at the same time make himself detestable in the eyes of the Israelites.

Exercise: Read 1 Samuel 27:8-12.

- Who did David raid?
- Why?
- What did he take from his raids?
- Who did David tell Achish he raided?

Recall the Amalekites from 1 Samuel 14 and 15. Saul was ordered to kill them all by Samuel, yet he disobeyed, thus in essence disobeying the very words of God Almighty. This episode, decades before the current one, began his descent. During his raids against the Amalekites, David "did not leave a man or woman alive."

This seems cruel to our modern sensibilities; however, these were dangerous times and David was fleeing and fighting for his life. It must be remembered that in ancient times, Israel, as she is in modern times, was surrounded by enemies on all sides.

Her neighbors showed no mercy in past altercations, thus, neither did David. God had his hand over David during these turbulent times. Under Moses, the Amalekites preyed on Israel's weak, sick, lame, and crippled citizens as they walked through the desert. This was why Saul was ordered to strike them all down in the first place. They were long overdue. David followed through on what Saul had not.

David was walking on a balance beam, with the Philistines on one side and Saul on the other. Every move he made required foresight, thoughtfulness, and much prayer. By this time in the narrative, David was a full-fledged fugitive. He was wandering from place to place, in exile from his own people, and living among strangers and foreigners. He was in a constant state of survival as his life was threatened on numerous fronts.

Yet it was during these times, perhaps even this time in Gath and Ziklag, that he wrote Psalm 23. Living in the land of the Philistines, and lying to the Philistine king about his actions, certainly qualified as walking through the valley of the shadow of death.

Exercise: Turn and read Psalm 23. Pay attention to the imagery David used.

- Relate this psalm to David's past experiences.
- Relate it to his present circumstances.
- In your opinion, what was the main theme or idea behind this Psalm?

It would not be too presumptuous to assume David thought often of his childhood, growing up a shepherd tending his father's flocks, the youngest of eight boys. Remember, David told Saul prior to his battle with Goliath, decades earlier from the current narrative, that he killed the lion and the bear in protecting his sheep, therefore he did not fear the Philistine champion. It was likely David often longed for this time when he was a youth and had the protection of his father, Jesse.

Now, however, David had turned into the sheep, and he was the one being pursued by the lion and the bear.

Exercise:

- Who was David's shepherd?
- What will this shepherd provide?

David expressed complete confidence in God—his Shepherd. What a great example for us to follow. We all have Philistines and Sauls in our lives. However, in the midst of our turmoil and frustrations we, like David, can be absolutely certain that "the Lord is my shepherd, I shall not want."

1 SAMUEL 28

THIS CHAPTER BEGINS THE FINAL days of Saul's reign, and his life. His forty-year reign as covered in 1 Samuel was quickly coming to an inglorious end. The Philistines under King Achish assembled for war near Mount Gilboa, located in the center of Jezreel Valley. They pitched their camp at Shunem while Saul and the Israelites were encamped in Gilboa.

In 1 Samuel 28:1–2, it's clear David and his men were to accompany Achish and the Philistines into this battle. David was apparently more than willing to go fight against Saul and his countrymen. Perhaps he saw this as an answer to his prayer in 1 Samuel 26:10.

David clearly made an impact on the Philistine king, though, for in 1 Samuel 28:2, the king tells David, "I will make you my bodyguard for life." David may have thought this was a way to protect himself and his men; or, perhaps he saw it as a chance to strike down Saul legitimately. God provided a means of protection for David, though it appeared as if he were going to fight against God's people. In this sense, however, David was in a much better state, for the Israelites under Saul faced imminent doom.

Exercise: Read 1 Samuel 28:3-5.

- Who did Scripture record as being dead in 1 Samuel 28:1?
- Why was this significant?

- What was Saul's reaction to the Philistines in 1 Samuel 28:5?

The Philistine force was larger in size, possessed far superior weaponry made of iron, wore bronze body armor and helmets, and had a large, heavily armored chariot force. The Israelites wore little to no armor; carried slings, swords, clubs, spears, and whatever else they could find; and possessed only infantry. The Philistines were warriors. The Israelites were farmers and herdsmen. Saul knew his chances were slim to none.

This was not an ideal battlefield for Saul and Israel either. Israel generally fought better in mountainous terrain where they could use guerilla tactics and where chariots were much less effective. The valley floor provided a perfect spot, however, for the Philistine chariot force to engage an enemy. Thus, the terrain heavily favored the Philistines, too, as their iron chariots were sure to slice through Israel's infantry. Israel was completely overmatched. And in fact, history proves this assessment correct.

At this time, circa 1100 B.C. (Iron Age), history shows Israel was an agricultural society, not one of war and conquest. Its technology was designed around farming and harvesting, not invasion. Archaeology, however, shows the Philistines were advanced in weaponry and technology and had highly sophisticated organization in their cities and army. They were a warrior society and possessed the cutting-edge technology of the time period, iron. Not only did the Philistines possess iron, but they controlled its usage in Canaan. They had every reason and opportunity to succeed in exterminating the tiny, powerless nation of Israel.

Exercise: Read 1 Samuel 28:6.

- Who did Saul turn to in 1 Samuel 28:6?
- What was the Lord's response to Saul?

Read Numbers 12:6 and Joel 2:28.

- How did God reveal himself in those days?

Some will think God's silence toward Saul was harsh. How could a loving God not answer Saul, the very king over his people? How could God ignore Israel in her greatest time of need? Does this mean we can fall out of God's grace? These are just a few of the difficult questions that arise when dealing with this difficult passage.

When dealing with passages that are difficult to understand, or don't fit into the nice boxes that theology, doctrine, and denomination provide, it is best to consider the words of Isaiah as recorded in Isaiah 55:8-9.

Exercise: Read Isaiah 55:8–9.

There is no doubt Saul knew God. The great prophet Samuel had anointed Saul in front of the people with the words, "Do you see him whom the Lord has chosen? Surely there is no one like him among all the people."

Saul prophesied with the prophets. He had been born an Israelite of the tribe of Benjamin, raised to follow God and live by his Word. Samuel instructed him in how to rule justly and obey God. Yet, Saul willfully disobeyed God's orders through Samuel on multiple occasions. His tendency was to turn to God only when it suited him.

Exercise: Turn and read Proverbs 1:24-31.

- Apply this passage to King Saul.
- Why does wisdom not respond to those in trouble?
- Who is wisdom?
- What is the ultimate fate for those who spurn wisdom and spurn God?

Jesus Christ spoke of similar situations in the New Testament. The *Parable of the Ten Virgins* is one example.

Exercise: Read Matthew 25:1-13. Notice Matthew 25:11–12.

Those who were not prudent knock on the door, crying, "Lord, lord, open up for us." However, the response from inside is, "Truly I say to you, I do not know you." This response perhaps summarizes God's attitude and reason for silence toward Saul in 1 Samuel 28:6.

Another example from the words of Jesus can be found in Luke 13:22-27.

Exercise: Read those verses and answer the following questions.

- Those knocking claim knowledge of "the head of the house." However, what is his response to them?
- What was it they said they did with him?
- What was his response?

We can draw parallels from Jesus's words in the New Testament and God's actions in the Old Testament. In the *Parable of the Ten Virgins*, it is important to take notice of Christ's words in Matthew 25:13, "Be on the alert then, for you do not know the day nor the hour." Though Saul was not living in the end times, he sought God's recognition and did not receive it. We should take notice of why Saul did not receive God's recognition so that we may not be found guilty of the same.

Like the five foolish virgins, Saul's actions throughout had not been prudent nor obedient. Saul, like too many others, turned to God only in times of hardship and crisis, yet forgot God's commands in times of prosperity. His pride overcame his humility.

God responds to faithful hearts, those who turn to him in times of good and bad. Though not perfect—in fact, fatally flawed—they continually acknowledge him and his mercy. They are found faithful in their belief. Hearts like these do not rush to the store for oil, because their oil is continually with them and upon their hearts.

Jesus taught in front of large crowds. Large crowds followed him from town to town. He likely had many companions who traveled with him and shared meals with him. Yet he only had twelve disciples. At his crucifixion, only three are mentioned by name. Hence Jesus's words in Luke 13:24, "For many, I tell you, will seek to enter and will not be able." Though Christ reconciled himself to his disciples, as he does to all mankind, too many accept that reconciliation halfheartedly, thus they are prevented from entering the kingdom of God.

This is where King Saul found himself, seeking to enter God's presence only to be denied. God had not even acknowledged Saul's request.

Exercise: Read 1 Samuel 15:26.

- What did Samuel accuse Saul of?

The consequences of Saul's past actions sealed his fate in God's eyes. God pronounced his judgment upon Saul in 1 Samuel 15.

Exercise: Read 1 Samuel 16:14.

Saul habitually gave himself over to his impulsive desires rather than pursue God's commands. God's silence drove Saul to further depravities. Rather than humble himself and seek God's forgiveness and mercy, Saul once again took matters into his own hands.

Exercise: Read 1 Samuel 28:6-19.

- Who did Saul turn to for help?
- Where was this person located?
- Who banned mediums from Israel?
- Who did Saul wish to summon from the dead?

Read Deuteronomy 18:10-11.

- What did Moses specifically prohibit that Saul was guilty of?

This encounter is a fascinating piece of biblical history. The implications of Samuel's appearance from the dead are far too great and lengthy for our current purpose to adequately cover. The Old Testament is very vague with its treatment of the afterlife. Sheol is frequently mentioned as the place souls go to after death, yet its function and nature is vaguely defined.

It is enough to say that Samuel (from wherever he came) was not happy about Saul's actions. Pay special attention to 1 Samuel 28:13. Saul was told "a divine being"—or "a ghostly figure" according to the NIV—arose from the ground. The medium informed Saul the figure "is wrapped with a robe," at which point Saul knew it to be Samuel.

Saul would never forget the image of Samuel's robe, torn, and the words Samuel spoke to Saul concerning his fate. The incident is recorded in 1 Samuel 15:27-28. Saul must have remembered those words in 1 Samuel 15 as the Philistine war machine glared from across the valley floor. He once again stood face to face with Samuel.

Exercise: Read their exchange in 1 Samuel 28:15-19.

- Did Samuel seem pleased to see Saul?
- What was Samuel's attitude toward Saul's plea?
- Why was the Lord angry with Saul? What was to be Saul's fate?

Who, or what, do you turn to in times of crisis and trouble? Many today turn to psychics and mediums. Many turn to wealth, sex, and possessions. We are wise to turn to God, in good times and bad. Saul had run out of time. Despite Saul's desperation, Samuel once again reminded him the Lord tore the kingdom from his hands and gave it to David. The Philistine chariot force would race across the valley floor and bring an end to not only Saul and his kingdom but to his sons as well.

Exercise: Read Titus 1:16.

- Relate this verse to King Saul's situation.

Saul's reaction was what one might expect. Though deserved and just, one cannot help but feel a tinge of sympathy for Saul. This was a tragic moment with a tragic figure in Scripture. Saul, as all of us will, came face to face with accountability. Judgment and accountability are two things God will require of every man and woman.

Exercise:

Read the following verses: Psalms 9:7-8; John 5:22, 24, 30; Romans 3:19; Revelation 20:12-13.

- In your opinion, what is/are the major theme(s) these verses have in common?
- What will every human eventually come face to face with?

Like Saul, we will one day be held accountable for our lives, choices, actions, and words. Saul's life showed the consequences of ignoring God and placing one's own desires and wishes above his. Even though many will prosper on this earth, as Saul prospered as king of Israel for forty years, a day of reckoning will come for every man. We are to take advantage of our time today and turn to God in prayer. No life is too messy, or dirty, or too far gone for God to change and use.

God simply wants the hearts of men, in whatever shape or state they comes in. Listen to the words of Ezekiel in Ezekiel 11:19-20.

"And I shall give them one heart, and shall put a new spirit within them. And I shall take the heart of stone out of their flesh and give them a heart of flesh... Then they will be My people, and I shall be their God."

1 SAMUEL 29

OFTENTIMES IN LIFE, IT SEEMS as if we are heading in one direction, only to find out we must turn around and head back the way we came. In times like these, one may begin to question God's plan. In 1 Samuel 29, we see just such an instance in the life of David.

David and his men were prepared to fight against Saul and their fellow Israelites. However, at the last moment, the Philistine king excused David and his men from fighting. They were sent packing back to Ziklag and spared from fighting. God's invisible hand was at work, for he could not have his future king of Israel fighting against Israel and with their arch enemies the Philistines. God's sovereignty extends to protect us even when we can't see it, know it, or acknowledge it. Such is the grace of God.

Exercise: Turn and read 1 Samuel 29:1-2.

- Explain the setting of this chapter. Where did it take place? With whom? Who was involved?
- Why do you think David and his men were in the rear, when clearly they were able and fierce warriors?

The Philistines gathered at Aphek. Aphek, one might recall, was the site of the battle with the Philistines in which they captured the ark of the covenant back in 1 Samuel 4:1. This battle took place before Saul's reign even began, decades prior to the current conflict in 1 Samuel 29.

It must be remembered that Israel and the Philistines fought for over a century throughout the Old Testament, stretching approximately from 1200 to 1000 B.C.

While the Philistines were encamped at Aphek, Israel was encamped at Jezreel in Jezreel Valley. As stated previously, David and his men were readying to fight against their own countrymen.

Exercise: Read 1 Chronicles 12:19.

- What did we learn about David from this verse?
- Where were the men that defected from?

Manasseh belonged to the ten tribes of the north, many of which would one day turn on David. However, this time the men from Manasseh joined David's forces. It was reasonable to assume the Philistines would have welcomed this large force of David's to fight on their behalf. However, the Bible paints a different picture.

Exercise: Read 1 Samuel 29:3-6.

- According to 1 Samuel 29:4, why did the Philistine commanders refuse to let David fight with them?

Defecting Hebrews were nothing new to the Philistines. This had been going on since the two nations had been fighting. In fact, the Bible depicts such an occurrence in 1 Samuel 14:21. This battle took place at the beginning of Saul's reign and was one of his major victories that helped legitimize his reign and unite Israel behind him as king.

The real hero of this battle, however, was Jonathan. It was Jonathan's exploits that sent the Philistine Army into panic and inspired his fellow Israelites to rise up and fight. In 1 Samuel 14:21, the Bible notes that "those Hebrews who had previously been with the Philistines and had gone up with them to their camp" turned on their Philistine friends and joined forces with their countrymen on the heels of Jonathan's heroics. The implication, however, is clear: many Hebrews had already defected over to the Philistines in an attempt to avoid being killed in battle.

These Hebrews, like David, joined the Philistine Army with the intent of fighting against their own country.

This situation, it would seem, was unacceptable to God—for he could not have his future king fighting against his own people. As we have already stated, nothing happens by accident. God has total control.

Had David fought in this battle, it would have been unlikely he would have had the support he needed to become king. He would have been branded a traitor and murderer for defecting.

Exercise: Read 1 Samuel 29:7-11.

- Did Achish want to get rid of David? Who was in favor of it?
- What did Achish call David in 1 Samuel 29:9?
- What did he instruct David to do? What did David want to do?

David was a warrior and it seemed as if he wanted to fight, even if it meant fighting against Israel. Perhaps at this point in David's life he resigned himself to the fact he was forever going to be an outlaw in his own country, or at least until Saul's death. Perhaps he had settled into the Philistine camp. In any case, he was not allowed to join in the battle.

Unknown to David at the time, God protected him with his invisible shield. He shielded David from fighting against his countrymen, for David was destined to be their king. Once the Philistines dismissed him, he and his men were abandoned by all but God.

Exercise:

Read Psalms 55:22. This was written by David and was echoed in 1 Peter 5:7.

- Do you believe David cast his burden upon God?
- What evidence from the text suggests such?

David's Psalms are full of references to God as a Rock and Deliverer. His change of fortune from one day to the next was surely an emotional roller coaster. God provided the stable foundation David so badly needed.

Exercise: Read Psalms 86:7

"In the day of my trouble I shall call upon Thee, for Thou wilt answer me."

David clung to these promises; in fact, he wrote many of them over the course of his adventurous and perilous life. In 1 Samuel 29:11, however, David and his men are kept from battle in an example of God shielding us from certain situations and circumstances. God was looking out for David's best interests overall, whereas David, like us, simply saw what was in front of him. God looks out for us, and David acknowledged this in Psalm 103.

Exercise: Read Psalms 103:13-14.

- Who is the Lord likened to?
- What, according to verse 14, is man?

God's role as a shield to us can be traced back to Genesis. In Genesis 15, Abram has just rescued Lot before he encounters the mysterious Melchizedek, king of Salem (Jerusalem).

Exercise: Turn and read Genesis 15:1.

- What did God tell Abram?

Psalms 103:19 tells us God's "sovereignty rules over all." His full knowledge of past, present, and future allows him to see and comprehend in ways we cannot imagine. He also protects us and looks over us in ways we cannot imagine. God is far more powerful and mysterious than we know, or want to admit.

Exercise: Read Deuteronomy 33:29.

- What was God compared to in this verse?

Not only is he Israel's defense ("shield of your help") but also Israel's offense ("sword of your majesty"). So he was for David, too, and so he is for us now. In Psalms 124:8, David said, "Our help is in the name of the

Lord, who made heaven and earth." The creator of all is keenly aware of his creation. Jesus reiterated this sentiment.

Exercise: Read Matthew 10:29-31.

- What was Jesus talking about in these verses?
- How aware is God of your life, struggles, successes, needs and desires, family or lack of family, wants and hopes, and goals?

God knows the very number of hairs on our head. He also functions in many ways over us. Some of these ways are mentioned in 2 Samuel 22:3.

This notion of God as our shield was carried over into the New Testament and expanded upon by Paul. God and faith in Jesus are likened to body armor worn in war. Our faith is our armor in our battle against the Adversary. While imprisoned in Rome, the very kingdom of the Adversary in the eyes of first-century Jews, Paul wrote his epistle to the Ephesians, probably circa 60-64 A.D.

Exercise: Read Ephesians 6:16-17.

- Based on the passage, fill in the blanks below.
  - Take up the _____ of faith.
  - Take up the _____ of salvation.
  - Carry the of _____ the Spirit.
- What is the shield of faith used for?
- What is our primary weapon?

David fully recognized this line of thought on God's role as protector and deliverer. David depended on it daily. Without God's shield in front of him, David would not have been King David. Without God's shield, he would have fought and killed some of his own countrymen. Without God's shield, it was likely Saul and his army would've found David and killed him. David's words reflected absolute dependency on God's protection and absolute trust in his sovereign plan.

Exercise:

Read the following Psalms and note similarities in themes and ideas: Psalms 3:3; Psalms 5:12; Psalms 7:10; Psalms 18:2, 30, 35; Psalms 28:7; Psalms 59:11; Psalms 115:9; Psalms 144:2.

Each of these Psalms was written by David. Each of these reflects his dependency.

God's relationship with David was centered on David's heart. His life was not one of perfect obedience. He was a warrior and a lover, among other things. But his heart was focused on God, and he knew his place in relation to the Lord. David gave full glory to God for his life and rose to the kingship. In 2 Samuel 22:36, David praises God for blessing him and protecting him.

"Thou hast also given me the shield of Thy salvation, and Thy help makes me great."

The word "help" is translated in some manuscripts as "answerings." God heard David's pleas as he hears ours. He protected David from not only Saul and the Philistines, but also from David himself by forcing him to withdraw from the fight. He was shielding David through the Philistine commanders, though at the time David did not know it.

We should keep this in mind the next time our plans change, or something doesn't work out like we wanted it to, or we question God's intervention or lack thereof. He sees the big picture, and if we live with our hearts dedicated to him, He will shield us from ourselves when need be, just as he did for David here in 1 Samuel 29. Once again, we can refer back to Jeremiah 29:11.

"'For I know the plans that I have for you,' declares the Lord, 'plans for welfare and not for calamity to give you a future and a hope.'"

Let us live this verse in faith, just as David did, and follow God blindly in trust and belief. His invisible shield surrounds us and protects us.

1 SAMUEL 30

THROUGH DAVID WAS A MAN of God, he was not above the trials, sufferings, and battles each and every human faces over the course of his or her life. David's life, in many ways, was one big conflict. God would later call David a man of bloodshed, which is why Solomon would build the temple. In the previous chapter (1 Samuel 29), he and his men were asked to leave the Philistine camp prior to the invasion of Israel. In 1 Samuel 30, Scripture opens to three days later, when they approach Ziklag after the journey back from the Philistine camp.

Exercise: Read 1 Samuel 30:1-2.

- How long was their journey home?
- What did they find upon returning?
- Who was responsible?

Can you imagine returning home to a devastated city, neighborhood, and home with your family no longer there? Many people can imagine such horrors, as many have suffered such a fate. For those who haven't, the world must feel as if it is being ripped apart. Perhaps David and his men saw the smoke rising from a distance before they encountered the burnt ash heap of their former homes. In 1 Samuel 30:4, we see the sorrow of David's band of men.

"Then David and the people who were with him lifted their voices and wept until there was not strength in them to weep."

David personally suffered much loss in the Amalekite raid. Times in southern Israel were as deadly then as they are now, perhaps more so. Rather than raiders on camels, however, now it's rockets and gunships. David lost both of his wives to the fiendish Amalekites.

Times took a turn for the worse for David and his men. When leaders encounter hardships and catastrophes, they are oftentimes blamed for them by those people they lead. Presidents are blamed, or praised, for the state of the economy and the country. When natural disasters strike, such as Hurricane Katrina or the Japanese tsunami, leaders are expected to act. When they do not, the people become unhappy.

In athletics, head coaches are held responsible for wins and losses. Too many losses result in the loss of a job. Whether they can do anything about it or not, leaders are held to a higher standard, sometimes unfairly. Such is the nature of leading from the top. David encountered such opposition from within his own ranks as a result of the Amalekite raid. However, it was not simply a job he was in danger of losing.

Exercise: Read 1 Samuel 30:6.

- What did the people talk of doing to David?

David's life, once again, was in danger. This time, it was his own people who spoke of stoning him. He was in a very vulnerable position and in danger of finally being killed. One can imagine David's state of mind. Fortunately, we do not have to imagine, for David wrote about it. Turn and read Psalms 25:15-17. David was lonely, caught in a net with nowhere to turn and nobody to turn to. His affliction was heightened by the fact it was his very own men who "were embittered, each one because of his sons and daughters."

David was not the only biblical figure to encounter such opposition from within.

Exercise: Turn to Exodus 17:1-4 and read of the great leader, Moses.

- What problem did the Hebrews face in this instance?
- How did the people respond to Moses?

- What was Moses afraid of?

Leadership exacts a high price at certain times. Notice Moses's response in Exodus 17:4, "So Moses cried out to the Lord."

Turn and read about another individual who encountered similar opposition in John 8:59.

- Who did this verse speak of?

Read John 8:57

- Identify who attempted to stone Jesus.

Christ encountered opposition on all fronts, but especially from his own people: the scribes, Pharisees, and teachers of the law, as well as the general Jewish population. He was even betrayed from within by one of his twelve disciples. He was eventually killed by the Romans. Jesus, like David, drew opposition from all sides. Like Moses, Christ, turned to the Father for strength. In fact, Moses, alongside Elijah, appeared to Christ in Mark 9. This appearance was certainly meant to strengthen and encourage Jesus for his upcoming death.

Exercise:

Now turn back to 1 Samuel 30:6. Notice David's first order of business after he found out people wanted to stone him.

- What did the last half of 1 Samuel 30:6 say David did?

David "strengthened himself in the Lord his God." A similar phrase was used in 1 Samuel 23:16, when Jonathan and David were united again, though only for a brief moment. The NASB translates 1 Samuel 23:16 using the term "encouraged." The Hebrew word used is *chazaq*. In 1 Samuel 30:6, the word is translated as "strengthened." Though different English translations, the same Hebrew word is used in both instances.

Chazaq literally translates as "to fasten upon, to seize, be strong, to fortify, harden, make hard, help, to be attached." The idea expressed in both verses is of David seizing the Lord, fastening his soul to God's. David was forced to refortify his heart after such a stressful ordeal. He sought renewal of his faith, which would harden his bond to God Almighty.

Scripture gave us excellent insight into this strengthening in the Lord. How do we strengthen ourselves in the Lord? The first encounter in 1 Samuel 23 involved two people, Jonathan and David. Godly friendship and companionship can energize a mired life. A friend can also kindly guide one back to the Lord as well. Jonathan was such a friend to David. He energized David and encouraged him to remain faithful to God.

In Proverbs 27:6, Scripture says, "Faithful are the wounds of a friend. But deceitful are the kisses of an enemy." Matthew 18:20 states that where "two or three have gathered together in My name, there I am in their midst." God's presence alone strengthens us, and he especially encourages us to gather together with our friends and family in his name. Our friends bring revitalization and energy into our lives.

David shed light on other ways to strengthen oneself in the Lord.

Exercise: Turn and read Psalms 27:14.

- According to this verse, what are we supposed to do?
- What are two qualities we must possess?

Similar words can be found in numerous passages throughout the Bible. In Nehemiah 8:16, Ezra is reading the law to the people as they attempt to rebuild Jerusalem in the fifth century B.C. We are told the Levites "calmed all the people saying, 'Be still, for the day is holy; do not be grieved.'" David told in Psalms 4:4, "tremble and do not sin; meditate in your heart upon your bed, and be still."

In Psalms 46:10, we are instructed to "cease striving and know that I am God." The prophet Zephaniah, writing around 630 B.C., also shared a similar message in Zephaniah 1:7. Zephaniah urged the people to "be silent before the Lord God!"

Silence and stillness seem to be associated with hearing God and letting him strengthen and renew you. We must set aside the many distractions of society and daily life and really listen. David spent much time in silence when tending his father's flock. It was likely those silent moments were now few and far between. However, he intentionally searched out times of silence so he might hear and meet God.

We must be intentional in our effort toward renewal and strengthening in the Lord. We must be silent and listen, setting aside the many daily distractions. Trout fishing on a secluded river in the earliest parts of the morning can provide such silence, as can hunting or hiking in the woods, separated from society, away from noise. Mountain climbing, hiking, camping, and a host of other activities all provide moments of silence.

Simply turning off the TV and picking up a Bible or shutting one's eyes and simply meditating are also examples of silence.

1 SAMUEL 31

IT IS PLAIN THAT SAUL'S encounter with Samuel in 1 Samuel 29 was not what he expected. King Saul learned of his final fate, and that day arrived. The scene of the battle was Mount Gilboa in Jezreel Valley.

Exercise: Read 1 Samuel 31:1–3.

- Which side was winning the battle?
- What happened to Jonathan and the other sons of Saul?
- How was Saul wounded?

Now turn back to 1 Samuel 15:28. Do you remember this exchange between Samuel and Saul? This event took place decades prior to Saul's death, yet Samuel predicted God would tear the kingdom from Saul. Turn back to 1 Samuel 28:19. Despite summoning Samuel from the dead, Saul's fate had not changed since 1 Samuel 15. The fate of his sons was directly tied to his own fate, thus all of them (save one) were to perish in the fight with the Philistines.

We must take from this account the fact that eventually our decisions and choices must be accounted for. The consequences that follow, whether positive or negative, are natural results of our choices and actions.

Saul, beginning in 1 Samuel 15, chose to disobey God.

Exercise: Turn back once more and read 1 Samuel 15:20-23.

- Who did Saul blame for his disobedience?
- What did Samuel tell Saul?

Samuel seems to indicate that Saul was more concerned with the appearance of worship and sacrifice than what the acts actually meant and represented. He said to Saul in 1 Samuel 22, "To obey is better than sacrifice." King Saul, however, obeyed his desires and sought the approval of his people rather than the approval of God. Saul's fate was sealed, and his refusal to submit to God's voice was a direct reflection of the state of his heart. He failed to give what God required.

What does God require? He told His servant Moses, who in turn told the people in Deuteronomy 10:12.

Exercise:

- According to Moses in Deuteronomy 10:12, what does God require of us?
- How are we to serve God?
- Does Saul fulfill this requirement?

Moses also laid forth how the people may restore their relationship with God if they wander from his voice.

Exercise: Turn to Deuteronomy 30:1-3.

- What does a return to God consist of?

Joshua, Moses's successor, reiterated his mentor's message to the tribes while they were east of the Jordan River in Joshua 22:5.

Exercise: Read this verse and answer the following questions.

- What did Joshua urge the people to do?
- How were they to serve God?
- What were they to take hold of?

God shielded David from capture. However, he abandoned Saul by withdrawing his protections. Psalms 7:10 states that God is a shield, "who saves the upright in heart." In Psalms 17:3, David prayed to God for protection, "Thou hast tried my heart... Thou has tested me and dost find nothing."

Exercise: Read and compare 1 Samuel 15:20–21 and 1 Samuel 17:45.

- When Saul was faced with questioning by Samuel, how did he reply? Compare his response with David's after being taunted by Goliath.

When the pressure is on, people become who they really are. Saul looked to blame the people, the very ones whom he obeyed and sought approval from, rather than obeying and seeking the God who anointed him. David's focus was on God's deliverance.

Exercise:

- What was the difference between Saul and David?
- What made David special in God's eyes, and what made Saul detestable?

Read the following passages: Psalms 44:21; Psalms 51:10; Proverbs 3:5; Proverbs 27:19.

- What do these verses primarily focus on?
- Relate Psalms 27:19 to the above verses on Saul and David.

David was not perfect by any means. Saul, however, showed repeated signs of disobedience. His heart had hardened, much like Pharaoh's during the time of Moses and Aaron. David, though not perfect, at least sought out God's presence and wisdom and displayed such on numerous occasions. The state of these two hearts is reflected in Ezekiel 11:19-20. In this passage, Ezekiel was speaking of the nation of Israel. However, it is applicable to us all.

Exercise:

- Who possessed the heart of stone, David or Saul? The heart of flesh?

- What does Ezekiel 11:20 state has to happen so that we will be God's people?

The message from God is clear: he desires the heart. And when we stray, we must adhere to the words of the prophet Joel in Joel 2:12.

"'Yet even now,' declares the Lord, 'Return to Me with all your heart.'"

A return to God requires a change of heart. Saul was unwilling to change. Thus, he fell to his own sword as a consequence. Saul pierced his own heart, taking his own life—a tragic death for sure. The very heart that refused to yield to God was destroyed by the ultimate act of selfishness—suicide.

After his death, Saul's body was captured and taken by the Philistines. They cut off his head and hung his body, along with the bodies of his sons, on the walls of Beth-shan. Saul's weapons were placed in the temple of Ashtaroth. Thus, Saul's death was cloaked in shame, much like his reign in many respects.

What had begun with such potential now hung headless and lifeless from the walls of Beth-shan. Fortunately, the city of Jabesh-gilead remained especially loyal to Saul. This was primarily because of his actions in 1 Samuel 11.

In 1 Samuel 11, Jabesh-gilead was besieged by Ammon. The Ammonite ruler Nahash was intent on partially blinding all of the men in the city. They petitioned the newly anointed King Saul for deliverance, at which point he rallied the men of Israel to their defense and drove off the Ammonites. Saul earned their undying loyalty as a result.

The men of Jabesh-gilead had not forgotten their pledge to King Saul. In 1 Samuel 31:11-12 they "walked all night" to reclaim the bodies of Saul and his sons to give them a proper burial. As Samuel's ghost correctly predicted, Saul fell in battle. His reign was over. A bloody war would begin between Saul's house and David for full control over Israel. Eventually David would prevail—a man after God's own heart.

Jesus spoke of the importance of a man's heart in Matthew 15:18-19.

Exercise:

- What two members of the body are mentioned in this verse?
- How are they connected?
- What defiles a man? What he does or does not do, or his heart?
- Acts 13:20-23 speaks of David and Saul. What was David called?

David was a clear example of 1 John 3:20-21. His life was full of bloodshed. He committed adultery. Yet, he remained humble before God and pure in his belief and willingness to honor God and repent of sin. In 1 John 3, we learn that "God is greater than our heart, and knows all things."

We would be wise to accept this and live in truth. For God knows all things anyway. Saul never accepted God's rule over his life. Saul refused God's sovereignty. His heart of stone refused instruction. God, thus, gave him over to his selfish desires, which proceeded from out of his heart. We must learn from Saul. We must listen to and take heed of the words of Jesus from Luke 12:34.

"For where your treasure is, there your heart will be also."

Where is your treasure?

Made in the USA
Monee, IL
19 September 2021